TRAITORS &
TURNCOATS

Twenty Tales of Treason,
from Benedict Arnold
to Ezra Pound

IAN CROFTON

Quercus

CONTENTS

INTRODUCTION

In his _Divine Comedy_, Dante put traitors – those who had betrayed their kin, their country, their God – into the ninth and lowest circle of Hell. Here all is silent, frozen, hopeless. All possibilities for life have been extinguished; a terminal spiritual entropy reigns. The ninth circle is where Satan himself resides, slowly beating his wings and gnawing for eternity on the head of Judas, the betrayer of Christ.

In the traditional view, treason is the most unnatural of crimes, a breaking of the bonds of society, of nature, of faith. The traitor, by acting against the monarch, God's representative on earth, has surrendered his or her humanity, and with it the right to be treated with the compassion due to a human being. In England, through to the 18th century, the most hideous punishment was reserved for those found guilty of treason: the victim, if male, was hanged, then slowly disembowelled while still alive, then cut into quarters; if female, they were burnt at the stake. Simple beheading or hanging was a merciful alternative.

Yet people have committed treason for all kinds of reasons – conscience, conviction, love, as well as pride, pique or greed. One man's traitor may be another man's hero, someone who has risked the most awful of deaths for something they believed in.

Turning traitor for money is perhaps the most despicable form of treachery – not for nothing is the term 'Judas' applied with such contempt. Judas himself was rewarded with thirty pieces of silver – a paltry sum compared to the $4.6 million received by the CIA officer Aldrich Ames for naming every US agent at work inside Russia. Equally contemptible in the eyes of some are those who change sides out of wounded pride, such as Coriolanus, the Roman general made famous by Shakespeare, or Benedict Arnold, whose name has become a byword for treachery in the United States. However, in both these cases some might argue that it was their own people who provoked the defection.

Politicians and others who have come to an accommodation with their country's enemies have been condemned to varying degrees by contemporaries and by posterity. Before the idea of the modern nation state became firmly established, the idea that loyalty to one's country was a moral imperative was largely irrelevant, as in the case of Pierre Cauchon, the French bishop who tried Joan of Arc; he just happened to support a different dynastic claimant to the throne of France, and remained loyal to the person he regarded as the rightful king. For both Charles I of England and Louis XVI of France, the country was embodied in the king, a notion that the subjects of both took exception to. The former raised an army against his own Parliament, while the latter connived with his country's enemies in an effort to reverse the republican tide. For these treasons both lost their heads. In civil wars and revolutions it is the losing side who become the traitors.

In 1940 Marshal Pétain believed he was saving France when he signed an armistice with the Nazis. But the France he sought to save was a conservative, authoritarian, Catholic France, not the democratic, secular, republican France established by the revolutionaries of 1789; *Liberté, égalité, fraternité* was replaced by *Travail, famille, patrie* ('work, family, fatherland'). Pétain was spared the firing squad at the end of the Second World War because of his military service in the First; his prime minister, Pierre Laval, was not so lucky.

Many have been convicted of treason for insurrection against the established authority. Of course, if that insurrection is successful, no one talks of treason. The unsuccessful rebel – such as the Earl of Essex in 1601 or the Duke of Monmouth in 1685 – dies a traitor's death. Those who are successful – Henry IV, Edward IV, Henry VII – take the crown. As the Elizabethan courtier Sir John Harington wittily observed:

> Treason doth never prosper, what's the reason?
> For if it prosper, none dare call it treason.

Some rebels, such as Essex, are no more than vainglorious fools, piqued that their stars are in decline, while others, like the Irish patriot Roger Casement, are noble spirits intent on the liberation of their nations. Sophie Scholl and her fellow students in the White Rose risked – and lost – their lives in demanding the overthrow of a terrible tyranny – that of Hitler in their native Germany. The Nazis called it treason; we call it heroic resistance.

We ascribe heroism to the likes of Sophie Scholl because, foolhardy though she was, she knew what she was doing. Other young women beheaded for treason, such as Anne Boleyn and Lady Jane Grey, have been the more-or-less unwitting victims of others' political ambitions. In Anne Boleyn's case, the ground for the charge of treason was adultery (a charge almost certainly without foundation); she was the victim of a treason law that identified sexual infidelity to the king with betrayal of country. Promiscuity may also have been the reason that Mata Hari was charged with aiding the enemy: someone who showed such a notorious absence of constancy in her personal life, the authorities may have calculated, could easily be depicted as someone capable of greater betrayals.

> **Any service rendered to the temporal king to the prejudice of the eternal king is, without doubt, an act of treachery.**
> Archbishop Stephen Langton, letter to the barons of England, 1207, expressing his opposition to King John

Ideology has often commanded a higher loyalty than country, from the Catholicism of Guy Fawkes to the abolitionism of John Brown, from the fascist beliefs of Ezra Pound and Lord Haw-Haw (William Joyce) to the communist sympathies of Julius and Ethel Rosenberg. More recently, Islamist jihadism in pursuit of an international caliphate is a phenomenon that ignores traditional national boundaries and loyalties. Certain groups of British-born Muslims, for example, think nothing of blowing up their fellow countrymen in pursuit of their goals – as happened in London on 7 July 2005. Guy Fawkes and his co-conspirators shared more than they would have cared to admit with these latter-day Gunpowder Plotters, their hatred fuelled by their faith and their thirst for martyrdom.

For some professional spies, such as the double agent Kim Philby and the East German spymaster Markus Wolf, the dangerous game itself seems to have been half the lure, although both stoutly maintained that they did what they did out of conviction. In his introduction to Philby's memoir, *My Silent War*, Graham Greene wrote:

> 'He betrayed his country' – yes, perhaps he did, but who among us has not committed treason to something or someone more important than a country? In Philby's eyes he was working for a shape of things to come from which his country would benefit.

Philby himself asserted that 'To betray, you must first belong,' and this has been the basis of the defence's argument in a number of treason trials. Roger Casement claimed the right (unsuccessfully) to be tried in an Irish, not an English, court. William Joyce's lawyers argued that he was not technically a British citizen, while those representing Markus Wolf after the fall of the Berlin Wall argued (successfully) on appeal that he could not, logically, be guilty of treason against a country – West Germany – that was not, at the time of his supposed betrayal, his own.

At the dawning of the third millennium, the concepts of loyalty and patriotism, principle and conscience continue to raise questions. Globalization, like jihadism, has blurred the borders of the nation state: not only do we see the emergence of supra-national organizations such as the European Union and the International Criminal Court, but also the increasing power of multinational corporations, cutting across jurisdictions and traditional national loyalties. Even as early as the 17th century the noted English jurist Sir Edward Coke wrote that corporations 'cannot commit treason', and today senior executives will always act first and foremost in the interests of the corporation and its shareholders, even where this conflicts with the interests of their own country.

Today, in the developed democracies, treason trials are few and far between. The very words 'treason', 'traitor', 'betrayal' and 'treachery' are so emotive that it becomes difficult to see how justice can be done when they are bandied about. The use over the centuries of treason laws to persecute dissidents, liquidate political rivals or suppress national liberation movements has meant that the whole concept of treason as a uniquely iniquitous crime has been somewhat debased. Henry VIII used the Treason Act of 1351 to eliminate those who stood in his way, just as Stalin, in an effort to snuff out any vestige of opposition to his personal rule, sent hundreds of thousands accused of treason to their dooms. William Wallace, the Scottish freedom fighter, was hanged, drawn and quartered in 1305 for opposing Edward I of England's attempt to conquer his country, and many of the heroes of Ireland's struggle for independence – right up to Roger Casement in 1916 – were executed for treason against the Crown. In 1956 the apartheid regime of South Africa charged Nelson Mandela and almost the entire executive of the African National Congress, together with scores of others, with treason – although that particular prosecution failed.

The last man to be hanged in the UK for treason was William Joyce in 1946, although the death penalty for treason was not abolished until the Crime and Disorder Act of 1998 – three decades after the UK had abandoned capital punishment for murder. The last prosecution for treason in the UK was in 1981, when Marcus Sarjeant, a disturbed teenager, was jailed for five years after he had fired blank shots at the Queen. He was prosecuted under the Treason Act of 1842, which made it treasonous to discharge a firearm near the sovereign – a case of breaking a butterfly upon a wheel. In 2005, in the wake of the 7/7 London bombings, there was talk of bringing treason charges against various Muslim clerics in the UK, but in the end the authorities settled on charges such as incitement to murder.

The US Constitution, to prevent the law of treason being used to shore up tyranny, gives the following narrow definition:

> Treason against the United States, shall consist only in levying War against them, or in adhering to their Enemies, giving them Aid and Comfort.

In consequence, most prosecutions are brought under the Espionage Act of 1917 or the Sedition Act of 1918. No prosecution for treason was brought in the USA between 1952 and 2006, when an indictment was brought *in absentia* against Adam Gadahn, a US-born propagandist on behalf of al Qaeda.

Today some place a greater value on loyalty to individuals than countries or corporations or faiths. 'If I had to choose between betraying my country and betraying my friend,' wrote the English novelist E.M. Forster in 1951, 'I hope I should have the guts to betray my country.' Certainly few today would blindly sign up to the old slogan, 'My country, right or wrong', and in a democracy we maintain the right to criticize the actions of our elected leaders, both in peace and in war. Although oaths of allegiance are required of new citizens, and also of office-holders and other servants of the state, in ordinary discourse few today express unquestioning fealty to disembodied abstractions such as 'the state' or 'the Crown'. Yet feelings of loyalty remain – to family and friends, and beyond that to communities, conceived of as collections of individuals like ourselves, and beyond that to all our fellow human beings. If we observe the principle 'Do unto others as you would have them do unto you', then it follows that if we harm another person, then we betray ourselves, and lose a part of our own humanity.

IAN CROFTON
London, January 2009

MY BIRTHPLACE
HATE I

The general who waged war on his native Rome

Men and women have turned traitor for many reasons: ideology, conscience, love, money, pride. The story of Coriolanus is a story of pride – and, indeed, Coriolanus, ever since Plutarch featured him in his *Parallel Lives* in the 2nd century AD, has through the ages become the archetype of the proud man, the noble yet haughty Roman general whose disdain for his fellow citizens drove him in the end to ally himself with Rome's enemies and to lead them against his native city.

> GAIUS MARCIUS
> CORIOLANUS
>
> *Born* late 6th century BC, in Rome (according to legend)
>
> *Died* murdered early 5th century BC, in the territory of the Volsci (again according to legend)

An account of the career of Gaius Marcius Coriolanus is given a century before Plutarch by Livy in his monumental history of Rome, *Ab Urbe Condite*, in which Livy refers to accounts of Coriolanus by earlier historians. However, the modern consensus is that Coriolanus may not have been a historical character at all, but rather a figure of legend, one created, in Dr Johnson's words, to 'point a moral, or adorn a tale'.

The capture of Corioli

Gaius Marcius makes his first appearance in Livy as a young man during the consulship of Spurius Cassius and Postumus Cominius. At this time, the early 5th century BC, Rome was at war with the Volscians, whose territory lay to the south of Rome, beyond the plain of Latium. As the Romans lay siege to the Volscian town of Corioli, they suddenly found themselves attacked simultaneously by a Volscian army from Antium and a force of Volscians sallying forth from Corioli itself. Livy recounts what happened next:

> 'My birthplace hate I, and my love's upon This enemy town.
>
> William Shakespeare, *Coriolanus* (1608), IV.iv

> Marcius at that time happened to be on guard. He, with a chosen body of men, not only beat back the attack of those who had sallied forth, but boldly rushed in through the open gate, and, having cut down all who were in the part of the city nearest to it, and hastily seizing some blazing torches, threw them into the houses adjoining the wall. Upon this, the shouts of the townsmen, mingled with the wailings of the women and children occasioned at first by fright, as is usually the case, both increased the courage of the Romans, and naturally dispirited the Volscians who had come to bring help, seeing that the city was taken.

OPPOSITE **This 1826 painting** by Giovanni Silvagni depicts Veturia pleading with her son Coriolanus to abandon his siege of Rome, while his wife Volumnia falls into a swoon.

THE TARPEIAN ROCK

THE *RUPES TARPEIA* OR TARPEIAN ROCK, a crag on the flank of the Capitoline Hill in Rome, took its name from the vestal virgin, Tarpeia, a figure from the legendary early history of Rome. When Rome's enemies, the Sabines, were besieging the city, Tarpeia offered to open the city gates to them in return for 'what they bore on their arms'. She had in mind their golden bracelets, but the Sabines ungratefully battered her to death with their shields, then threw her body off the rock that bears her name. Subsequently, being thrown from the Tarpeian Rock became the fate for Rome's most egregious traitors and murderers, notably patricides. Plutarch describes how Coriolanus almost shares their fate at the hands of the outraged populace, prior to going into exile in the land of the Volscians. However, there is no mention of this in Livy, so it may be a poetic embellishment on Plutarch's part.

Thus Marcius earned the honorific name Coriolanus. (This at least is the legend, although the Roman custom of naming men after the sites of their victories did not emerge for almost another two hundred years, so it is more likely that the reason for the name was that the Marcius family originated in Corioli.)

Coriolanus reappears in Livy's history some years later, during the consulship of Marcus Minucius and Aulus Sempronius. This time he does not take the role of defender of Rome, but of defender of the privileges of his own class, the patricians.

Patricians vs plebeians

The last king of Rome, the tyrannical Tarquin the Proud, had been expelled from Rome in 510 BC, but the establishment of a republic had not benefited the majority of the population, the so-called plebeians, who remained both poor and powerless. Power and wealth were in the hands of the patricians – the Roman nobility – and only they could become senators and consuls. However, in the 490s the plebeians, outraged that some of their number who had fallen into debt were being sold as slaves, successfully pressed for an improvement in their status. They established as their representatives the tribunes, who had the power to veto the decisions of the consuls and the Senate, and who could also propose legislation.

The patricians resented this erosion of their power, and in the late 490s used the threat of famine in an attempt to reassert their hegemony. 'Many were of opinion that the time was come for crushing the commons [i.e. the plebeians],' writes Livy, 'and recovering those rights which had been wrested from the senators by secession and violence.' The Senate had

> SECOND CITIZEN: Would you proceed especially against Gaius Marcius?
> FIRST CITIZEN: Against him first; he's a very dog to the commonalty.
> SECOND CITIZEN: Consider you what services he has done for his country?
> FIRST CITIZEN: Very well, and could be content to give him good report for't but that he pays himself with being proud.
>
> William Shakespeare, *Coriolanus* (1608), I.i
> (commonalty = the ordinary people)

purchased grain from abroad to feed the population, but Coriolanus argued that subsidized grain should only be handed out if the plebeians abolished the tribunate:

> If they desire corn at its old price, let them restore to the senators their former rights. Why do I, like a captive sent under the yoke, as if I had been ransomed from robbers, behold plebeian magistrates, and Sicinius [a tribune] invested with power? Am I to submit to these indignities longer than is necessary? Am I, who have refused to endure Tarquin as king, to tolerate Sicinius? Let him now secede, let him call away the commons.

Even the Senate felt this was too harsh; as for the people, their outrage well-nigh drove them to arms:

> They complained that they were now being attacked with famine, as if they were enemies, that they were being robbed of food and sustenance, that the corn brought from foreign countries, the only support with which fortune had unexpectedly furnished them, was being snatched from their mouths, unless the tribunes were delivered in chains to Gaius Marcius, unless satisfaction were exacted from the backs of the commons of Rome. That in him a new executioner had arisen, one to bid them either die or be slaves. He would have been attacked as he was leaving the Senate house, had not the tribunes very opportunely appointed him a day for trial.

CORIOLANUS [*addressing the plebeians*]:
You common cry of curs, whose breath I hate
As reek o' th' rotten fens, whose loves I prize
As the dead carcases of unburied men
That do corrupt my air ...
                              ... Despising
For you the city, thus I turn my back;
There is a world elsewhere.
William Shakespeare, *Coriolanus* (1608), III.iii

Coriolanus did not deign to appear before the court appointed to try him, and was condemned in his absence. Instead he went into exile among the Volscians, who were still threatening Rome.

Going over to the enemy

The Volscians welcomed him warmly, 'and treated him still more kindly every day, in proportion as his resentful feelings toward his countrymen became more marked'. Together Coriolanus and the Volscian chief, Attius Tullius, hatched a plan to attack Rome. Patriotically, Livy claims that it was in Coriolanus that the greater hopes of the Volscians reposed. 'These hopes,' he continues, 'he by no means disappointed, so that it was clearly seen that the Roman commonwealth was powerful by reason of its generals rather than its military force.' Under Coriolanus' command, says Livy, the Volscians proceeded to take from the Romans a succession of towns that they had recently conquered, and subsequently marched on Rome, pitching their camp only five miles from the city. (Some modern historians have suggested that the story of Coriolanus' leadership of the enemy was generated by the Romans, who could not endure the thought that a foreign general could have been so successful; alternatively, Coriolanus may simply have been a mercenary.)

The Volscians set about ravaging the land round about, causing fear and discord within the city – although Coriolanus ordered that any lands belonging to the patricians should escape harm. Rome panicked. Envoys were sent to treat for peace, but brought back a 'haughty answer':

> If their lands were restored to the Volscians, the question of peace might then be considered; if they were minded to enjoy the plunder of war at their ease, he, remembering both the injurious treatment of his countrymen, as well as the kindness of strangers, would do his utmost to make it appear that his spirit was irritated by exile, not crushed.

When the envoys went once more to treat with Coriolanus, they were refused entry to the camp.

At this point the matrons of Rome gathered round Veturia, the mother of Coriolanus, and Volumnia, his wife, and prevailed upon them to go with them to the camp of Coriolanus to 'defend the city by entreaties and tears, since men were unable to defend it by arms'. (In Shakespeare's play, Volumnia is Coriolanus' mother, not his wife; the latter is called Virgilia.)

When his mother, wife and children appear before him, Coriolanus, bewildered to the point of distraction, offers to embrace Veturia, but she angrily rebuffs him:

> Before I permit your embrace, let me know whether I have come to an enemy or to a son, whether I am in your camp a captive or a mother? Has length of life and a hapless old age reserved me for this – to behold you first an exile, then an enemy? Have you had the heart to lay waste this land, which gave you birth and nurtured you? Though you had come in an incensed and vengeful spirit, did not your resentment abate when you entered its borders? When Rome came within view, did not the thought enter your mind – within those walls are my house and household gods, my mother, wife and children? So then, had I not been a mother, Rome would not now be besieged: had I not a son, I might have died free in a free country. But I can now suffer nothing that will not bring more disgrace on you than misery on me; nor, most wretched as I am, shall I be so for long. Look to these, whom, if you persist, either an untimely death or lengthened slavery awaits.

Then his wife and children embrace him, and this and the wailing and lamentation of the women soften his heart, and he withdraws his camp from the city.

Livy notes that there are different versions of Coriolanus' ultimate fate. The oldest source he can find, Fabius, asserts that Coriolanus lived to an advanced old age in exile; other versions have him being put to death by the outraged Volscians. This

'While the force and vigour of his soul, and a persevering constancy in all he undertook, led him successfully into many noble achievements, yet, on the other side, also, by indulging the vehemence of his passion, and through an obstinate reluctance to yield or accommodate his humours and sentiments to those of a people about him, he rendered himself incapable of acting and associating with others. Those who saw with admiration how proof his nature was against all the softnesses of pleasure, the hardships of service, and the allurements of gain, while allowing to that universal firmness of his the respective names of temperance, fortitude, and justice, yet in the life of the citizen and the statesman, could not choose but be disgusted at the severity and ruggedness of his deportment, and with his overbearing, haughty, and imperious temper. Education and study, and the favours of the muses, confer no greater benefit on those that seek them than these humanizing and civilizing lessons, which teach our natural qualities to submit to the limitations prescribed by reason, and to avoid the wildness of extremes.'

Plutarch, *Life of Coriolanus* (2nd century AD), translated by John Dryden

last is the fate of Shakespeare's Coriolanus, condemned by the Volscian leader Tullus Aufidius, who addresses his fellow countrymen thus:

> You lords and heads o' the state, perfidiously
> He has betray'd your business, and given up,
> For certain drops of salt, your city Rome,
> I say 'your city', to his wife and mother;
> Breaking his oath and resolution like
> A twist of rotten silk, never admitting
> Counsel o' the war, but at his nurse's tears
> He whined and roar'd away your victory …

Some of the Volscians want to put Coriolanus on trial, but others cry 'Kill, kill, kill, kill, kill him!' They are as good as their word.

Political resonances

Today, the story of Coriolanus is known largely through Shakespeare's version, itself closely modelled on Plutarch. *Coriolanus* is one of Shakespeare's least performed but most political works, and seems to resurface particularly at times of political turbulence. A 1719 adaptation by John Dennis, entitled *The Invader of His Country, or The Fatal Resentment*, was a clear attack on the claim to the throne of the Old Pretender, James Francis Edward Stuart, who in 1715 had mounted an abortive

Shakespeare's *Coriolanus* has often aroused strong political passions from both right and left. In this 1995 West Yorkshire Playhouse production, Steven Berkoff played the title role as a cross between a gangster and a Mussolini-like dictator.

French-backed rebellion in Scotland, followed by a lesser effort that same year, 1719, this time backed by Spain. Similarly, James Thomson's 1745 version (only loosely based on Shakespeare) coincided with the Jacobite rising then in progress, in which the Young Pretender, Charles Edward Stuart, raised the Highland clans against the Hanoverian monarchy.

The tension in Shakespeare's play between democratic and autocratic values came to the fore in the 20th century. For Marxists, the play clearly illustrates the class struggle, with the proletarian plebeians defending their rights against the oppressions of the patrician ruling classes; Coriolanus' loyalty to the latter proves stronger than his loyalty to his country. The play particularly appealed to directors in the communist bloc of Eastern Europe; at the time of his death in 1956 Bertolt Brecht was working on a rewritten version, in which the tribunes organize the plebeians into an effective military force, and Coriolanus is dissuaded from attacking Rome not by his mother's pleas but by the smoke belching from the newly organized armouries. The moral is that no one man is indispensable; strength lies in collective endeavour – a riposte to Livy's assertion that 'the Roman commonwealth was powerful by reason of its generals rather than its military force'.

For the hard right, in contrast, Coriolanus embodies all that they admire, and the mob all that they despise. A production at the Comédie Française in Paris in 1934 became the focus of demonstrations against the left-wing French government by royalists and fascists, and the resultant riots led the police to shut down the theatre. In Germany during and after the First World War the play had been interpreted as an attack on militarism, but once the Nazis came to power in 1933 they adopted the play as a text for schoolchildren, with Coriolanus as a Roman Führer struggling to lead his people to a healthier society, 'as Adolf Hitler in our days wishes to lead our beloved German fatherland'. After the Second World War, the US occupying forces banned all performances of the play, a ban only lifted in 1953.

At the end of Laurence Olivier's 1955 production the murdered Coriolanus was suspended upside down, in a deliberate reference to the fate of Mussolini, who, after his execution, was slung head-down from a meat hook in Milan. There are uncanny resemblances, in fact, between the ancient Roman general and the fascist dictator, beyond their arrogant, vicious authoritarianism. In July 1943, following the Allied invasion of Sicily, the king of Italy demanded Mussolini's resignation, and the new government proceeded to negotiate an armistice with the Allies. Germany, once Italy's ally, now became its enemy, and German troops poured over the Brenner Pass and down the peninsula. Mussolini, held under house arrest on the Gran Sasso, high in the Apennines, was rescued by German paratroopers, and until the end of the war headed a puppet republic in the north of Italy, effectively controlled by the Nazis. In the spring of 1945, as the Germans faced defeat, Mussolini attempted to escape to neutral Switzerland, from where he hoped to take a plane to fascist Spain. But on 27 April his car was stopped by partisans on the shores of Lake Como, and, despite being disguised in a German officer's uniform, he was immediately recognized as the detested Duce, and was shot the next day. His body was taken to Milan, where it was put on display in the Piazzale Loreto and suffered the angry assaults of the populace, before being buried in an unmarked grave.

AT THE
HOT GATES
EPHIALTES
Betraying the Three Hundred at Thermopylae

The Pass of Thermopylae, above the Gulf of Malis on the eastern coast of Greece, guards the route south from Thessaly to Lokris, Athens and the Peloponnese. Nowadays the route is taken by the main highway linking the north and south of the country; the many bends in the road have resulted in numerous traffic accidents, and the passage is nicknamed the 'horseshoe of death'. In ancient times the pass was known as the 'Hot Gates', because of the thermal springs that gave the place its name.

Today, petrol fumes and the roar of lorries drown the scent of thyme and the relentless chirping of the cicadas. In the past the pass has echoed more than once to the clash of arms, while the earth has soaked up the blood of many men. Here Greeks have fought Macedonians, Gauls, Romans and Turks, but the most famous battle at Thermopylae was that fought in August 480 BC between a small force under King Leonidas of Sparta and the mighty army of the Persian emperor, Xerxes.

EPHIALTES OF TRACHIS

Born late 6th century BC, possibly in Malis, Greece
Died murdered c. 470 BC, possibly in Trachis, Greece

The Persian invasion

In 480 BC Xerxes led a vast army into mainland Greece, determined to put an end once and for all to Greek resistance to Persian expansion in the eastern Mediterranean. The Greeks at this time were far from united: there were numerous rival city-states, which sometimes acted in concert, but more often did not. On this occasion many of them did come together, rallying round the two major players, Athens and Sparta. A plan evolved, by which the Athenian navy would block the sea route south, while an allied Greek army held the Pass of Thermopylae.

The plan was hampered by the fact that the Olympic Games were in progress, and by tradition all the Greek city-states ceased fighting for the duration of the games. The Spartans themselves – regarded as the military elite of ancient Greece – were celebrating their own religious festival, and the magistrates would only allow Leonidas to take with him 300 warriors. The king chose only men with sons old enough to take the place of their fathers should they not return. He himself had consulted the Delphic Oracle, and had been told that only the sacrifice of a king descended from Hercules could save Sparta. By tradition, Leonidas traced his ancestry back to the great hero, and thus became convinced that he would die at Thermopylae. As he left his queen he told her that after his death she should 'marry a good man and have good children'.

OPPOSITE Ephialtes, having been promised Persian gold, shows the enemy the mountain track that enables them to outflank the Greeks defending the pass at Thermopylae.

The struggle for Thermopylae

Leonidas was joined by contingents from other city-states as he marched north, and by the time he reached Thermopylae he commanded an army of some 5,000 men. However, he faced a Persian army that the Greek historian Herodotus numbered at over 2 million; although it was probably only a tenth of this size, it still vastly outnumbered the Greeks.

Leonidas stationed the bulk of his army at the 'Middle Gate', the narrowest section of the pass, while posting a thousand Phocians to guard the path through the mountains that bypassed the pass, in case the Persians discovered it and attempted to outflank the main Greek force. When Xerxes sent an ambassador to demand that the Greeks lay down their arms, Leonidas told the Persians: 'Come and get them.'

For two days the Greeks threw back wave after wave of Persians, including the elite 10,000 known as the Immortals. At this point, let Herodotus take up the story:

PLEASANT NEWS

FIGHTING IN THE HEAT OF AUGUST was desperately hard work, but to the toughened, laconic Spartans it was all one. When told shortly before the start of the battle that the air would soon be dark with Persian arrows and spears, one Spartan, a man called Dieneces, responded: 'This is pleasant news … for if the Persians hide the sun, we shall have our battle in the shade.'

> How to deal with the situation Xerxes had no idea; but while he was still wondering what his next move should be, a man from Malis got himself admitted to his presence. This was Ephialtes and he had come, in hope of a rich reward, to tell the king about the track which led over the hills to Thermopylae – and the information he gave was to prove the death of the Greeks who held the pass.

The following day Xerxes dispatched a force to follow the path through the mountains. The Phocians who guarded it were alerted of the Persian approach by the rustling of oak leaves, and, believing the whole Persian army was upon them, fled to defend their native city. Hearing that the Phocians had abandoned their allies, Leonidas ordered the bulk of his army to retreat. He himself remained with his 300, plus 700 Thespians and 400 Thebans – although the latter deserted to the Persians as soon as the opportunity arose.

> 'I was neither at the hot gates
> Nor fought in the warm rain ...
> T.S. Eliot, 'Gerontion' (1920)

The fate of Leonidas and his men was sealed. Herodotus describes what happened next:

> The Greeks, who knew that the enemy were on their way round by the mountain track and that death was inevitable, fought with reckless desperation, exerting every ounce of strength that was in them against the invader. By this time most of their spears were broken, and they were killing Persians with their swords. In the course of that fight Leonidas fell, having fought like a man indeed. Many distinguished Spartans were killed at his side – their names, like the names of all the three hundred … deserve to be remembered.

Herodotus also records that when the Spartans no longer had swords, they resisted with 'their hands and their teeth'.

The name Ephialtes came in Greece to be synonymous with 'traitor'. It also means 'nightmare'. The man himself never received his reward, as the following month the Persians were decisively beaten at the great naval battle at Salamis, and Ephialtes fled north to Thessaly with a price on his head. Some ten years later he was killed by Athenades of Trachis. Although Athenades had his own reasons for killing Ephialtes, he was nevertheless handsomely rewarded by the Spartans.

As for Leonidas and the Three Hundred, they were commemorated by one of the world's most famous epitaphs, inscribed on a stone at the site of the battle:

> Go tell it in Sparta, stranger passing by,
> That here, obedient to their laws, we lie.

FOR A HANDFUL OF SILVER

JUDAS

The greatest sinner in Dante's Hell

The poet William Cowper, while suffering one of his frequent fits of depression in the 1770s, wrote of himself as 'damned below Judas; more abhorred than he was'. Such was the depth of his misery, Cowper latched on to the most extreme exemplar of sinfulness and worthlessness that he could think of – Judas, the man who betrayed Jesus. Cowper's 'lines written under the influence of delirium' continue:

> Man disavows, and Deity disowns me,
> Hell might afford my miseries a shelter;
> Therefore, Hell keeps her ever-hungry mouths all
> Bolted against me.

Hell is very firmly where Dante, in the *Inferno*, places Judas. The betrayer of Jesus suffers the worst torments in the ninth and lowest circle, the fate of those who have committed treachery against their family, their masters, their country or their God. Here the damned are not warmed by fire, as befits the

> ### JUDAS ISCARIOT
> *Born* c. 10 BC?, possibly in Kerioth, southern Judaea
> *Died* committed suicide? c. AD 30, in Jerusalem

passionate sinner, but frozen in contorted positions in the ice – for treachery is a cold, calculated crime. It is, apart from the slow flapping of Satan's wings, a place of stillness, lifelessness, hopelessness, where every spiritual possibility is deadened. At the foot of the pit is Satan himself, part-encased in ice, and in each of his three mouths he chews upon a traitor. In the outer mouths are Brutus and Cassius, the assassins of Julius Caesar, whom Dante reveres as the founder of the Roman Empire. In the central mouth is Judas, stuffed in head-first, with his back eternally skinned by the Devil's claws. This is the fate of the man Dante considers the greatest sinner in the world.

> From six eyes he wept, and from three chins
> Dripped tears and blood-red dribble.
> His teeth, like an iron comb
> Mangling flax, chewed a sinner
> In each mouth, making three at once in torment.
> For the foremost this gnawing was as nothing
> To the clawing as again and again
> His back was stripped of every shred of skin.
> 'The soul up there, he in the greatest pain,'
> My master said, 'That is Judas Iscariot.
> His head's inside, his legs flail helplessly without.'
> Dante, *Inferno* (1308–21), Canto XXXIV (trans. author)

OPPOSITE **Judas betraying Jesus** with a kiss, as depicted by Giotto in one of his frescoes for the Scrovegni Chapel, Padua, painted between 1303 and 1310.

Who was Judas?

One of the twelve disciples of Jesus, Judas was surnamed Iscariot to distinguish him from the other disciple called Judas, the 'good' Judas, also known as Thaddaeus. Iscariot probably means 'man from Kerioth', a village in southern Judaea; this would mean that Judas was not a Galilean like the other disciples, which may have marked him out as an outsider, 'the other'. An alternative theory is that the name 'Iscariot' is a corruption of Latin *sicarius*, meaning 'murderer', indicating that he might have been a member of the Sicarii, one of the most radical of Jewish sects, who believed in direct, violent action against the Roman occupiers; alternatively, the name might reflect his role in the death of Jesus.

Judas is identified as the guardian of the purse of the disciples (John 12:6). In the same chapter, John recounts how when Mary, sister of Martha, anoints the feet of Jesus with 'a pound of ointment of right spikenard, of great price', Judas objects, saying 'Why was not this ointment sold for three hundred pence, and given to the poor?' (John 12:5). Judas's radical questioning of this extravagant gesture of devotion to Jesus is rapidly dismissed in John's Gospel – the last of the Gospels to be written, and the most overt in giving a theological spin to the basic narrative: 'Now he said this, not because he cared for the poor; but because he was a thief' (12:6). No further evidence of Judas's thievery is adduced; but it is all part of the pattern in which his name is retrospectively blackened.

> 'In ancient shadows and twilights
> Where childhood had strayed,
> The world's great sorrows were born
> And its heroes were made.
> In the lost boyhood of Judas
> Christ was betrayed.'
> Æ (George William Russell), 'Germinal' (1931)

Betrayed by a kiss

There is no clear reason why the chief priests should have required the services of Judas to arrest Jesus. But the synoptic Gospels (Matthew, Mark and Luke) all describe how Judas approaches the priests and offers to betray his master for money: 'What will ye give me, and I will deliver him unto you? And they covenanted with him for thirty pieces of silver.' (Matthew 26:14–16) Luke adds the detail that Judas does this because Satan has entered into him (22:3), an assertion repeated by John (13:2).

At the Last Supper, Jesus predicts 'One of you which eateth with me shall betray me' (Mark 14:18), and says 'it had been good for that man if he had not been born' (Matthew 26:24). John recasts Jesus' speech at this point to suggest that the whole story of Jesus, including his betrayal by Judas, is a fulfilment of Old Testament prophecy:

> I speak not of you all: I know whom I have chosen: but that the scripture may be fulfilled, He that eateth bread with me hath lifted up his heel against me. John 13:18

This is a deliberate echo of Psalm 41:9:

> Yea, mine own familiar friend, in whom I trusted, which did eat of my bread, hath lifted up his heel against me.

The synoptic Gospels all describe how, in the Garden of Gethsemane, Judas comes to Jesus with 'a great multitude with swords and staves, from the chief priests' (Mark 14:43), and identifies Jesus with a kiss:

> And he that betrayed him had given them a token, saying, Whomsoever I shall kiss, that same is he; take him, and lead him away safely. Mark 14:44

There is no kiss in John. Instead, Jesus identifies himself to the officers of the chief priests, saying 'I am he' (18:5).

The fate of Judas

The biblical accounts of the fate of Judas vary. In Matthew, Judas repents and tries to return the thirty pieces of silver to the chief priests, saying 'I have sinned in that I have betrayed the innocent blood.' But they say, 'What is that to us?' (27:4). Judas throws the silver down in the temple, and goes off and hangs himself (by tradition from a tree – the Judas tree, *Cercis siliquastrum*). The chief priests decide it is not lawful for them to put the money into the treasury, 'because it is the price of blood'. Instead, they use it to buy 'the potter's field, to bury strangers in' (27:7), a place there-after known as the 'field of blood'.

In the Acts of the Apostles, the field of blood gets its name for a more literal reason:

> Now this man [Judas] purchased a field with the reward of iniquity; and falling headlong, he burst asunder in the midst, and all his bowels gushed out. Acts 1:18

The suicide of Judas depicted in a fresco (*c.*1530) by an unknown artist in the Église Saint-Sébastien in Plampinet, near Briançon, southeast France.

Whether this indicates that Judas had an accidental fall, or threw himself off a rock, or suffered divine punishment, is unclear.

A third account of the fate of Judas is found in a fragment from the hand of the 2nd-century Christian leader, Papias:

> Judas walked about in this world a sad example of impiety; for his body having swollen to such an extent that he could not pass where a chariot could pass easily, he was crushed by the chariot, so that his bowels gushed out.

Divine punishment of the eternal variety is certainly what most subsequent theologians had in mind for Judas. But one of the key issues the story and its interpretation raises is the tension between predestination and free will. Judas is condemned for his decision to accept money to betray Jesus, even though that betrayal is, according to the Gospels, foreordained, and Jesus himself anticipates it. It is not only John who makes connections to the Jewish scriptures of the Old Testament: the link between thirty pieces of silver and the potter's field comes in Zechariah (11:12–13), while Acts (1:16, 20) says that Judas's end is predicted in the Psalms (69:25 and 109:8). Judas thus plays a necessary and predetermined role in the fundamental Christian narrative in which Christ comes to earth to die for the sins of humankind.

The Gnostic interpretation

In the 1970s a codex was discovered in Egypt that contained a Coptic translation of a text called the Gospel of Judas. This had been known of for millennia – it had been condemned by St Irenaeus of Lyon in AD 180 – but the text had been lost for centuries. The manuscript spent two decades in a bank vault, but in 2006 the text and a translation were eventually published. The Gospel of Judas is almost certainly a Gnostic text; the Gnostics, who flourished between the 2nd and 5th centuries, emphasized the importance of the revelation of esoteric knowledge. For them, two worlds existed simultaneously: that of the good and the divine on the one hand, and that of the evil and the material on the other. Thus the body was regarded as the enemy of spiritual life.

In the Gospel of Judas, Judas is Jesus' favourite disciple, and it is to Judas alone that Jesus reveals his secret knowledge of God, the cosmos and the creation of men and angels. The Gospel records the conversations between Jesus and Judas in the days before the Last Supper, and in these dialogues Jesus tells Judas that he will exceed all the other disciples, 'For you will sacrifice the man that clothes me.' Thus, in helping to engineer the death of Jesus the man, Judas helps to liberate Jesus the god.

> 'There is one eternally true legend – that of Judas.'
> Joseph Stalin, at the treason trial of
> Karl Radek during the Great Purge, 1937

The archetypal traitor

Despite the ambivalence and the contradictions found in the Gospels, the name Judas soon became synonymous with treachery – particularly spiritual, ideological or intellectual treachery. The identification of Judas as the man who betrayed his God also helped to seed the growth of Christian anti-Semitism, in which the Jewish people are held responsible for the murder of Jesus (conveniently forgetting that Jesus was himself a Jew).

The story of Judas, and the iconography associated with him, pervade Western art and literature. There are many pictorial representations of the kiss of Judas, from Giotto on, and the kiss that kills has provided a poignant, paradoxical image for many writers, for example Oscar Wilde in *The Ballad of Reading Gaol* (1898):

> Yet each man kills the thing he loves,
> By each let this be heard,
> Some do it with a bitter look,
> Some with a flattering word.
> The coward does it with a kiss,
> The brave man with a sword!

Wilde also asserted, in his essay 'The Critic as Artist' (1891), that: 'Every great man nowadays has his disciples, and it is always Judas who writes the biography.'

One of the most powerful allusions to the Judas legend is Robert Browning's poem 'The Lost Leader', written in 1843 on the occasion of William Wordsworth's acceptance of the poet laureateship. Browning was dismayed at this last betrayal of his former radical republicanism by the grand old man of English Romantic poetry, who in his youth had been an enthusiast for the French Revolution. Was it not Wordsworth who had written of that time:

> Bliss was it in that dawn to be alive,
> But to be young was very heaven!

AND THE HECKLERS SHOUTED JUDAS

WHEN BOB DYLAN ABANDONED HIS ACOUSTIC GUITAR for an electric one, those of his followers who felt he had betrayed the purity of folk music were aghast. Appearing with his amplified band at the Free Trade Hall in Manchester on 17 May 1966, a member of the audience shouted 'Judas!'. Another yelled 'I'm never listening to you again, ever!' Dylan replied, 'I don't believe you.' Then, after a pause, he added, 'You're a *liar*.' And then, whispering to his band to 'Play it ****** loud', he launched into a particularly visceral rendition of 'Like a Rolling Stone'.

The Napoleonic Wars had narrowed Wordsworth's outlook, and stolid reactionary patriotism began to replace his earlier enthusiasms. To celebrate Napoleon's final defeat at Waterloo in 1815 – and the restoration of the *anciens régimes* across Europe – Wordsworth and his fellow poet Robert Southey sat on the summit of Skiddaw in the Lake District and feasted on roast beef and plum pudding, washed down with punch. Thereafter, Wordsworth was to become a pillar of the Established Church and the Tory Party, and his acceptance of the laureateship from the Crown was for the young Robert Browning the last straw:

> Just for a handful of silver he left us,
> Just for a riband to stick in his coat …

Thus Wordsworth, having taken his 'handful of silver', becomes a new Judas, betraying the progressive cause. Like Judas among the other disciples, Wordsworth is cast out and isolated, the despised 'other':

> Shakespeare was of us, Milton was for us,
> Burns, Shelley, were with us, – they watch from their graves!
> He alone breaks from the van and the free-men,
> – He alone sinks to the rear and the slaves!

In the end, though – despite condemning Wordsworth's acceptance as:

> One more devils'-triumph and sorrow for angels,
> One wrong more to man, one more insult to God!

– Browning draws back from the brink. Instead, he sentimentally pictures Wordsworth 'Pardoned in heaven, the first by the throne!' It is a far cry from Dante's image of Judas clamped head-first and forever between the fangs of Lucifer in the lowest circle of hell – but it illustrates well the shift from late-medieval visions of divine justice to the Victorian belief that to forgive is not so much divine as just plain good manners.

WHEN HEAVEN AND EARTH ARE SILENT

PIERRE CAUCHON

The bishop who burnt Saint Joan

Thomas de Quincey, the English essayist and opium-eater, imagined a merciful end for Pierre Cauchon, the French bishop who sent his country's national heroine, Joan of Arc, to the stake. At the end of his 1847 essay on Joan, de Quincey conjures up the bishop on his deathbed, 'haunted and waylaid by the most frightful of his crimes'. In his dreams Cauchon finds himself once more in Joan's native village of Domrémy, where he sees a woman seated by a fountain, her face hidden, but as he draws nearer the woman raises her wasted features. 'Would Domrémy know them again for the features of her child? Ah, but *you* know them, bishop, well! Oh, mercy! what a groan was *that* which the servants, waiting outside the bishop's dream at his bedside, heard from his labouring heart ...'

PIERRE CAUCHON, BISHOP OF BEAUVAIS AND OF LISIEUX

Born 1371, in Reims, France
Died of natural causes, 15 December 1442, in Rouen, France

The bishop seeks rest and respite in the forest beyond the village, but finds there instead a tumult of armies and nations assembling, while 'towering in the fluctuating crowd are phantoms that belong to departed hours'. They are gathering around 'a tribunal that rises to the clouds', and in the dock is Cauchon himself, who must, like Joan, face his accusers alone, without counsel.

> Alas! the time is short, the tumult is wondrous, the crowd stretches away into infinity; but yet I will search in it for somebody to take your brief; I know of somebody that will be your counsel. Who is this that cometh from Domrémy? Who is she in bloody coronation robes from Rheims? Who is she that cometh with blackened flesh from walking the furnaces of Rouen? This is she, the shepherd girl, counsellor that had none for herself, whom I choose, bishop, for yours. She it is, I engage, that shall take my lord's brief. She it is, bishop, that would plead for you; yes, bishop, *she* – when heaven and earth are silent.

An unconscionable scoundrel?

De Quincey is kinder to Cauchon than many have been. Generations have represented the bishop, in the words of George Bernard Shaw in his preface to *Saint Joan*, as 'an unconscionable scoundrel', and have asserted that all the

PREVIOUS PAGE Bishop Cauchon interviews Joan in this engraving after the French painter Paul Delaroche (1797–1856).

OPPOSITE A Vichy French poster intended to stir up hatred of the English after the Allied bombing of Rouen, 1944. The slogan reads 'The assassins always return to the scene of their crimes', referring to the fact that Joan of Arc was burnt in Rouen.

questions he and others put to the Maid during her 1431 trial were traps. The process of vilifying Cauchon began with the inquiry that rehabilitated Joan a quarter-century after her death. But, Shaw argues,

> This rehabilitation was as corrupt as the contrary proceeding applied to Cromwell by our Restoration reactionaries. Cauchon had been dug up, and his body thrown into the common sewer. Nothing was easier than to accuse him of cozenage, and declare the whole trial void on that account. That was what everybody wanted, from Charles the Victorious, whose credit was bound up with The Maid's, to the patriotic Nationalist populace, who idolized Joan's memory. The English were gone; and a verdict in their favour would have been an outrage on the throne and on the patriotism which Joan had set on foot.

The political circumstances had changed, and Cauchon himself was dead (although he had not literally been dug up and thrown in the common sewer). The Inquisitor General's court of inquiry concluded in 1456 – shortly after the English had finally been expelled from their strongholds in Normandy and Gascony   that Joan was a

martyr who had been unjustly executed for heresy by a court that held no proper jurisdiction. Joan – the memory and legend of Joan – had now become a useful means to bolster a newly emerging French national identity.

This process was to gain momentum over the years, and by the 19th century there was growing public pressure in France to have Joan canonized; she was eventually declared a saint on 16 May 1920. During the Second World War, both the pro-German Vichy government of France and their enemies, the Gaullist Free French, claimed Joan as their own. The anti-British collaborationists could point out the perfidious role of the English in Joan's martyrdom, while the Maquisards could point out how French collaborators such as Cauchon had allied themselves with the foreign invaders and betrayed the interest and honour of France.

War of independence or dynastic tussle?

As is so often the case, the stories of Joan and Cauchon have been hijacked by those who have their own agendas. During the Hundred Years War France was as divided as it was to be during the German Occupation half a millennium later. Although Joan was later painted as the leader of the patriotic French resistance to the English invaders, and Cauchon as a treacherous collaborator, the Hundred Years War was in many ways a French civil war, with the country divided between the supporters of two rival dynastic claimants. In fact, in the context of feudal western Europe, in which nobles in one country also frequently held land in other countries and could thus owe fealty to more than one king, it is misleading to think of France at this stage as a country at all, in the sense of a fully fledged nation state. It is thus also problematic to think in terms of patriotism and its antithesis, treason.

The difficulties had begun a century before, in 1328, when with the death of Charles IV of France the Capetian dynasty had died out in the direct male line. Edward III of England, as a maternal grandson of Philip the Fair of France and a nephew of Charles IV, claimed the French throne, but it went instead to another of Charles's nephews, Philip of Valois, who became Philip VI. As dukes of Aquitaine, the kings of England – native French-speakers since the time of the Norman Conquest – had for generations ruled large areas of France as notional subjects of the French Crown, a situation that had often given rise to tension and conflict.

Edward III began his campaign against Philip VI in 1337 in Flanders, whose inhabitants were subjects of the French Crown but whose valuable cloth-weaving industry depended on imports of English wool; thus the Flemish supported the English claim. Things became even more complicated after 1384, when Flanders and Artois came into the possession of the powerful dukes of Burgundy, representatives of a junior branch of the French royal house; although subjects of the French Crown, the dukes of Burgundy ruled their vast lands in eastern and northern France as virtually independent princes. The mental incapacity of Charles VI of France (ruled 1368–1422) led to a fierce struggle for control between, on the one hand, Philip the Bold and his son John the Fearless of Burgundy, and, on the other, another junior branch of the French royal family, the dukes of Orléans. This instability was exploited by the English soldier-king, Henry V, who in 1415 won a stunning victory at Agincourt. The murder of John the Fearless in 1419, in which the French dauphin, the future Charles VII, was implicated, pushed John's son, Philip the Good, firmly into the English camp. Within a year, by the Treaty of Troyes, Charles VI had named Henry V as his successor, and given Henry the hand of his daughter Catherine in marriage. That might have been that, had not Henry died of a fever, aged 34, in 1422, two months before Charles VI. Henry's heir, Henry VI, was only nine months old; the baby's uncle, the Duke of Bedford, took over as regent.

> ❝You, the English captains, must withdraw from the kingdom of France and restore it to the King of Heaven and his deputy, the King of France, while the Duke of Burgundy should return at once to his true allegiance. Take yourself off to your own land, for I have been sent by God and his angels, and I shall drive you from our land of France. If you will not believe the message from God, know that wherever you happen to be, we shall make such a great Hahaye as has not been made in France these thousand years.❞
>
> Joan of Arc issues her challenge to the English and the Burgundians, March 1429

Enter the Maid

If Henry V had lived, the Anglo-French union would have been cemented. Even so, the Anglo-Burgundian regime controlled Paris, most of northern France and parts of the southwest. Reims, the traditional site for French royal coronations, was occupied by the Burgundians, so Charles VII could not even be crowned. Orléans, the only city north of the Loire still loyal to Charles, was under siege by the English. It was during these dark days that a peasant girl from the village of Domrémy in Lorraine, eastern France, announced that she had on several occasions heard the voices of Saints Michael, Catherine and Margaret telling her to rid France of the English invaders. In 1429 Joan, disguised as a man and now aged about nineteen, made her way through hostile Burgundian territory to Charles's court with an extraordinary proposal.

It is a measure of the desperation of his situation that Charles acceded to Joan's request to be provided with all the accoutrements of a knight, and to be put at the head of his army struggling to relieve the siege of Orléans. Within a matter of days she had led the French to victory; historians are divided as to whether her role was primarily one of raising morale, holding aloft her famous banner, or whether she was in fact a bold and skilled tactician. The 'Maid of Orléans' went on to lead, or inspire, a succession of further French victories, including the capture of Reims, where Charles was duly crowned on 17 July. Bishop Cauchon had been visiting the city, his birthplace, but slipped away before Joan and Charles – whom he had always opposed – arrived. When, the following May, Joan was captured by the Burgundians, Cauchon played a key role in negotiating her transfer to the English – for a price. He was to go on to become the chief agent of her destruction.

A political cleric

Pierre Cauchon, the son of a recently ennobled bourgeois family, was born in Reims in 1371. In her 1981 study of Joan of Arc, Marina Warner asserts that 'he had both the self-made man's characteristic impatience with the decadent aristocracy represented by the Valois court and a natural affinity with the fundamental hard-headedness of the court of Burgundy'. As a young man, Cauchon attended the

University of Paris, where he proved a brilliant student. He was selected to present the university's case to the Parlement regarding the Great Schism, the period of rupture in the Church during which the French Crown supported the alternative pope in Avignon, while the English and the Burgundians – and the University of Paris – supported the pope in Rome. Thereafter, Cauchon firmly identified himself with the Anglo-Burgundian cause, and patronage from John the Fearless then Philip the Good aided his ecclesiastical advancement. In 1407 he attempted to negotiate an ending to the Great Schism, raising his profile as an astute diplomat, and in 1414 Philip the Good selected him

> 'And this whole devilish war was continued and prolonged by three bishops: the Chancellor, a very cruel man, who was Bishop of Thérouanne; the then Bishop of Lisieux, formerly of Beauvais [i.e. Pierre Cauchon]; and the Bishop of Paris. There is no doubt that it was through their madness that many people were pitilessly killed, secretly and openly by drowning and by other means, not counting those who died in battle.'
>
> Anon., *Journal d'un bourgeois de Paris, 1405–99*, Lent 1435

to be his ambassador to the Council of Constance, which eventually ended the rift. In 1420 Cauchon was involved in the marriage negotiations between Henry V and Princess Catherine as part of the Treaty of Troyes, and as a reward was appointed Bishop of Beauvais. By now he held a number of benefices, including the archdeaconry of Chartres and the chaplaincy of the Duke of Burgundy's chapel in Dijon. His total income was now in excess of 2,000 livres per year.

The brief period of amity ended with the deaths of Charles VI and Henry V in 1422. Cauchon, who opposed the claims of Charles VII in favour of those of Henry VI, then returned to his diocese and from 1423 was a well-paid member of the Duke of Bedford's council. For some years the Valois cause looked hopeless, until its fortunes were revived by the appearance of Joan of Arc. In 1430, after accompanying the young Henry VI from London to Rouen, seat of the English government in France, Cauchon learned that Joan had been captured by the Burgundians near Compiègne. As Compiègne was in his diocese of Beauvais, Cauchon claimed the right to try her case. The charge was heresy.

Due process or entrapment?

Cauchon was paid 756 livres for his part in negotiating the transfer of Joan from the Burgundian vassal John of Luxembourg, and for the work he put into gathering evidence against her. He was not the only Frenchman involved in prosecuting her; more than a hundred 'assessors' attended her trial, and the vast majority of them were French-born, mostly members of the pro-Burgundian University of Paris or clerics in English-occupied areas.

The trial, which took place in Rouen, began in January 1431. An examination of Joan by the Duchess of Bedford confirmed her virginity, so her claims to purity could not be denied. But that still left the charge of heresy, on two grounds: her claim to hear the voices of saints and her habit of wearing men's clothing. Joan was given no counsel, and complained that there were no 'ecclesiastics of the French side' present. Nevertheless, she managed to avoid falling into various theological traps set for her, partly by refusing to testify on a number of matters. The court considered using torture, and she was shown the implements that might be used against her, but in the end the court decided against it. She had been weakened by fasting during Lent, and then, after eating a carp sent to her by Cauchon after Easter, she became ill. Those who wished to discredit her did not want her dying in prison before a verdict could be returned: that would make her a martyr, rather than a heretic or a hoaxer.

Cauchon meticulously went through all the procedures of due process, including requests to the clerics at the University of Paris for their opinions. He was determined to give the appearance that justice was being done; it was the only way to discredit Joan and the Valois cause she represented. But the Duke of Bedford grew impatient, and in May put pressure on Cauchon to bring things to a satisfactory conclusion.

Cauchon then came up with what hagiographers of Joan have regarded as a cunning plan, but quite how deliberate it was is difficult to assess; most of the evidence comes from the inquiry that rehabilitated Joan 25 years later. If he could get Joan to abjure her heresy – to admit that she had made up the voices, and to reject male attire – then she would be shown to be a fake, and she and her cause would be fatally damaged. He thus had Joan taken, on 24 May, to a cemetery in Rouen and placed upon a scaffold, where, before an audience that included Bedford, the Earl of Warwick, the Cardinal of Winchester and a clutch of bishops, she was preached at from a text in St John's Gospel: 'the withered branch must be thrown in the fire else the tree cannot flourish'. Thus threatened with burning, she put her mark on a declaration of recantation. As she could not read, it is unclear if she understood what she had signed.

> And in general, having cast aside all womanly decency, not only to the scorn of feminine modesty, but also of well instructed men, she had worn the apparel and garments of most dissolute men, and, in addition, had some weapons of defence.

Extract from the charges brought against Joan at her trial in 1431

Nevertheless, her recantation condemned her to imprisonment for the rest of her life, in solitary confinement, on a diet of bread and water. Legally, if convicted as a simple heretic, she could not be handed over to the secular authorities for burning; only a relapsed heretic – one who had recanted and then gone back to their heresy –

Bishop Cauchon looks on as Joan is tied to the stake, in this book illumination from *Vigiles de Charles VII* (1484) by Martial d'Auvergne.

could be sent to the stake. Thus Bedford and Warwick were furious with Cauchon. They wanted Joan – whom they believed to be a witch, a 'limb of the fiend' – dead. What is not clear is whether Cauchon did; nor is it clear to what extent he manipulated Joan to achieve her destruction.

But whatever Cauchon's intentions, within a few days Joan was wearing male attire again; it has been suggested that the clothing was left with her as a temptation, and some of the witnesses at the 1456 inquiry said that her women's clothes were actually taken away from her. Joan then sealed her fate by telling Thomas de Courcelles, the rector of the University of Paris, that she still heard her voices, and that she had only recanted 'for fear of the fire'. Perhaps faced with a lifetime in prison, and with the realization that all the ecstasy and glory of her previous life was now to be counted as nothing but a sham, she concluded that the flames offered a preferable fate.

On 30 May 1431 Joan was taken to the Vieux-Marché in Rouen. An anonymous contemporary Parisian journal-writer described her execution, and the divided opinion it inspired:

They bound her to a stake on the platform, which was made of plaster, and lit the fire under her. She died quickly, and her clothes were burned away; then they raked back the fire and showed her naked body to all the people so that they could see the secret parts that a woman should have, and there were no doubts left in their minds … Many people there and elsewhere said that she had died a martyr for her own true lord. Others said this was not so, and that the men who had supported her for so long had done wrong. That is how people talked, but whatever good or ill she had done, she was burnt that day.

In fact, she was burnt not just once, but three times. Her body was thus reduced to dust, and her ashes thrown into the River Seine. There were to be no relics left for those who might wish to begin a cult of the Maid of Orléans. Her executioner later admitted that he 'greatly feared to be damned'.

As for Cauchon, he continued his career in the Church, accompanying Henry VI to his coronation in Paris in 1432, and acquiring the bishopric of Lisieux, where in the cathedral he financed the building of a splendid vault. He failed to prevent the reconciliation of Philip the Good and Charles VII in 1435, and, as the English fortunes in France went into a terminal decline, he divided his later years between Rouen and Lisieux. He died suddenly, in Rouen on 15 December 1442, aged 71, probably of a heart attack, and is buried in his magnificent vault at Lisieux.

> 'My lord: I apologize to you for the word used by Messire John de Stogumber. It does not mean in England what it does in France. In your language traitor means betrayer: one who is perfidious, treacherous, unfaithful, disloyal. In our country it means simply one who is not wholly devoted to our English interests.'
>
> The Earl of Warwick to Cauchon, in Shaw's *Saint Joan* (1923)

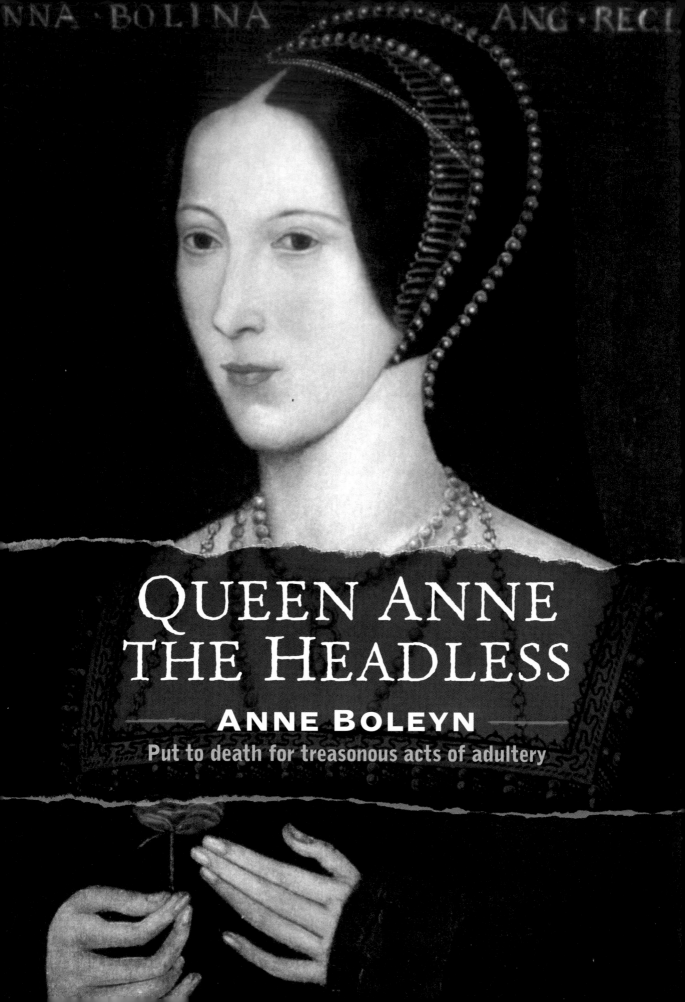

NNA · BOLINA   ANG · REGI

QUEEN ANNE
THE HEADLESS

ANNE BOLEYN

Put to death for treasonous acts of adultery

When Princess Diana gave her famously frank television interview to the BBC's *Panorama* programme in 1995 she may not have realized the danger she was courting. In admitting to an adulterous affair with Captain James Hewitt between 1987 and 1992, she was unknowingly admitting to high treason. Both she and her lover, if tried and found guilty, would have been liable to the death sentence.

Of course, no such charges were brought, but the law that could have made that possible is still on the statute book of the United Kingdom. The Treason Act of 1351 sought to codify all existing laws relating to treason, and among the offences that constitute high treason under the act is the violation of 'the King's companion, or the King's eldest daughter unmarried, or the wife of the King's eldest son and heir'. The notable jurist Sir William Blackstone wrote in his *Commentaries on the Laws of England* (1765–9) that 'the plain intention of this law is to guard the Blood Royal from any suspicion of bastardy, whereby the succession to the Crown might be rendered dubious'. Diana was, until her divorce in 1996, the wife of the monarch's eldest son and heir, Prince Charles, and the law specifies that if the sexual intercourse is consensual, then both parties are guilty of high treason, which, at the time of her affair, was still a capital offence. It was under this provision that two of the wives of Henry VIII, Anne Boleyn and Catherine Howard, lost their heads. In the case of Anne – the woman for whom Henry had moved heaven and earth to marry – the charges were almost certainly without foundation.

> **ANNE BOLEYN OR BULLEN, MARCHIONESS OF PEMBROKE**
>
> *Born* 1501 or 1507, possibly at Blickling, Norfolk, England
> *Died* beheaded 19 May 1536, in the Tower of London, England

> **'When a Man doth** compass or imagine the Death of our Lord the King, or of our Lady his Queen or of their eldest Son and Heir; or if a Man do violate the King's Companion or the King's eldest Daughter unmarried, or the Wife of the King's eldest Son and Heir; or if a Man do levy War against our Lord the King in his Realm, or be adherent to the King's Enemies in his Realm, giving to them Aid and Comfort in the Realm, or elsewhere …'
>
> Some of the offences comprising high treason, according to the Treason Act of 1351 (25 Edw. III St. 5 c. 2). Slaying the chancellor, treasurer or the king's justices was also considered high treason.

OPPOSITE **This portrait of Anne Boleyn,** by an unknown 16th-century English artist, can be seen at Hever Castle in Kent, where Anne spent her early childhood.

Learning to turn the heads of kings

Anne Boleyn was the daughter of Sir Thomas Boleyn, a courtier and diplomat, and Lady Elizabeth Howard, sister of the Duke of Norfolk. Around the age of twelve or thirteen she was sent to the Habsburg-ruled Low Countries, where her father was ambassador, as maid-of-honour to Margaret, Archduchess of Austria, who found her 'bright and pleasant for her young age'. Shortly afterwards she moved to France, where she served first Henry VIII's sister Mary, briefly betrothed to Louis XII, and then Queen Claude of France. While abroad, Anne not only learnt French but also acquired a good knowledge of literature, and also of French fashions and court culture. Although her dark eyes, black hair and olive skin were compelling, she was no conventional beauty, so her learning, wit and style stood her in good stead. She was graceful on the dance floor, lively in conversation and sang and played skilfully. A contemporary wrote that 'no one would ever have taken her to be English by her manners, but a native-born Frenchwoman'.

Back in England in 1521, Anne took up a position as maid-of-honour to Henry VIII's first wife, Catherine of Aragon, and quickly established herself as a leader of fashion at court. Another contemporary commented on her 'charm, style and wit, and will and savagery which make her a match for Henry'. That was still to come, however; at this stage the king had taken Anne's sister, Mary Boleyn, as his mistress, while Anne herself attracted a number of admirers, including Henry Percy, later 6th Earl of Northumberland, and the poet Sir Thomas Wyatt. The Percy match was barred by Percy's father, while Wyatt, who was already married, had become a victim of the popular pastime at court in which men and women played the roles of passionate lover and disdainful object of affection. The game of courtly love was intended as just that, an exercise in elegant public flirtation with no real emotional – let alone sexual – involvement. It seems, however, that Wyatt found that his heart had become ensnared – although there is no evidence that Anne reciprocated his feelings.

It was during these games of courtly love that Henry's interest in Anne was first aroused, and at some point in the mid-1520s he began his pursuit. Anne played

> 'Whoso list to hunt, I know where is an hind,
> But as for me, *hélas*, I may no more.
> The vain travail hath wearied me so sore,
> I am of them that farthest cometh behind.
> Yet may I by no means my wearied mind
>   Draw from the deer, but as she fleeth afore
>   Fainting I follow. I leave off therefore,
> Sithens in a net I seek to hold the wind.
> Who list her hunt, I put him out of doubt,
>   As well as I may spend his time in vain.
>   And graven with diamonds in letters plain
> There is written, her fair neck round about:
> *Noli me tangere*, for Caesar's I am,
> And wild for to hold, though I seem tame.'

Sir Thomas Wyatt, 'Whoso List to Hunt', in which the 'hind' is Anne Boleyn, whom Wyatt at one time courted. 'Caesar' is, of course, Henry VIII.

for the highest stakes. It was clear to everybody that Queen Catherine had failed to fulfil her dynastic duty: a series of confinements had only provided the king with a single heir, Princess Mary; the rest had ended in miscarriages or stillbirths. What the king needed was a boy, but with the queen now past childbearing age there seemed little hope of that.

So when Henry began to play the game of courtly love with Anne, and found like Wyatt his heart had become ensnared, she spurned his physical advances. She was not going to settle for the position of royal mistress as her sister had done; she wanted more than that. She wanted to be queen.

The king's 'great matter'

It was this combination of dynastic and personal desires that led Henry to pursue his 'great matter', his quest for a divorce from his wife, Catherine of Aragon. But Catherine was the aunt of the Habsburg emperor, Charles V, and at the time Charles's armies occupied Rome. The pope was thus no more than an imperial pawn, and was obliged to do the emperor's bidding – which in this instance was to deny Henry a divorce. For years Cardinal Wolsey, Henry's lord chancellor, worked on Henry's behalf to achieve an annulment, but to no avail; and his failure led to his fall.

In the end Henry's lust for Anne and desire for a son led to the momentous break with Rome. The death in August 1532 of William Warham, Archbishop of Canterbury, removed a major obstacle: Warham had increasingly resisted Henry's attempts to subject the Church to the will of the state. Sometime after this Henry and Anne began to sleep together, and she was already pregnant when they married in secret on 25 January 1533. On 30 March Thomas Cranmer was consecrated as Archbishop of Canterbury on the clear understanding that he was to solve Henry's marital difficulties, and on 10 April he duly obliged by declaring Henry's marriage to Catherine null and void. In June Anne was crowned as queen consort, and the following month Henry was excommunicated by the pope. The Act of Supremacy of 1534 made Henry supreme head of the Church in England, so retrospectively lending legal respectability to all that had gone before. The political management of all this had been handled by Henry's new fixer and chief minister, Thomas Cromwell.

So far to fall

But it did not all turn out as happily as either Henry or Anne might have wished. On 7 September 1533 Anne had given birth to a baby girl, Elizabeth. It was a bitter disappointment to Henry, who had gone to all this trouble just for another female heir. The irony of it gave comfort to many conservatives; there was still much sympathy for Catherine and her bastardized daughter Mary at court, and in the country at large. The Boleyns and their faction had been in the ascendant at court for some years: Anne's father, Sir Thomas, had been created Earl of Wiltshire in 1529, and her brother George was a member of the privy chamber, the king's influential inner circle; Anne herself was now Marchioness of Pembroke in her own

HENRY'S OTHER VICTIMS

DURING HENRY'S REIGN treason charges were brought against many whom the king regarded as enemies or potential rivals – or who simply stood in his way. Often the grounds were spurious, and the evidence thin or non-existent. Some of Henry's more prominent victims are noted below.

SIR RICHARD EMPSON and **EDMUND DUDLEY**, whose activities as collectors of taxes and fines for Henry's father, Henry VII, had made them deeply unpopular. On assuming the throne Henry set about ingratiating himself with his subjects by having his father's two loyal servants executed for treason in 1510.

EDWARD STAFFORD, 3rd Duke of Buckingham, a proud young magnate whose extravagant lifestyle, royal blood and powerful connections made Henry suspicious. An anonymous letter accused him of treasonable talk, and he was executed in 1521.

CARDINAL WOLSEY, who failed to obtain a divorce for Henry from the pope, died in 1530 on his way to London to face treason charges. 'If I had served God as diligently as I have done the king,' he remarked bitterly, 'He would not have given me over in my grey hairs.'

SIR THOMAS MORE, who resigned as Henry's lord chancellor in 1532. His conscience prevented him from acknowledging Henry as supreme head of the Church in England, and he was beheaded in 1535.

HENRY COURTENAY, 10th Earl of Devon, a grandson of Edward IV and a cousin of Henry. He was executed in 1539 on the basis of a few unwise remarks, having fallen out with Thomas Cromwell.

THOMAS CROMWELL, Henry's minister who had engineered Anne's death, was himself executed in 1540 after his own fall from grace.

MARGARET POLE, Countess of Salisbury, who was the niece of Edward IV and Richard III, and therefore a potential dynastic rival to the Tudors, although she was 67 at the time of her death in 1541, and her eldest son had been executed in 1539. She violently resisted when the time came for her own sentence to be carried out, and, as she struggled, the first blow of the axe missed her neck and instead hit her shoulder. It took the executioner, 'a wretched and blundering youth', several more blows to finish her off.

CATHERINE HOWARD, Henry's fifth wife, who was beheaded for adultery in 1542. Young and indiscreet, she had certainly had lovers before her marriage, and possibly afterwards.

HENRY HOWARD, Earl of Surrey, the poet and soldier, who was executed in 1547 after he had fallen out of favour. The only charge against him was that he had included the arms of Edward the Confessor in his own heraldry, which the paranoid old king saw as a threat to the Tudor line.

right. Such an ascendancy inevitably instilled jealousy among those who were not so highly favoured. This discontent might have rumbled on harmlessly had not Cromwell, and the king himself, eventually turned against the queen.

Anne had so long played the game of courtly love before becoming Henry's wife that she found it difficult to adapt from the role of coquette to that of submissive and dutiful wife. Indeed, it was not in her character to do so. Her relationship with Henry continued to be turbulent, full of tantrums and reconciliations. A miscarriage in August 1534 appears to have dented Henry's sexual confidence (Anne herself dropped a hint to this effect), and it was not until 1535 that she conceived again, only to be delivered of a stillborn son in January 1536 (later Catholic propagandists insisted that she had miscarried a 'shapeless mass of flesh', but there is no evidence of this). Henry – an egotistical, mean-spirited, self-deluded monster, pious when it suited him – convinced himself that God had somehow been offended. He was equally sure that it could not have been him who had caused the offence.

It was around this time that the king's eye came to rest on a young woman at court called Jane Seymour, one of the queen's maids-of-honour. Jane was Anne's opposite in every respect: fair, pale-skinned, demure, pliant; she was also some years younger. Henry's heart skipped another beat. He was hooked; and Anne was doomed.

Anne was especially doomed because Henry had married her for love, not political or financial expediency – the usual basis of royal marriages. Following her miscarriage her enemies saw their chance. Jane's family encouraged her to reciprocate the king's interest, while holding out for the big prize: marriage. The powerful Seymours, who aligned themselves with the religious reformers, made common cause with the conservatives, and deliberately and subtly set about poisoning the mind of the king against Anne. They also lobbied Cromwell, who had hitherto seen a convergence between his and the queen's interests.

A victim of *Realpolitik*

There were four reasons for the ambitious Cromwell to move against Anne. The first was his master's need for a son; Anne had shown herself incapable of providing one, so the king must have a new, younger, more fecund wife – and had already publicly shown his interest in Jane Seymour. The second reason was Anne's opposition to Cromwell's handling of the dissolution of the monasteries, which Cromwell primarily intended as a means to fund the king's many extravagances; Anne, who had been influenced by the new humanism while in France, believed the resources yielded by the dissolution should be directed to the establishment of charitable educational foundations. Thirdly, although the Boleyn faction in the privy chamber had hitherto been Cromwell's allies, they also constrained his room for manoeuvre. Finally, Cromwell and others wanted to achieve a foreign-policy realignment, shifting from the existing alliance with France to a rapprochement with the Habsburgs. Henry was determined to get the Emperor Charles V to recognize Anne as his queen; Charles's refusal to do this was an obstacle in the way of diplomatic realignment – so long as Anne was still on the scene. Some time in the early spring of 1536 Anne and Cromwell openly quarrelled.

If ever there was a victim of *Realpolitik* it was Anne. But the queen was a woman of spirit, and was not going to go down without fighting. On 2 April 1536 her almoner, John Skip, preached a sensational Passion Sunday sermon, undoubtedly with

her approval, in which he openly criticized the attacks and depredations of Cromwell and the reformers. His words were reported thus by someone in the congregation:

> He wished that men would therein use a more temperance and first amend their own lives before they taxed other men's … Nowadays many men … rebuke the clergy … because they would have from the clergy their possessions.

Even more sensationally, he made an implied comparison of King Henry with King Solomon, who

> … in the latter end of his reign … became very un-noble and defamed himself sore by sensual and carnal appetite in taking of many wives and concubines and also by avaricious mind in laying too great or sore burdens and yokes upon his subjects, over-pressing them too sore thereby.

Thus Anne set herself up as effective leader of the opposition. She also set herself up for a fall.

Cromwell's coup

Cromwell's move against Anne came with great rapidity. He knew that Henry was a tyrant, but a tyrant who liked to tyrannize within the framework of the law. So Cromwell through his career made sure that the king's wishes were fulfilled through

Greenwich Palace, also known as the Palace of Placentia ('pleasant place'). It was here that Anne Boleyn and Henry VIII were seen having a row shortly before her arrest.

due legal process, in particular by deploying the law of treason against anyone who appeared to stand in the king's way. Skip had preached his sermon on 2 April; just three weeks later, on 24 April, the court to try Anne had been set up. Henry himself had not yet terminally turned against his queen; on 25 April he was writing to his ambassador in Rome of 'the likelihood and appearance that God will send us heirs male', and referred to 'our most dear and most entirely beloved wife, the queen'.

The charges that were to be brought against Anne were adultery, incest and high treason, but at this stage none of this was made public. First, Cromwell needed to assemble the 'evidence' – and quickly. To this end he rounded up a number of the Boleyn faction and their retainers and had them accused of having carnal knowledge of the queen. What may have prompted Cromwell to pursue this line was the ambience of public flirtation in Anne's circle, where the game of courtly love was a popular pastime. And if the queen were shown to be an adulterer, then that would explain why God had decreed she should not provide Henry with a male heir. Cromwell knew how to pander to Henry's enormous capacity for self-pity.

The queen did not help herself. Either on Saturday 29 April or the following day she was seen to be engaged in an emotional argument with Henry Norris, groom of the stool and the most influential member of the Boleyn faction, who may well have

> ‘Never prince had wife more loyal in all duty and in all true affection than you have ever found in Anne Bullen – with which name and place I could willingly have contented myself, if God and your grace's pleasure had so been pleased.’
>
> Anne Boleyn protests her innocence to Henry from the Tower of London, 6 May 1536. The original of this letter is lost; it appears in *Scrinia Sacra: Mysteries of State and Government in Letters of Illustrious Persons* (1691), and may not be authentic.

> 'A time thou haddest above thy poor degree,
> The fall where of thy friends may well bemoan:
> A rotten twig upon so high a tree
> Hath slipped thy hold, and thou art dead and gone.'

Extract from an elegy attributed to Sir Thomas Wyatt, mourning the fate of the men condemned with Anne. These lines refer to Mark Smeton.

become infatuated with the queen. Shortly after this, Anne and Henry were seen to be having a row at Greenwich Palace. The same day as the argument between Norris and the queen, a young musician on the fringes of Anne's circle, a commoner called Mark Smeton, was seen mooching about the queen's presence chamber. She asked him why he was so sad, and he replied that it was no matter. 'You may not look to have me speak to you as I should do to a nobleman, because you are an inferior person,' Anne told him. 'No, no, Madam,' Smeton replied, 'A look sufficeth, thus fare you well.' This exchange was promptly reported to Cromwell, who must have rubbed his hands with glee. In no time Smeton found himself at Cromwell's house in Stepney. It seems unlikely that Smeton was tortured, but psychological pressure applied to this vulnerable young man (and perhaps the threat of the thumbscrew and the rack) did the trick: after 24 hours of questioning he eventually crumbled and confessed to adultery with the queen.

The unwitting dominoes lined up by Cromwell now fell. Henry's suspicions of Norris were vindicated by Smeton's confession, and Norris was arrested on 1 May. The following day Anne herself was taken to the Tower, where she appears to have suffered some kind of breakdown and babbled in a way that her accusers took as self-incriminatory. Shortly afterwards three other men of the Boleyn faction were arrested and charged with adultery with the queen: Sir Francis Weston, William Brereton (a groom in the privy chamber) and Anne's own brother, George Boleyn, Viscount Rochford. In the meantime, Henry had worked himself up into a lather of morbid self-pity, claiming that Anne had slept with more than a hundred men, weeping and thanking God that he and his sister had 'escaped the hands of that cursed and poisoning whore who had planned to poison them'. None of this, of course, dulled his ardour for Jane Seymour, with whom he keenly continued his dalliance, while she played hard to get.

Justice in the service of the king

On 12 May Norris, Weston, Brereton and Smeton were tried at Westminster Hall, all but the last maintaining their innocence. As was standard in Tudor treason trials, the defendants were given no advance notice of the evidence against them, nor

> 'When the queen first came into the tower, she said, 'Master Kingston, shall I die without justice?' and he answered 'The poorest subject the king hath has justice;' and therewith she laughed.'

Charles Knight, *Popular History of England* (1857)

were they allowed defence counsel. The imperial ambassador, Eustace Chapuys, summarized the proceedings for his master, Charles V, in a letter dated 19 May:

> Only the groom [Smeton] confessed that he had been three times with the said *putain* [whore] and Concubine. The others were condemned upon presumption and certain indications, without valid proof or confession.

Cromwell made sure that the jury comprised men who owed him or the king favours (or one of the accused money), and they returned the required verdict. Although all four men were sentenced to be hanged, drawn and quartered, the king (perhaps in belated but unstated acknowledgement that the men were innocent stooges) commuted this to a simple beheading, and they thus escaped the horrors of castration and disembowelment while still alive.

Anne and her brother George were tried on 15 May in the King's Hall in the Tower before a jury of peers presided over by their uncle, the Duke of Norfolk, and some two thousand spectators. Although Cromwell could not pack a jury of peers, he knew they knew their duty to the king.

Anne had recovered her composure, as one of those present later attested: 'She made so wise and discreet answers to all things laid against her, excusing herself with her words so clearly as though she had never been faulty to the same.' The 'things laid against her' were summarized by Chapuys in his letter to the emperor:

> What she was principally charged with was having cohabited with her brother and other accomplices; that there was a promise between her and Norris to marry after the King's death, which it thus appeared they hoped for; and that she had received and given to Norris certain medals, which might be interpreted to mean that she had poisoned the late Queen [Catherine of Aragon, who had died on 7 January that year] and intrigued to do the same to the Princess [Mary]. … She was also charged, and her brother likewise, with having laughed at the King and his dress, and that she showed in various ways she did not love the King but was tired of him.

In addition to making mock of her husband, there was also the tricky charge of slandering the king's virility:

> I must not omit, that among other things charged against him [George] as a crime was, that his sister had told his wife that the King '*nestoit habile en cas de soy copuler avec femme, et quil navoit ne vertu ne puissance*' [i.e. he was impotent]. This he was not openly charged with, but it was shown him in writing, with a warning not to repeat it. But he immediately declared the matter, in great contempt of Cromwell and some others, saying he would not in this point arouse any suspicion which might prejudice the King's issue. He was also charged with having spread reports which called in question whether his sister's daughter was the King's child. To which he made no reply.

Detail from Edouard Cibot's 1835 painting of Anne Boleyn in the Tower of London, where she was imprisoned, tried and beheaded.

George and Anne were duly condemned, a verdict that they accepted with dignity – even though analysis of the details of the charges relating to Anne's supposed adultery reveal that in most cases either Anne or her alleged lover were not at the location specified on the date in question. In addition, none of Anne's ladies, who would know about all the intimate comings and goings around the queen, were produced as witnesses for the prosecution. Nor were any other witnesses called.

The Earl of Northumberland, who had courted Anne so many years before, collapsed after he had joined his fellow peers in returning a verdict of guilty; and the judge, the Duke of Norfolk, wept as he handed out the sentences of death to his nephew and niece.

A JUDICIAL PARADOX

ON 17 MAY 1536, two days after Anne was found guilty of adultery, Archbishop Cranmer declared that her marriage to Henry was null and void. This meant not only that her daughter Elizabeth was now illegitimate, but that Anne had never been properly married to Henry in the first place – thus she could not, by definition, be guilty of adultery. Needless to say, no one at the time cared to point this out.

At the king's pleasure

Anne was to be 'burnt or beheaded at the king's pleasure'. Burning was the standard sentence for female traitors, but Henry, having crushed the woman for whose love he had once risked eternal damnation, now saw fit to be merciful. Not only did he opt for beheading, but he employed the executioner of Calais, a master of the Continental style, in which the victim knelt upright as the headsman took a single horizontal swipe with a heavy sword. This was neater than the normal English method, in which the victim placed their head upon a block while the executioner made one or more attempts to sever their neck with his axe.

Knowing of the method by which she was to die, Anne mockingly styled herself 'Queen Anne the Headless' – her levity perhaps deriving from relief that she was not to burn. 'I heard say the executioner was very good,' she told the constable of the Tower, 'and I have a little neck.' With this she put her hands round her throat and gave a laugh. But although she spent her remaining time reconciling herself with her sentence and with her God, on the night before her execution she twice swore on the sacrament that she was innocent.

The end came on 19 May within the Tower, in front of an audience of a thousand. George Boleyn died first, followed by his sister. A contemporary Spaniard left the following account:

> The said Queen (unjustly called) finally was beheaded upon a scaffold within
> the Tower, with the gates open. She was brought by the captain upon the said
> scaffold, and four young ladies followed her. She looked frequently behind her
> and when she got upon the scaffold was very much exhausted and amazed. She

begged leave to speak to the people, promising to say nothing but what was good. The captain gave her leave, and she began to raise her eyes to heaven, and to cry mercy to God and to the King for the offence she had done [in fact, she never admitted guilt], desiring the people always to pray to God for the king, for he was a good, gentle, gracious and amiable prince. She was then stripped of her short mantle furred with ermine, and afterwards took off her hood, which was of English make, herself. A young lady presented her with a linen cap with which she covered her hair, and she knelt down, fastening her clothes about her feet, and one of the said ladies bandaged her eyes.

Immediately the executioner did his office, and when her head was off it was taken by a young lady and covered with a white cloth …

The executioner received his generous fee of £23 6s 8d and returned to France. The next day Henry became betrothed to Jane Seymour, and their marriage took place on 30 May. The following year Jane gave birth to a son, but within a fortnight she herself was dead from puerperal fever. Cromwell's ascendancy did not last: although raised to the peerage as the 1st Earl of Essex in July 1536, his desire for an alliance with the Protestant princes of Germany led him to arrange for the king to marry Anne of Cleves, whom he portrayed as a great beauty. But when in 1540 she arrived in England Henry was revolted by this 'Flanders Mare', and Cromwell's many enemies took the opportunity to poison the king against him. Henry showed Cromwell none of the killing kindness he had bestowed on Anne: instead, he ordered that the execution of his faithful servant be carried out by an inexperienced youth, who only succeeded in severing the head on the third attempt.

As for Anne Boleyn, for years little was said or remembered of her. But in 1544 Henry decreed that his son Edward, if he had no issue, was to be succeeded by Princess Mary, and if she died without issue, the crown was to pass to Anne's daughter, Princess Elizabeth, bastardized in the wake of her mother's conviction. As fate would have it, both Edward and Mary proved to be childless, and in 1558 Queen Elizabeth I ascended the throne, so beginning what many of her subjects believed to be one of the most glorious reigns in British history.

> 'To all other sinister judgements and opinions, whatsoever can be conceived of man against that virtuous queen, I object and oppose again (as instead of answer) the evident demonstration of God's favour, in maintaining, preserving, and advancing the offspring of her body, the lady Elizabeth, now queen.'
>
> John Foxe, *Acts and Monuments* (1563). Early in the reign of Elizabeth I, the Protestant martyrologist begins the rehabilitation of the young queen's mother, Anne Boleyn.

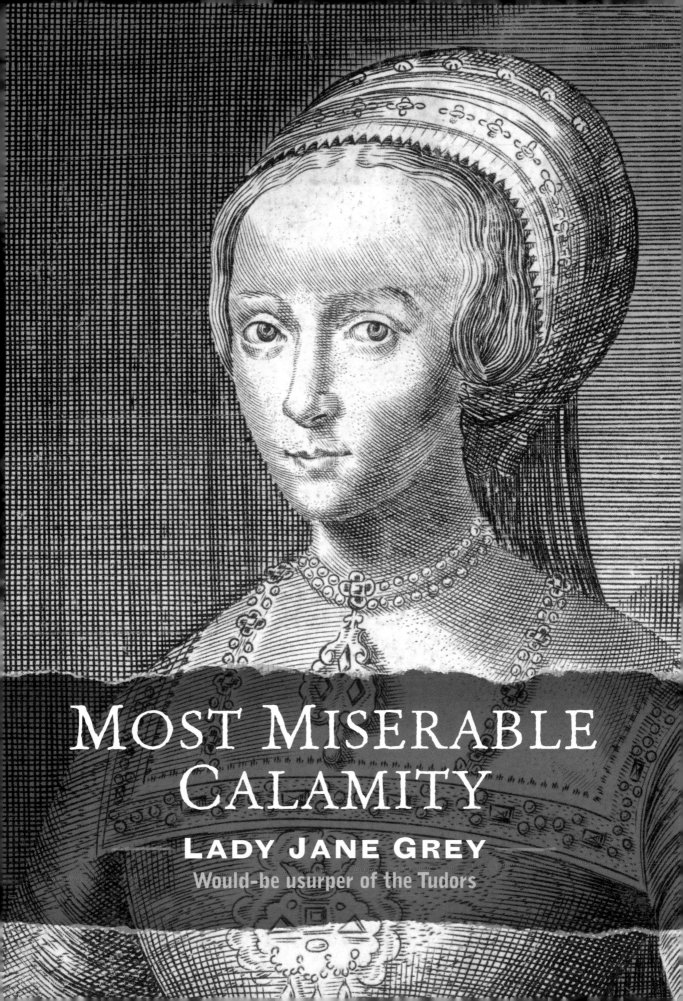

Most Miserable Calamity

Lady Jane Grey

Would-be usurper of the Tudors

Few today mention 'Queen Jane of England', whose nine-day reign was the shortest in English history. She was just fifteen at the time, reluctantly pushed onto the throne by her ambitious father-in-law, the Duke of Northumberland, who, in order to preserve his own power, tore up the Act of Succession put in place by Jane's great-uncle, Henry VIII. Jane's claim to the throne was at best tenuous, and her unwilling usurpation of the legally sanctioned heir, Henry's Catholic daughter Mary, opened her up to the charge of treason – for which she was to lose her head. She was only sixteen when she died.

LADY JANE GREY

Born October 1537, at Bradgate, Leicestershire, England
Died beheaded 12 February 1554, in the Tower of London, England

Lady Jane Grey – a young woman renowned for her intelligence, her beauty and her devout Protestant faith – was the daughter of Henry Grey, Marquis of Dorset and later Duke of Suffolk, and Frances Brandon, daughter of Mary Tudor, the sister of Henry VIII. In the Act of Succession of 1544, Henry had laid down that he should be succeeded by his son Edward; then, if Edward died childless, he was to be succeeded by Henry's daughter Mary; and if she died childless, she was to be succeeded by Henry's younger daughter, Elizabeth (the future Elizabeth I). In his will Henry had named the heirs of his sister Mary as next in the line of succession after his own children and their heirs. Jane's mother gave up her claim in favour of her daughter, whom she trained up to attract the highest bidder.

A pawn in the power play

As a young girl Jane baulked at the severe treatment she received from her parents, who expected perfection in everything she did. It must have been some relief when, at the age of nine, she was sent to live in the household of Catherine Parr, the sixth and last wife of Henry VIII. Here she received instruction in the kind of evangelical Protestantism of which Catherine was an adherent, as well as a sound education in both modern and ancient languages, including Hebrew. When she was only twelve or so, the humanist scholar Roger Ascham found her reading Plato in the original Greek 'with as much delight as some gentlemen would read a merry tale in Boccaccio'. She was no goody-goody, though, and could show a rough edge to her tongue. When one of her tutors returned to Catholicism, she did not hesitate to denounce him as a

PREVIOUS PAGE Line engraving (1648) of Lady Jane Grey, by William Marshall, after Willem and Magdalena de Passe.

> '... when I am in presence either of father or mother, whether I speak, keep silence, sit, stand or go, eat, drink, be merry or sad, be sewing, playing, dancing, or doing anything else, I must do it, as it were ... even so perfectly as God made the world, or else I am so sharply taunted, so cruelly threatened, yea presently some times with pinches, nips and bobs ... that I think myself in hell.'

Lady Jane Grey, complaining as a girl of her treatment at the hands of her parents, for whom she was a means to further their own ambitions

'deformed imp of Satan' and an 'unashamed paramour of Antichrist'.

On his death, Henry VIII was succeeded by his nine-year-old son, Edward VI. Henry's widow, Catherine Parr, married Thomas Seymour, the Lord Admiral, who was the brother of the regent, Edward Seymour, Duke of Somerset, and of the late Jane Seymour, mother of the young king. After Catherine Parr's death in childbirth, Thomas Seymour, an ambitious man, began to pay court to Princess Elizabeth, although this came to nothing. He also made Lady Jane his ward (paying her parents a large sum of money for the privilege), and planned to marry her to the priggish King Edward, whose Protestant fervour was, if anything, stronger than her own. (On one occasion, aged only eleven, he wrote to his uncle, the Protector Somerset, condemning those who waste their time 'on the follies and vanities of this world – spending it in trifling sports and diversions, from whence comes no profit or benefit to themselves or mankind'. As for himself, young Edward set about writing *A Small Treatise against the Primacy of the Pope*.)

But Thomas Seymour overreached himself, and in March 1549 was executed for treason after he had plotted to overthrow his own brother. Somerset himself fell from favour in October, and three years later, on 22 January 1552, the young king coolly noted in his journal that: 'The Duke of Somerset had his head cut off upon Tower Hill between eight and nine o'clock in the morning.'

The agent of Somerset's downfall was another fiercely ambitious Protestant magnate, John Dudley, Earl of Warwick and later Duke of Northumberland. Northumberland, a rapacious and power-hungry man, became the new regent, and his policy of religious intolerance seems to have been principally aimed at getting his hands on the wealth of the Church.

The last days of Edward

Northumberland's position came under threat in 1552, when Edward contracted both measles and smallpox. Should the young king die he would, according to the Act of Succession, be succeeded by the Catholic Mary, who would undoubtedly have had Northumberland's head. Although Edward appears to have recovered, by early the next year he was showing the symptoms of consumption – 'a tough, strong, straining cough' accompanied by 'a weakness and faintness of spirit'. Around this time Edward drew up a 'Device for the succession', whether as a school exercise or at the behest of Northumberland is unclear, but in it Edward specified that if he died without issue, the succession should go to 'the heirs male' of his fellow-Protestant, Lady Jane Grey, rather than his Catholic half-sister, Mary. The 1544 Act of Succession was thus brushed aside.

To put the last piece of the jigsaw in place, Northumberland then arranged for his son, Lord Guildford Dudley, to marry Jane; she was reluctant, young Dudley being her inferior both in intellect and character, but her father overrode her wishes and 'compelled her to accede to his commands by blows'. The marriage took place on 21 May 1553, but immediately afterwards Jane returned to live with her parents.

Not long afterwards, a medical student attached to the royal household was reporting on the king's condition:

> He does not sleep except he be stuffed with drugs … The sputum which he brings up is livid, black, fetid and full of carbon; it smells beyond measure … His feet are swollen all over. To the doctors these things portend death, and that within three months.

Around this time Edward asked his law officers to incorporate the terms of his 'Device' regarding the succession into a will. Perhaps because Lady Jane showed no signs of producing an heir (her relations with Dudley had not improved), in Edward's will the phrase 'the heirs male of the Lady Jane' was changed to read 'the Lady Jane and her heirs male'. This alteration was probably made by Northumberland – but almost certainly with the agreement of Edward, who was desperate to ensure the Protestant succession. Edward only lasted until 6 July, and with his last breath he reputedly prayed, 'O my Lord God, defend this realm from papistry, and maintain Thy true religion.'

The Nine Days Queen

As was customary, the king's death was kept secret for two days. There was a problem: as the dead king had been a minor, his will was technically invalid, and the changes to the succession the will proposed would anyway need the consent of Parliament. But Northumberland had the backing of the council, and, as the Imperial envoy Simon Renard observed at the time, 'The actual possession of power is a matter of great importance, especially among barbarians like the English.' Northumberland sent a party of men to arrest Mary, but the princess had retreated to her estates in Norfolk, where she had many loyal followers. Mary heard rumours of the king's death, but she had to make absolutely sure of it – for to declare herself queen while the king still lived would have been treason. Once she was certain, she wrote to the council in London, demanding their allegiance. They replied by asserting their allegiance was to Queen Jane, and by demanding Mary's submission.

On 9 July, the same day as Mary had declared herself queen, Jane – who had earlier feared she was being poisoned – was taken to Syon House, to the west of London, by one of Northumberland's daughters. Here she was formally told that

Edward had nominated her as his successor, and that she was therefore queen. By her own account, she was 'stupefied and troubled', and collapsed in tears, declaring herself insufficient to the task. But she also prayed that God would help her to govern the realm to his greater glory. The next day she travelled in state down the Thames to the Tower of London, where she was publicly proclaimed queen. To the intense annoyance of the Dudleys, she refused to make her husband king, protesting that 'the crown was not a plaything for boys and girls'.

Mary's counter-coup

It is clear that Northumberland had under-estimated the strength of will of his protégée, who was beginning to realize just how much she was being exploited. Northumberland had also badly miscalculated in other ways: although he had secured the support of the council, the populace at large were less than enthusiastic about Jane's accession. There was no public rejoicing, no bonfires, no ringing of bells. Many still felt sympathy for Princess Mary, despite her Catholicism, and remembered with distaste the ill treatment of her mother, Catherine of Aragon, by Henry VIII.

Mary herself was building up a following of armed men in Norfolk, and as the days passed many more flocked to her cause. As yet, Mary had no experienced commander, but neither did Northumberland, apart from himself. Aware that if he left London to take on Mary the unanimity of the council might collapse, he found that by 14 July he had no alternative, and rode out at the head of 1,500 men. But his army was soon melting away, as were some of the great lords who had at first supported Jane's accession.

> [The Queen was] very short and thin, but prettily shaped and graceful. Her hair was nearly red, her complexion good but freckled, and her teeth, when she smiled, white and sharp.

An Italian spectator describes Jane as she arrives in London to be publicly proclaimed queen, 10 July 1553

By 18 July Mary had 30,000 men at her disposal, and all across the country she was being proclaimed queen. In London, the council split, and the majority came out in favour of Mary – to great popular acclaim. The French ambassador was astonished: 'I have witnessed the most sudden change believable in men,' he wrote, 'and I believe God alone has worked it.' Even Jane's father, the Duke of Suffolk, realized the game was up, and on 19 July told his daughter she was no longer queen.

The failure of Northumberland's coup has been attributed to his universal unpopularity: not even ardent Protestants came out in support of him. But the popular consensus that Mary should succeed was not primarily due to Northumberland's unpopularity, nor to a widespread desire to restore the old religion. It was simply that Mary had been named as next in line to the throne in an act of Parliament, and the great body of opinion was that statute law outweighed the personal preferences of a king.

The fate of the Dudleys and the Greys

Jane's overthrow can thus be seen as a significant milestone on the road to democracy – even though Mary herself was to prove to be, by inclination, an absolutist. But for Jane herself the outcome was tragic.

Her father, remarkably, escaped scot-free, his swift-footed change of allegiance being rewarded with a pardon. Northumberland can never have expected anything other than the axe, which duly fell on 22 August, his last-minute conversion to Catholicism having failed to avert this doom. Jane was shocked at his apostasy: 'I pray God,' she exclaimed, 'I, nor no friend of mine, die so.' She and her husband were also sentenced to death for treason after a short trial on 19 November, although Mary had declared that her conscience prevented her from putting her cousin to death. The couple were confined to the Tower.

They might have lived, had not Mary made the most unpopular decision of her unpopular reign. This was her choice of husband, Philip II of Spain. Philip, leader of Catholic Europe, was anathema to Mary's fellow countrymen, who were incensed that England was to be put under the thumb of a foreign king. But Mary was obdurate. In protest, early in 1554 Sir Thomas Wyatt came out in rebellion, a rebellion in which

> 'Woe worth him! He hath brought me and our stock in most miserable calamity by his exceeding ambition.'
>
> Lady Jane Grey, on hearing of her father-in-law Northumberland's execution on 22 August 1553

Jane's father, the Duke of Suffolk, also took part – but in which Jane appears to not have participated. The rebellion was successfully suppressed, but Mary realized that she could no longer allow Jane – a possible figurehead for any future Protestant discontent – to live. Mary made one last attempt to save Jane's life, offering her a pardon if she converted to the Catholic faith. Jane refused, declaring: 'The faith of the Church must be tried by God's word, and not God's word by the Church; neither yet my faith.' Mary granted her cousin a private execution on Tower Green, a privilege usually reserved for royalty, and gave her the opportunity to see her husband one last time before his execution. Jane declined the latter offer.

Jane was calm on the day of her execution, 12 February 1554, adhering to the last to her Protestant faith, while her weeping attendants handed her a blindfold. The anonymous author of the contemporary *Chronicle of Queen Jane* reports on her last moments thus:

> She tied the kercher about her eyes; then feeling for the block said, 'What shall I do? Where is it?' One of the standers-by guiding her thereto, she laid her head down upon the block, and stretched forth her body and said: 'Lord, into thy hands I commend my spirit!' And so she ended.

After death Jane continued to be manipulated. Following the burnings of Mary's reign, and the anti-Catholic reaction that followed, Jane became numbered among the Protestant martyrs in works such as Foxe's *Acts and Monuments*, first published

The Execution of Lady Jane Grey, by Paul Delaroche, 1833. Queen Mary granted Jane a private execution, a privilege usually reserved for royalty.

in 1563. Her role as tragic Protestant champion continued through to the 19th century, when a sentimentalizing strain entered the Jane-ite discourse, emphasizing her innocence, youth and piety – an image encapsulated in Paul Delaroche's famous 1833 painting of her execution, in which the pale-skinned victim is dressed all in white for the sacrifice. This re-imagining necessitated the suppression of the real Jane. Innocent victim of *Realpolitik* she may have been, but this should not blind us to her undoubted intellectual gifts, her feistiness, her fervent faith, and her fearsomely strong will.

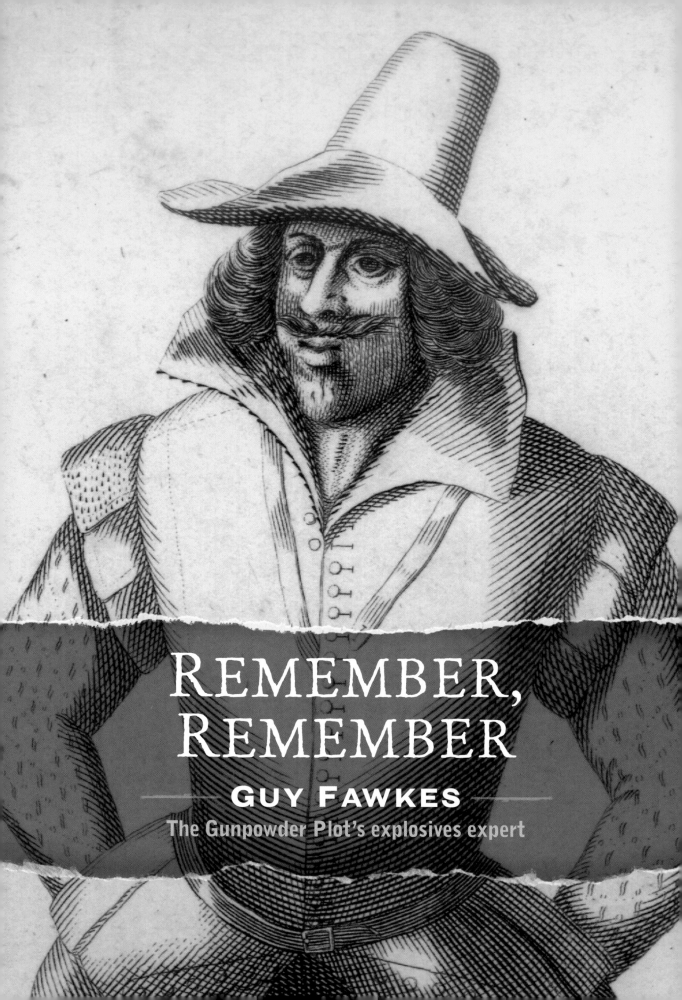

Remember, Remember

Guy Fawkes

The Gunpowder Plot's explosives expert

On one night every year, as the first fogs and chills of winter creep over the South Downs and up the River Ouse, the peace of the historic market town of Lewes in East Sussex is shattered as the streets fill with bands and banners and thousands of figures in fancy dress. Some carry flaming torches, others burning crosses, while others again bear elaborately constructed tableaux and grotesque effigies, some with their heads stuck on pikes. Eventually the crowds find their way to any of five enormous bonfires, where the effigies – of locally or nationally unpopular figures – are either burnt or blown apart by fireworks.

The identity of the figures to be destroyed varies from year to year – since the mid-19th century victims have included the Indian mutineer Nana Sahib, Cardinal Manning, the Mahdi, the Boer leader Paul Kruger, the Kaiser, the Russian Bear, Archbishop Makarios, Prime Minister Margaret Thatcher, Ayatollah Khomeini and Osama bin Laden. But two figures always feature: Pope Paul V, who became pontiff on 16 May 1605, and a man called Guido or Guy Fawkes, of whom nothing would be remembered had he not been caught attempting to blow up the king and Parliament on 5 November that same year.

> ### GUY OR GUIDO FAWKES
>
> *Born* 1570, in York, England
> *Died* hanged 31 January 1606, in Old Palace Yard, Westminster, England

Most towns and villages in Britain have long abandoned such violent and unashamedly anti-Catholic celebrations on 5 November – known as Guy Fawkes Night, Bonfire Night or Firework Night – and have replaced them with tightly controlled public firework displays or small private affairs in people's back gardens. Many places still burn on top of a big bonfire a crude dummy stuffed with straw or rags known as a 'guy', but few share in the spirit of bigotry and xenophobia that originally marked the celebrations, or remember that until 1859 it was a legal requirement to attend a special church service every 5 November to commemorate the foiling of what became known as the Gunpowder Plot.

> ‘Remember, remember
>   the Fifth of November,
> Gunpowder treason
>   and plot.
> I see no reason why
>   gunpowder treason
> Should ever be forgot.’
> Traditional English rhyme

OPPOSITE **An engraving c.1606** of Guy Fawkes, the man remembered in Britain every 5 November with bonfires and firework displays.

A century of turmoil

The century leading up to the Gunpowder Plot had seen much religious turmoil in England. When in the 1530s Henry VIII had made himself head of the English Church in order to obtain a divorce from Catherine of Aragon and marry Anne Boleyn, he unwittingly unleashed the Protestant Reformation in England. After his death, his sickly young son, Edward VI, pushed forward the Protestant agenda, but when he died, aged only fifteen, in 1553, he was succeeded by his fervently Catholic half-sister, Mary. Mary was a zealot, more interested in theological purity than good governance, and immediately set about the task of extirpating Protestantism from England. During her five-year reign some three hundred Protestant martyrs went to the stake – including seventeen in Lewes, and it is in memory of these local martyrs that the people of Lewes carry seventeen fiery crosses through the streets every Bonfire Night.

> We do, out of the fullness of our apostolic power, declare the foresaid Elizabeth to be a heretic … [and] to be deprived of her pretended title to the aforesaid crown …
>
> Pope Pius V, *Regnans in Excelsis* (1570)

The accession of Mary's Protestant half-sister Elizabeth in 1558 brought to the throne a very different character. Where Mary was driven into unwisdom by her faith, Elizabeth was an altogether shrewder, more pragmatic figure. 'I would not open windows into men's souls,' she famously said regarding her religious policy, which required outward conformity while not inquiring too closely as to private beliefs and practices. People were simply required to attend the services of the Church of England; those who did not were branded recusants.

Thus, in a few great houses up and down the country – mostly in the north, but also nearer London – a handful of powerful aristocrats and their extended families and retainers continued to hear the Mass. But even private adherence to the old faith became increasingly risky after the Catholic Mary Queen of Scots – thrown out of her own kingdom – sought refuge in England in 1568. The trouble was that the Roman Catholic Church recognized Mary – like Elizabeth, a granddaughter of Henry VII – as the rightful queen of England, and before long Mary became the focus of a number of plots against Elizabeth.

In 1570 Pope Pius V, following the failed rebellion in the north of England of the Catholic Earls of Northumberland and Westmorland, issued his bull *Regnans in Excelsis*. This excommunicated Elizabeth and deposed her from the throne, which gave her subjects licence (as far as the Roman Catholic Church was concerned) to disobey her authority and her laws, and to seek her overthrow. As can be imagined, this did not go down well, and when a Catholic barrister called John Felton nailed a copy of the bull to the door of the Bishop of London's residence, he was hanged.

In 1571 an international conspiracy known as the Ridolfi Plot came to light, after which the Duke of Norfolk, an ally of Mary Queen of Scots, was executed. In

France, thousands of Protestants were mercilessly put to death in the St Bartholomew's Day Massacre of 1572, while in the Netherlands the Dutch Protestants rose against their Catholic Spanish rulers. The atmosphere of paranoia and conspiracy thickened, and English Catholics were obliged by a new law to refute 'the power of the Bishop of Rome' and to swear an oath of allegiance to Elizabeth; failure to do so was treason. From 1580, the Jesuits began to infiltrate exiled English priests back into England to preach in secret; frequently this preaching was more political than theological, and government spies and *agents provocateurs* came up with considerable evidence of conspiracies: in 1583 the Throckmorton Plot was exposed, while in 1586 the Babington Plot was incontrovertibly linked to Mary Queen of Scots. The following year Elizabeth was eventually persuaded to sign Mary's death warrant. Within two months, the Spaniards had assembled an invasion fleet, but when it did eventually sail in 1588, the Armada was defeated and dispersed by the English navy and the English weather.

> 'The plot was to have blown up the king at such time as he should have been set in his royal throne, accompanied with his children, nobility and commoners, and assisted with all the bishops, judges and doctors, at one instant – a blast to have ruined the whole state and kingdom of England.'
>
> Sir Edward Hoby, letter to Sir Thomas Edmondes, English ambassador in Brussels, 19 November 1605

Catholic resistance

Mary's cause had attracted a number of romantically minded young men, struck by her beauty, her tragic history and her perilous situation. Such men were prepared to go to extreme lengths for her sake, convinced that their deaths would be but a moment of transition to eternal life. Their passionate devotion was in marked contrast to the majority of English Catholics, who restricted their activities to 'cogitations and inward opinions', and who, despite increasingly punitive measures against them, were content to obey the law of the land. Even this majority represented only a tiny section of the total population; the Armada had had the effect of cementing a sense of national solidarity among the English, an essential element of which became the rejection of Rome.

> 'Thus you see this crown [of England] is not like to fall to the ground for want of heads that claim to wear it, but upon whose head it will fall is by many doubted.'
>
> Thomas Wilson, *The State of England* (1600)

In the last decade of her life, speculation grew as to who would succeed the childless Elizabeth. The queen herself was silent on the matter, but many believed her most likely successor was James VI of Scotland, son of Mary Queen of Scots; unlike his mother, James was a Protestant.

In 1599 representatives of the pope had approached James to offer the support of English Catholics in return for religious toleration, but he had rejected this; in 1602 the pope offered James his support if he were to bring up his eldest son as a Catholic, but again James demurred. As it turned out, he did not need any of this proffered support; when Elizabeth died in 1603 James had the backing of the key players in England: Elizabeth's chief minister, Sir Robert Cecil, and the entire Privy Council. The fact that some of the more moderate English Catholics favoured Lady Arabella Stuart, a cousin of James, as their queen, and the more extreme ones gave their loyalty to the Infanta Isabella, daughter of Philip II of Spain, was neither here nor there.

Catholic resistance in England had been worn away by changes in public opinion and by the assiduous intelligence operations orchestrated by Elizabeth's cool-headed spymaster, Sir Francis Walsingham. But on mainland Europe there remained a rump of discontented, desperate Catholic exiles, hardened successors to the impressionable young men who had once sought to lay down their lives for Mary Queen of Scots. Many of them were effectively soldiers of fortune with Sir William Stanley's English regiment, which served alongside the Spanish against the Dutch rebels in the Low Countries. There was talk of an invasion of Alderney, a small island of no strategic significance in the Channel Isles; other exploits included attempts to counterfeit English coinage, and there was a successful theft of jewels and plate from Winchester Cathedral. It was a world of free-booters, of impoverished no-hopers, of younger sons looking for advancement. It was also a world of agents and double-agents, many of them – such as the Irishman Michael Moody, who had once planned to assassinate Queen Elizabeth by detonating gunpowder under her bed – willing to sell their services to the highest bidder.

> 'These things were the spurs that set those gentlemen upon that furious and fiery course which they afterwards fell into.'
> Father John Gerard, in his account of the Gunpowder Plot

Desperate diseases require desperate remedies

Among these exiled adventurers was an expert in military mining – the art of tunnelling under the enemy and then blowing him up – called Guy Fawkes. Fawkes, whom contemporaries described as 'highly skilled in matters of war', was a tall man of powerful build and striking appearance, with thick auburn hair, flamboyant moustache and full beard. He was also a man of strong character and great stead-fastness, courage and loyalty.

Fawkes was born in York, most probably in 1570 (the year of his baptism). Although his father, Edward Fawkes, appears to have been a convinced Protestant, two or three years after Edward's death in 1579 his widow married into a staunchly Catholic family, and it is presumed that Guy converted some time after that. He was educated at St Peter's School, York, which appears to have been something of a hotbed of recusancy. (The school still exists, and does not celebrate Bonfire Night.)

'He told me the nature of the disease required so sharp a remedy.'

Thomas Winter recalls, in his confession, how Robert Catesby informed him of his plan

In 1592, having sold up the small estate he had inherited from his father, Guy Fawkes went to seek his fortune fighting with Stanley's regiment in the Low Countries, where he changed his first name to Guido. Although a dedicated and courageous soldier, not much in the way of advancement or riches seems to have come his way: in 1599 he was reportedly 'in great want', and by 1602 he had risen no higher than the rank of ensign. Nevertheless, Stanley gave 'very good commendations of him' when in 1604 he was approached by a man called Thomas Winter, who was looking for an explosives expert. After establishing that Fawkes was trustworthy, Winter told him that there was 'a resolution to do somewhat in England, if the peace with Spain helped us not'. However, he added that he and his colleagues were 'as yet resolved upon nothing'.

A contemporary engraving of the Gunpowder Plotters by Crispijn van de Passe the Elder. The text is in Latin, French and German, indicating the international interest in the events described.

The Guy Fawkes of France

ON 5 JANUARY 1757 Robert-François Damiens, a man of humble origins in the throws of a religious mania, attacked King Louis XV with a knife. Although the wound was only slight, Damiens became notorious as the 'Guy Fawkes of France', and was the last man to suffer the traditional French punishment for regicides. The place appointed for his gruesome end was the Place de Grève in Paris, where he was tormented with red-hot pincers, and the hand that had wielded the knife was burnt with sulphur, molten lead and boiling oil. Then a horse was attached by ropes to each of his limbs, with the intention of tearing him apart; however, after several hours the desired effect was not achieved, so his ligaments were cut to make the job easier for the horses. Finally, his limbless trunk, apparently still with some life left in it, was burnt at the stake.

'The day (we all know) was meant to be the day of all our deaths ... It is our Passe-over.'

Bishop Lancelot Andrewes, preaching the first of his annual 'Gunpowder sermons' in 1606

This was not in fact the case. Winter was acting as a representative of a leading dissident Catholic, a young man called Robert Catesby, who at a meeting in London had already confided to Winter his plan to blow up Parliament, and asked Winter to go over to the Low Countries and bring back a trustworthy gentleman 'such as you shall understand best for this business'. Catesby explained his choice of target to Winter thus: 'In that place have they done us all the mischief and perchance God hath designed that place for their punishment.' Winter, in his confession after his arrest, recalled that Catesby then 'told me the nature of the disease required so sharp a remedy, and asked me if I would give my consent. I told him Yes, in this or what else soever, if he resolved upon it, I would venture my life …' The language – as is so often the case among religiously inspired terrorists – is of purging, of purification, of sacrifice and death.

It was, indeed, a desperate, hopeless gesture. With Spain and England conducting peace negotiations, the chance of a Spanish army landing in England to restore Catholicism was reduced to zero. Catesby concluded that there was only one thing for it: to act without outside aid. He seems to have believed that with the king and aristocracy spattered in bits across the City of Westminster the English would see the error of their ways, rise up against the Protestant establishment and return to Rome. Whether Guy Fawkes was so naïve it is difficult to tell; some historians believe he may have been in it at least partly for the money.

Shall we always talk and never do anything?

At first, Fawkes did not know any more than that there was 'a resolution to do somewhat in England'. When he arrived in London in the spring of 1604, Winter took him to see Catesby at a house in Lambeth. At this stage only Winter, Catesby and a third conspirator, John Wright, knew Catesby's purpose, but when Thomas Percy, a cousin of the Earl of Northumberland, joined them in May – angrily asking 'Shall we always, gentlemen, talk and never do anything?' – Catesby decided the time was ripe to let Fawkes and Percy in on the plan. But first they all had to swear an oath of secrecy, which they did in an upper room of a house in Butcher's Row, near the church of St Clement Danes:

> Ye shall swear by the Blessed Trinity and by the Sacrament ye now prepare to receive never to disclose directly or indirectly by word or circumstances the matter that shall be proposed to you to keep secret nor desist from the execution thereof until the rest shall give you leave.

Father John Gerard, who was at this stage unaware of the plot, then administered communion in a neighbouring room, after which they returned to the room where they had sworn the oath. Here Percy and Fawkes, having blindly committed themselves, were let in on Catesby's plan.

The first requirement was to find a property to rent near the Houses of Parliament. They found premises on the river side of the buildings, which they rented in Percy's name, and to which they obtained access in December. Meanwhile, on the other side of the Thames, in Catesby's lodgings in Lambeth, they had begun to accumulate the necessary stores – gunpowder, firewood and mining tools – which they could easily ferry across the river to Westminster in the dead of night. The plan was to dig a passage through the walls to a cellar under Parliament, then a rambling maze of buildings. Tunnelling began before Christmas – hard work for gentlemen unused to physical labour. They soon realized the need for reinforcements, and three more men were recruited: John Wright's brother Christopher, Thomas Winter's brother Robert, and John Grant. Without proper plans of the complex of buildings, it was difficult to establish quite where their tunnel was taking them, but by a stroke of luck they found that a vault beneath the chamber of the House of Lords had become vacant, and immediately secured the lease. They could thus abandon their tunnel, and build up their supplies of explosives and combustibles in the vault. The barrels – possibly containing as much as two and a half tons of gunpowder, enough to blow up Parliament some five times over – were covered with hundreds of faggots of firewood. All they had to do now was wait until Parliament reconvened in the autumn.

'This pale miner in the infernal regions, skulking in his retreat with his cloak and dark lanthorn, moving cautiously about among his barrels of gunpowder, loaded with death ...'
William Hazlitt, writing on Guy Fawkes in 1821

The plot is blown

Fawkes spent the summer in Flanders, keeping a low profile – although not sufficiently low that his encounters with other English recusants there were not noticed by English government spies. Catesby, who had borne all the cost of the enterprise so far, was running out of funds, and by the late summer he had involved others in the plot – Ambrose Rookwood, Sir Everard Digby and Francis Tresham – in the hope of raising more cash. This was particularly needed to pay for Catesby's planned uprising of Catholic gentlemen in the Midlands to follow the blowing up of Parliament. Tresham did his best to dissuade Catesby from his rashness, but the latter was set on his plan, which now seemed to involve capturing young Prince Charles and/or his sister Princess Elizabeth after the explosion (on the assumption that their elder brother Prince Henry would perish in Parliament with the king). As the Victorian historian S.R. Gardiner commented in his *History of England 1603–1642* (1883–4), 'With the advantage of having an infant sovereign in their hands, with a little money and a few horses, these sanguine dreamers fancied that they would have the whole of England at their feet.'

Fawkes returned to England in September, disguised as Thomas Percy's servant John Johnson. He and Winter replaced some of the gunpowder in the vault, fearing that it might have become damp. Around this time anxiety grew among some of the conspirators that the Catholic peers – some of them relatives of the plotters – would perish with the Protestant lords when the House of Lords was destroyed. Catesby overruled these qualms, declaring 'The innocent must perish with the guilty, sooner than ruin the chances of success.' By this stage it seems likely that the government had some idea that something was afoot, but no clear idea as to what it was. Some of the plotters heard that various peers had received warnings to keep away from Parliament; some believed that Tresham had already betrayed them, and they kept a ship at anchor in the Thames to make good their escape should they be discovered. It had always been planned that Fawkes, after he had lit the powder train, should ride to Greenwich and there take ship to the Continent; he was not expected to take part in the uprising, which again suggests that he might have been acting primarily on a professional basis.

The date for the state opening of Parliament was now set for 5 November. At the end of October Fawkes was confident enough to go to check on the condition of the gunpowder, and found no sign that anyone had interfered with it. He subsequently returned to the vault, this time with a watch and a slow match. The government by this stage, having heard about the warnings sent to the peers, had put two and two together, but had not quite made four. On the afternoon of 4 November the Earl of Suffolk, in his role as lord chamberlain, led a search of the Lords' chamber, and then of the vaults beneath. They came across the firewood covering the barrels of

> 'The innocent must perish with the guilty, sooner than ruin the chances of success.'
>
> Robert Catesby, October 1605

> 'The world has no instrument or means so pernicious as gunpowder, and capable of effecting such mischief.'
>
> Thomas Barlow, *The Gunpowder Treason* (1679)

Guy Fawkes is caught red-handed in the vault under the House of Lords in this engraving after a painting by Robert Smirke (1752–1845).

SEARCHING THE VAULTS

TO THIS DAY, on the eve of the annual state opening of Parliament, the vaults of the House of Lords are subjected to a ritual search. Such searches were, in the 17th century, in deadly earnest: in 1678, in the atmosphere of fevered superstition generated by the fabricated Popish Plot, there were reports of coal and firewood being discovered in the cellars, and, even more alarmingly, it was said that 'a great knocking and digging' had been heard under the ground. By the 18th century the searches had become ritualized, and since the beginning of the 20th century they have been conducted by the colourfully costumed Yeoman of the Guard carrying lanterns and wearing their Tudor-style hats. They finish the business in hand by drinking a ceremonial glass of port – originally supplied in 1760 by a patriotic wine merchant called Old Bellamy. These days, with the high level of terrorist threat in London, a more assiduous search is carried out by officers of the Metropolitan Police.

'There is a treason discovered, in which the King and the Lords should have been blown up.'

Remark overheard in the streets of London by Thomas Winter, one of the conspirators, in the early morning of 5 November 1605

gunpowder, but were reassured when Fawkes, still disguised as John Johnson, told them the wood belonged to his master, Thomas Percy, a familiar figure at court.

But some doubts seem to have been sown, especially as Percy was a known Catholic. When these suspicions were drawn to the attention of the king, James – having spent much of his minority in Scotland in fear for his life – ordered a further search. This was conducted that evening by Sir Thomas Knyvett, keeper of the Palace of Westminster. Around midnight he and his men entered the 'Vault of Villainy', where they found Fawkes in his outdoor clothes and his boots – a suspicious circumstance at so late an hour. Fawkes was apprehended, and the firewood pulled aside, to reveal the 36 barrels of gunpowder. On Fawkes's person were found the watch and slow match. 'The Devil,' Fawkes was later to declare, 'and not God, was the discoverer.' Those members of the Privy Council who could be found were alerted, and at around four in the morning of 5 November Fawkes was taken to the king's bedchamber for the interrogation to begin.

The devil of the vault

Within hours of Fawkes's arrest, word had got out that the plot had been discovered. But Fawkes remained largely silent, apart from boasting that he would have blown the king and his fellow Scots back to their native mountains. He was almost certainly subjected to torture – the king had instructed 'The gentler tortures are to be first used unto him' – but he refused to name his colleagues, saying, 'You would have me discover my friends.' This gave the conspirators time to fly from London to the Midlands, where they attempted to mount the planned rising. It turned out to be a damp squib, and during the course of a skirmish in Staffordshire on 8 November Catesby, the Wright brothers and Percy were all killed. Winter was taken alive. The following day King James addressed Parliament: 'It may well be called a roaring,' he said, 'nay a thundering sin of fire and brimstone, from the which God hath so miraculously delivered us all.'

The trial of eight of the surviving plotters, including Fawkes, took place on 27 January 1606. Long before this, the Dean of Chester, preaching at Paul's Cross, had anticipated the verdict by denouncing

THE HEART OF A TRAITOR

ON 30 JANUARY 1606 one of the Gunpowder conspirators, Sir Everard Digby, was hanged, drawn and quartered. According to John Aubrey's *Brief Lives*, compiled later in the century and known more for its gossip than its reliability, 'When his heart was pluct out by the Executioner (who, *secundam formam*, cryed, "Here is the heart of a Traytor!") it is credibly reported he replied, "Thou liest!"'

Fawkes as 'the devil of the vault'. The prosecutor was Sir Edward Coke, who already had a reputation for his savage way with those in the dock. The trial of the Gunpowder Plotters was no exception: he described the accused as 'most perniciously seduced, abused, corrupted and jesuited'. Indeed, it was the Jesuits at whom Coke pointed the finger: 'the seducing Jesuits ... men that use the reverence of Religion ... to cover their impiety, blasphemy, treason and rebellion, and all manner of wickedness'. The fact that the plotters had been at work under the ground and with gunpowder gave Coke and other government propagandists a gift, for did not Satan have his sulphurous dwelling place in the underworld? So were not these 'Moles', these 'Miners', no more nor less than minions of Hell? Coke conjured up an apocalyptic vision for the court: 'Lord, what a wind, what a fire, what a motion and commotion of earth and air would there have been!' The trial took only a day, and, to no one's surprise, guilty verdicts were unanimously returned.

Four of the conspirators were executed on 30 January, in St Paul's Churchyard. The other four, including Fawkes, met their ends the following day, in Old Palace Yard, Westminster, in sight of the Parliament buildings they had planned to destroy. As was customary for those convicted of high treason, the condemned were to be hanged by the neck until half conscious, then 'drawn' – a hideous process by which the executioner would slowly pull out their intestines while they still lived – and finally quartered, their bodies dismembered with the headsman's axe and their heads mounted on poles. But Fawkes, the last to mount the ladder, and now 'weak with torture and sickness', cheated the crowd of their vicious pleasure by jumping from the scaffold and breaking his neck before the full agony of his sentence could be carried out.

LOST TO ALL
SENSE OF HONOUR

BENEDICT ARNOLD
America's hero-turned-villain

For over two centuries the name 'Benedict Arnold' has in the United States been a synonym for 'traitor'. It was Benedict Arnold – perhaps the finest general of the American Revolution after George Washington – who became so piqued that his merits had not been sufficiently recognized by the political establishment that he offered to betray his fellow patriots to the British, in return for a substantial sum of money and a brigadier's commission. But the question remains: did Arnold betray his country, or did his country betray him?

Despite fearlessly demonstrating his brilliance as a soldier – and almost losing a leg in the process – Arnold was consistently overlooked for promotion by the Continental Congress in favour of those with better political connections. Furthermore, Congress not only refused to pay the expenses he had incurred in funding some of his campaigns, but went on to accuse him of corruption. 'Having become a cripple in the service of my country,' Arnold complained to George Washington, 'I little expected to meet [such] ungrateful returns.' Arnold was, like Coriolanus, a proud man, and in the end it was the succession of blows to his *amour propre* that pushed him into the arms of his country's enemies.

> ### BENEDICT ARNOLD V
>
> *Born* 14 January 1741, in Norwich, Connecticut, USA
> *Died* of natural causes, 14 June 1801, in London, England

From apothecary's apprentice to brigadier general

Benedict Arnold was born in Norwich, Connecticut, into a well-established colonial family, one of his great-grandfathers having been a governor of Rhode Island. Arnold's father, a merchant, drank heavily, especially after suffering considerable losses in a number of ill-judged enterprises; things only got worse after the death of his wife. In an attempt to recover the family's failing fortunes, the young Arnold was apprenticed to two of his mother's cousins who had an apothecary business. Young Arnold found it difficult to settle, and at the age of fifteen he ran off to enlist with

> 'Good God; are the Americans all asleep and tamely giving up their liberties, or are they all turned philosophers, that they don't take immediate vengeance on such miscreants?'
>
> Benedict Arnold, reacting to the Boston Massacre of 5 March 1770

OPPOSITE **Benedict Arnold**, after a portrait by John Trumbull (1756–1843), well known for his historical paintings of the American Revolutionary period.

the Connecticut militia to fight in the French and Indian War. After the cessation of hostilities he resumed his career as an apothecary, and also set himself up as a merchant, trading down the coast of North America and around the Caribbean. Energetic and restless, he was also quick to take offence: when a British sea captain in Honduras called him a 'd—d Yankee, destitute of good manners or those of a gentleman', Arnold challenged him to a duel, and succeeded in wounding him. The captain later apologized.

Like many of his fellow merchants in the American colonies, Arnold found the restrictions placed on his ability to trade by Parliament back in Britain both oppressive and damaging to business, and at the outbreak of the Revolution in 1775 he volunteered the services of his local militia, of which he had been elected captain. Possessed of a bold strategic vision, Arnold proposed a campaign to capture Fort Ticonderoga on Lake Champlain, which would not only prevent a British advance down the Hudson River, but also secure the fort's much-needed supplies of cannon and gunpowder.

En route to the fort, Arnold, now promoted to colonel, encountered Ethan Allen and his Green Mountain Boys, and insisted that these wild irregulars be placed under his command – something that Allen resisted. As it transpired, Fort Ticonderoga fell without a shot being fired; the garrison were sound asleep when the patriot force marched in. Successful campaigning in up-state New York and over the border into Canada continued, as did the squabbling between Arnold and Allen. Arnold was further incensed when the Continental Congress ordered him to serve under the newly arrived Colonel Benjamin Hinman. Arnold, protesting that 'he would not be second to any man', resigned his commission and returned to Massachusetts.

But before long Arnold was lobbying to lead a second force in the proposed expedition to Canada, where he hoped the French settlers would revolt against the British. Washington and Congress backed his plan, and he was commissioned as colonel. It turned out to be a desperately difficult campaign, involving long river voyages in badly built boats and a hard portage over the Appalachians, not to mention storms and starvation – at one point the men resorted to eating candles, dogs and even their own shoes. Arnold reached Quebec City in November 1775, declaring that the journey he had just made was 'not to be parallelled in history': many of his men were sick, and 'almost naked and wanting every thing to make them comfortable' – but the fact that they had reached their destination at all was largely thanks to Arnold's inspiring leadership. Arnold was subsequently joined by General Montgomery and his men, and the two forces attacked the city on 31 December, hoping that a blinding snowstorm would give them a vital element of surprise. It didn't, and they were violently repelled. Montgomery was killed, and Arnold wounded in the leg – although he refused to leave the field before his men.

> **'Few men ever met with so many hairbreadth escapes in so short a time.'**
>
> General Horatio Gates, referring to Arnold's rearguard actions on Lake Champlain in 1776

Arnold's division attacking Quebec in a snowstorm, 31 December 1775. The attack was repulsed, and Arnold was hit in the knee by a musket ball.

Arnold's role in the campaign earned him promotion to brigadier general, and during the late summer of 1776 he led a fighting retreat down Lake Champlain, preventing the British from advancing down the Hudson River. 'It has pleased Providence to preserve General Arnold,' wrote his commander, General Horatio Gates. 'Few men ever met with so many hairbreadth escapes in so short a time.' Later in the year Arnold was made deputy commander of the Eastern Department, but in July 1777 Congress again appointed a less experienced (but better connected) commander over his head, and once more Arnold resigned his commission. However, George Washington, who recognized Arnold's merits, persuaded him to withdraw his resignation, and asked Congress to send him north to play what turned out to be a key role in defeating a British invasion force led by General Burgoyne.

Victory and disappointment

Arnold threw himself into his task with his usual enthusiasm, and succeeded in relieving Fort Stanwix by spreading rumours that a vastly superior American army was on its way. He then joined General Gates for the decisive Saratoga campaign, but was frustrated by Gates's insistence on conducting a defensive operation; by the time of the final, crucial battle at Bemis Heights on 7 October, the two were not even on speaking terms. In defiance of his orders, Arnold led the attack that culminated in

THE SOFTER SIDE OF A TURNCOAT

WE KNOW LITTLE OF ARNOLD'S FIRST WIFE, Margaret (née Mansfield), whom he married in 1767, beyond the fact that she bore him three sons. She died on 19 June 1775, while Arnold was away on the Ticonderoga campaign, and thereafter Arnold's sister Hannah looked after his children.

In 1776, during a lull in the fighting, Arnold began to court 'the belle of Boston', Betsy Deblois, whom one contemporary described thus: 'She was much celebrated as a beauty ... sociable and agreeable, though not wholly destitute of that kind of vanity which is so naturally the companion of beauty. She puckers her mouth a little, and contracts her eyelids a little to look very pretty, and is not wholly unsuccessful.' Arnold set about his courtship with the same single-mindedness he applied to his soldiering, and his flowery epistolary efforts are in marked contrast to the terseness of his military communications. 'Twenty times have I taken my pen to write to you,' he wrote:

> ... and as often has my trembling hand refused to obey the dictates of my heart.
> A heart which has often been calm and serene amidst the clashing of arms and
> all the din and horrors of war trembles with diffidence and fear at giving offence
> when it attempts to address you on a subject so important to its happiness.

But his efforts were in vain; Miss Deblois rejected his suit, not once, but twice.

After a period of amatory tranquillity, Arnold turned his guns on the eighteen-year-old Miss Peggy Shippen of Philadelphia. In this second epistolary campaign, Arnold drew on many of the phrases that he had previously addressed to Miss Deblois, presumably reluctant to waste his resources. There were new, darker notes too, as Arnold railed against the increasing hostility that he found around him:

> I daily discover so much baseness and ingratitude among mankind that I almost
> blush at being of the same species, and could quit the stage without regret was it
> not for some gentle, generous souls like my dear Peggy, who still retain the lively
> impression of their Maker's goodness; and who, with smiles of benignity and
> goodness, make all happy round them. Let me beg of you not to suffer the rude
> attacks on me to give you a moment's uneasiness. They can do me no injury ...

The campaign was a success, and the two married on 8 April 1779. It seems to have been a very happy marriage, despite all the vicissitudes of their life together; after his death she wrote that 'his affection for me was unbounded'. Peggy herself, twenty years his junior, outlived him, according to some sources, a mere three years, but according to other accounts she returned incognito to America, where she died on 14 February 1836.

victory, and in the process was shot in the same leg that had been wounded at Quebec. The leg was a terrible mess, but he refused to allow it to be amputated, calling the surgeons 'a set of ignorant pretenders'. Arnold eventually recovered, but his damaged leg ended up 2 inches shorter than the other. To add insult to injury, Arnold never received the public recognition for his part in the victory that he deserved, largely because of the enmity of Gates, who denounced his subordinate for disobeying orders. Perhaps Arnold anticipated something of this during the battle. When a fellow officer anxiously asked him where he had been shot he replied, 'In the leg.' Then he added, 'I wish it had been my heart.' It has often been remarked that if Arnold *had* been killed at Saratoga, his reputation as an American national hero would have been secure.

Recovery was slow and painful, but by the following June Arnold was well enough to take up the post of military commander of Philadelphia, following the British withdrawal. Here he courted and wed Peggy Shippen, an elegant young woman from one of the leading families of the city, with known loyalist sympathies (Arnold's first wife had died in 1775). After the wedding, Arnold and his new wife moved into the house of Governor Penn, the finest in the city, and this he

> 'It is but justice to confess, that by his military frenzy, or romantic heroism, Arnold contributed to the honour and success of the day.'
>
> James Thacher, MD, *Military Journal, during the American Revolutionary War from 1776 to 1783* (1823), grudgingly admitting to Arnold's part in the victory at Saratoga

furnished 'in a rich and splendid style', according to the military surgeon James Thacher, who published a hostile biographical sketch of Arnold in 1823. 'His carriage and equipage were equally splendid,' Thacher continues, 'and he rioted in the luxury and pageantry of a nobleman.' Arnold, relishing his new position in society, threw extravagant parties, and began to accumulate large debts. His financial position was not helped by his involvement in a number of shady schemes, nor by Congress's refusal to reimburse him for his considerable expenses in mounting the Canadian expedition of 1775. There is no doubt that his haughtiness and extravagance had elicited enmity in various quarters, just as his earlier military successes had provoked jealousy among some of his fellow officers. Another hostile writer, Mrs M. Warren, in her 1805 *History of the American Revolution*, describes Arnold as 'Proud of the trappings of office, and ambitious of an ostentatious display of wealth and greatness,' which, she censoriously adds, is 'the certain mark of a narrow mind'; furthermore, in Philadelphia 'his rapacity had no bounds':

> He deliberately seized every thing he could lay his hands on in the city, to which be could affix an idea that it had been the property of the disaffected party, and converted it to his own use.

This was the sort of thing his enemies were saying in 1779. That year the Pennsylvania Council, urged on by a man whom Arnold had earlier stripped of his command, accused him of corruption. Although a committee of Congress concluded that Arnold was guilty of no such thing, Congress itself disregarded the committee and ordered that Arnold face a court martial. This found Arnold guilty of two misdemeanours, and Washington was reluctantly obliged to issue a reprimand.

Dealing with the enemy

In May 1779 Arnold began to send secret military intelligence to Sir Henry Clinton, the British commander-in-chief. His motives were complex. He himself later justified his actions on

> If your Excellency thinks me criminal, for Heaven's sake let me be immediately tried, and, if found guilty, executed. I want no favour; I ask only for justice.
> Benedict Arnold, letter to George Washington, 5 May 1779

political grounds: firstly, he was opposed to America's new alliance with France, a country he denounced as a Catholic autocracy, ideologically at odds with America's Protestant, democratic traditions; secondly, he claimed that he had never supported full independence, and had fought only to achieve an end to the unjust treatment by the British government of its colonies. But Arnold had never mentioned these reservations prior to his final defection in 1780: the Declaration of Independence was by then four years old, while the French had joined the war in 1777, after Arnold's victory at Saratoga showed them which way the wind was blowing.

The real reason was more to do with Arnold's damaged pride, and what he must have seen as the bottomless ingratitude of Congress. The last straw had been the fiasco in Philadelphia. However, Arnold kept the depth of his disaffection concealed: revenge, as the old saw goes, is a dish best served cold. In 1780 he successfully lobbied Washington for the command of the strategically important fort at West Point, and took up his post in August. He then secretly offered to surrender the fort to the British, for the vast sum of £20,000 and a senior commission in the British army. However, his plan was exposed on 23 September when Major André, the British officer acting as intermediary between Arnold and Clinton, was captured in possession of documents detailing the plot. Hearing of the arrest, Arnold fled, being carried on board the British ship *Vulture* to the safety of New York City. André was not so fortunate: on 2 October the Americans hanged him as a spy.

> … he evinced a mind destitute of both moral principle and political integrity. Rebuffed and mortified in his vicious pursuits, he became soured and disaffected to our government and cause, and the most malevolent and rancorous spirit agitated his unprincipled bosom.
> James Thacher, MD, *Military Journal, during the American Revolutionary War from 1776 to 1783* (1823)

On 25 September Arnold had written to Washington in an attempt to justify his actions:

> The heart which is conscious of its own rectitude, cannot attempt to palliate a step which the world may censure as wrong. I have ever acted from a principle of love to my country, since the commencement of the present unhappy contest between Great Britain and the colonies; the same principle of love to my country actuates my present conduct, however it may appear inconsistent to the world, who very seldom judge right of any man's actions.

His main reason for writing to Washington, however, was to request that his wife be given the commander-in-chief's protection, and in due course Mrs Arnold was permitted to rejoin her husband.

As West Point remained in American hands, Arnold only received the reduced sum of £6,315 from the British, plus a pension of £360 per annum and the rank of brigadier general. For a year he led a loyalist regiment, the American Legion, in operations in Virginia and Connecticut, but in December 1781 he set sail for London. Thereafter he resumed his earlier mercantile operations, and from the mid-1780s ran his shipping business from Canada, trading with the West Indies. But in the words of a former lieutenant governor of Upper Canada, Arnold was 'a character extremely obnoxious to the *original* loyalists of America', and his unpopularity was such that in 1791 he returned to England. He continued to feel hard done by, and petitioned the government to grant him and his family 50,000 acres of Upper Canada, arguing that 'there is no other man in England, who has made so great sacrifices as I have done of property, rank, prospects &c., in support of government, and no man who has received less in return'. Eventually he was given an award of 13,400 acres, but financial difficulties were never far away, and his last years were unhappy and dogged by ill-health: gout in his good leg, pain in the bad one, his body bloated by dropsy and, at the end, his brain racked by delirium. His death on 14 June 1801 came as a relief, at least according to his wife:

> For his own sake the change is a most happy one, as the disappointment of all his expectations, with the numerous vexations and mortifications he has endured, had so broken his spirits and destroyed his nerves, that he has been for a long time past incapable of the smallest enjoyment.

And yet, she affirmed, 'He was the best of husbands.'

A blackened name

'I am mistaken,' Washington wrote to a friend shortly after Arnold's defection, 'if at this time Arnold is undergoing the torments of a mental hell. From some traits of his character which have lately come to my knowledge, he seems to have been so hackneyed in crime – so lost to all sense of honour and shame – that while his faculties still enable him to continue his sordid pursuits, there will be no time for remorse.' Alexander Hamilton held up his hands in horror at Arnold's alleged corruption: 'This man,' he said, 'is in every sense despicable.' In his biographical sketch of Arnold, the American military surgeon James Thacher quotes 'a respectable officer', who wrote to a friend:

> It is not possible for human nature to receive a greater quantity of guilt than he possesses. Perhaps there is not a single obligation, moral or divine, but what he has broken through. It is discovered now that, in his most early infancy, hell marked him for her own, and infused into him a full proportion of her own malice. His late apostasy is the summit of his character.

Thacher himself lists 'the crimes of this unprincipled conspirator', to wit, 'treason, avarice, hypocrisy, ingratitude, barbarity, falsehood, deception, peculation and robbery'. He continues: 'He aimed to plunge a dagger into the bosom of his country, which had raised him from the obscurity in which he was born, to honours which never could have been the object even of his hopes.' Thacher goes on to describe the reactions of the populace at large:

> An effigy of Arnold, large as life, was constructed by an artist at Philadelphia, and, seated in a cart, with the figure of the devil at his elbow, holding a lantern up to the face of the traitor to show him to the people, having his name and crime in capital letters. The cart was paraded the whole evening through the streets of the city, with drums and fifes playing the Rogue's March, with other marks of infamy, and was attended by a vast concourse of people. The effigy was finally hanged, for the want of the original, and then committed to the flames.

There were even those in England who could not stand the thought of a traitor in their midst. Edmund Burke spoke up in Parliament, demanding that Arnold should not be given high command in the British army, lest 'the sentiments of true honour, which every British officer [holds] dearer than life, should be afflicted'. Lord Surrey, rising to speak in the House of Commons, spotted Arnold in the public gallery, and promptly sat down. 'I will not speak,' he declared, pointing at Arnold, 'while that man is in the house.' On another occasion Lord Lauderdale, after seeing Arnold on the right hand of the king as he addressed Parliament, declared that 'however gracious the language he had heard from the throne, his indignation could not but be highly excited at beholding, as he had done, his majesty supported by a traitor'. This occasioned Arnold to issue a challenge, but the resulting duel saw no blood shed.

There is a story that, after switching sides, Arnold asked a captured American officer what the patriots planned for him should they get him into their hands: 'Cut off your right leg,' the man answered, 'bury it with full military honours, and then hang the rest of you on a gibbet.' This ambivalence towards Arnold is reflected in the memorial erected in 1887 in the Saratoga National

Historical Park. Shaded by trees in a quiet corner of a meadow, the memorial takes the form of a single boot, attached to the barrel of a cannon, and bears the following words:

In memory of
the most brilliant soldier of the
Continental Army
who was desperately wounded
on this spot …
winning for his countrymen
the Decisive Battle of the
American Revolution
and for himself the rank of
Major General.

It is the only war memorial in the United States that docs not bear the name of the person it commemorates, and stands witness to America's equivocal feelings towards the haughty hero who became its blackest villain.

The memorial to **Benedict Arnold** at Saratoga National Historical Park pointedly omits his name, but commemorates the leg that was wounded at Quebec, then shattered at Saratoga.

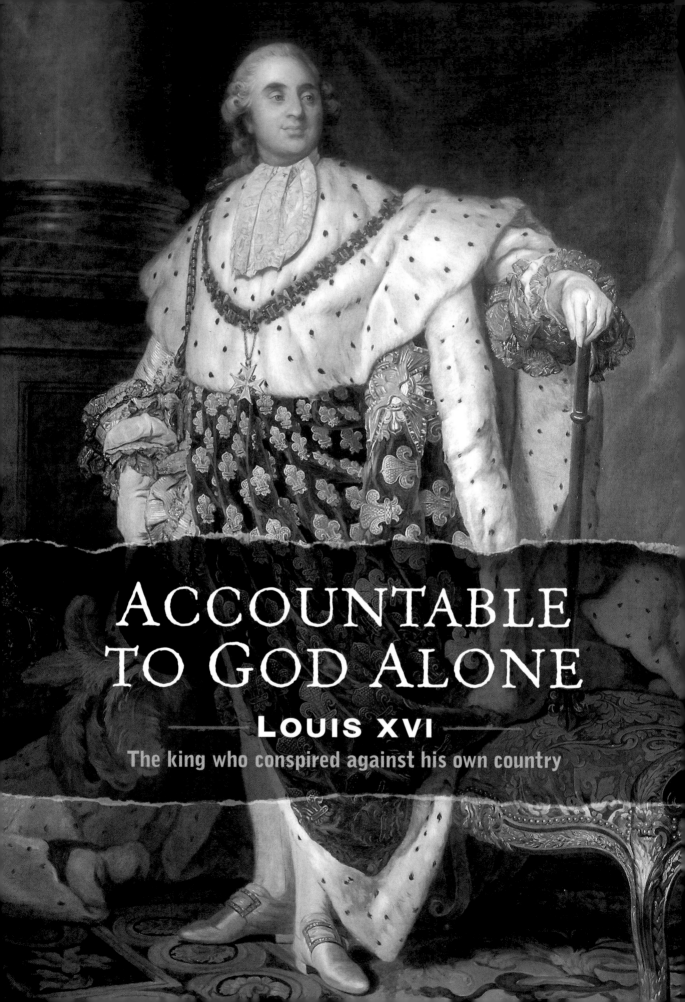

ACCOUNTABLE TO GOD ALONE

LOUIS XVI

The king who conspired against his own country

'L'État c'est moi' – 'I am the state.' So Louis XIV – the most absolute of Europe's absolute despots – had declared to the Parlement de Paris in 1655. Over a hundred years later, in 1787, his great-great-great-grandson, Louis XVI, was giving the Parlement much the same message. 'To the king alone belongs sovereign power in his kingdom,' he pronounced via his minister, Chrétien-François de Lamoignon. 'He is accountable to God alone for the exercise of supreme power. The bond that unites the king and the nation is indissoluble by its very nature.' This being the case, it was by definition illogical – insane, blasphemous – to think that the king, who embodied the nation, could ever be guilty of treason.

But the nation in question had a different view of matters. Within two years, its people – exasperated by the incompetence of the king and his ministers – had risen up and reduced Louis to the role of constitutional monarch. In August 1789 they drew up the *Declaration of the Rights of Man and of the Citizen*, in which they asserted that:

> Men are born and remain free and equal ... The fundamental source of all sovereignty lies in the nation. No institution, no individual may wield authority that does not explicitly stem from it ... The law is the expression of the general will.

> ### LOUIS-AUGUSTE DE FRANCE
>
> *Born* 23 August 1754, at the Palace of Versailles, France
> *Died* guillotined 21 January 1793, in the Place de la Révolution (now the Place de la Concorde), Paris, France

Thus the king was reduced from absolute ruler to citizen, and, as such, liable to charges of treason if he conspired against the nation and the general will. In the end, this is what Louis was charged with, for it looked to many as if the king had invited the other crowned heads of Europe to invade France in order to oust the elected representatives of the people and to restore him to his former power. If that wasn't treason, they argued, nothing was.

A disaffected people

It was Louis XIV who had begun the process of isolating the king and the nobility of France from the common people. In the wake of the civil wars of the early 17th century, in which a fractious aristocracy had threatened the Crown from their castles and fiefdoms across France, Louis set about concentrating power at the centre – himself. To this end, he recreated himself as *le Roi soleil*, the Sun King,

OPPOSITE **Painting of Louis XVI** in his coronation robes, by Joseph-Siffred Duplessis, the official *peintre du roi*, c.1777.

the image of earthly and perhaps even heavenly glory, and built the vast, ornately decorated Palace of Versailles, where he required the nobility to take up residence so he could keep an eye on them. At Versailles Louis established a sumptuous court devoted to pomp, and ceremonial and lavish entertainments, where the aristocracy could vie with each other over precedence and all the other petty jealousies that surround an all-powerful king. As far as Louis was concerned, petty court politicking was preferable to rebellion and unrest in the provinces, but the long-term effect was that the nobility rarely visited their estates, and had nothing to do with their feudal underlings apart from extracting rents from them. 'If the French *noblesse* had been capable of playing cricket with their peasants,' the English social historian G.M. Trevelyan famously observed in 1942, 'their chateaux would never have been burnt.' A further cause of resentment was that the *noblesse* were bribed into submission by the Crown by being exempted from taxation, the burden of which fell on the bourgeoisie and the peasantry.

Throughout the 18th century, as France sought to establish itself as the leading power in Europe by military means, and built (and lost) its first empire, this burden steadily increased. The last straw was the decision by Louis XVI and his ministers to support the Americans in their war of independence against the British. The vast expenditure involved nearly bankrupted the country and in May 1789 the king was obliged to summon, for the first time since 1614, the Estates-General, the legislative assembly of the three estates: the clergy, the nobility and the bourgeoisie. The Second Estate, the nobility, was paralysed and obdurate, unable to adapt to changing times or to deal with the crisis. It was the Third Estate, the bourgeoisie – long critical of unfair taxes, royal monopolies in commerce and the extravagance and decadence of the court – who now took power, declaring itself to be the National Assembly. In a few short months the king had lost much of his executive authority; the storming by the mob of the Bastille on 14 July to free a handful of political prisoners symbolized a revolution that had already taken place. As Lord Dorset, the British ambassador in Paris, wrote two days later:

Rien

Louis' journal entry – in its entirety – for 14 July 1789, the day of the storming of the Bastille. *Rien* means 'nothing'. The king was referring to the day's hunting.

> The greatest Revolution that we know anything of has been effected with, comparatively speaking, if the magnitude of the event is considered, the loss of very few lives: from this moment we may consider France as a free country; the King a very limited Monarch, and the Nobility as reduced to a level with the rest of the Nation.

Louis the Lacklustre

In the early 1780s Thomas Blaikie, a Scottish gardener employed at Versailles, described Louis XVI as 'a good, rough, stout man, dressed like a country farmer'. Although well-educated, Louis was not one to show off whatever intelligence he might have had. His wife, the Austrian princess Marie Antoinette, confided in a letter to Count Rosenberg in April 1775 – a year after Louis had succeeded to the throne – that 'my tastes are not the same as the King's, who is only interested in hunting and his metal-working. You will agree that I would cut an odd figure at a forge; I am not one to play Vulcan there and if I played the role of Venus that would displease him a great deal more ...'

> ‘The Dauphin is not a man like others!’
> Empress Maria Teresa, mother of Marie Antoinette, referring to Louis' lack of amatory interest in her daughter

The queen was referring, wistfully, to their as-yet-unconsummated marriage. The wedding had taken place in 1770, when Louis, then the Dauphin (heir apparent), was fourteen and Marie Antoinette twelve. Although she was generally considered attractive (apart from a hanging lower lip, a gift of her inbred Habsburg heritage), she was to remain a virgin for another seven years. Louis, described as 'cold, sulky, listless' during the wedding ceremony, was more interested in stuffing himself with sweet pastries than in fulfilling his dynastic duty, and the pastries gave him stomach upsets which made him even less interested in the mysteries of the bedchamber. Lack of interest was matched by lack of knowledge of the basic mechanisms – as his brother-in-law, the Emperor Joseph II, was to discover when he visited the couple in April 1777, alarmed at the non-appearance of an heir.

After castigating his sister – fifteen years his junior – for appearing 'cold, bored, even disgusted' in her husband's presence, Joseph then took Louis for a walk and a

One of numerous prints suggesting that Queen Marie Antoinette was insatiably promiscuous. In this engraving entitled *My Constitution*, attributed to Villeneuve, 1790, she is depicted *in flagrante* with the Marquis de Lafayette.

man-to-man talk. What his brother-in-law was doing wrong the emperor described to his brother, the Archduke Leopold, in graphic terms:

> Imagine, in his marriage bed – this is the secret – he has strong, perfectly satisfactory erections; he introduces his member, stays there without moving for about two minutes, withdraws without ejaculating but still erect, and bids goodnight. It's incredible because he sometimes has night-time emissions; it is only when he is actually inside and going at it, that it never happens. Nevertheless the King is satisfied with what he does … Oh if only I could have been there! I could have seen to it. The King of France would have been whipped so that he would have ejaculated out of sheer rage like a donkey.

Whipping proved unnecessary; the emperor's advice was sufficient to bring about his sister's first pregnancy the following spring. But such was the growing unpopularity of the doltish king and his spoilt foreign queen, that the *libellistes* – the French satirical pamphleteers who avoided prosecution by publishing in England or the Netherlands – suggested a variety of fathers for the unborn child.

L'Autrichienne

Marie Antoinette – often referred to simply as '*l'Autrichienne*', the Austrian woman – was suspected by many in France, including Louis himself, of attempting to manipulate French policy in favour of Austria. This suspicion appears to have been largely unfounded; indeed, Marie Antoinette's brother, the Emperor Joseph, expressed his frustration with her for not doing more for the land of her birth.

> '*Vera incessu patuit dea*: by her gait she revealed that she was in truth a goddess.'
>
> Horace Walpole quotes Virgil in reference to Marie Antoinette

Although at first Marie Antoinette was admired for her beauty and charm, and, surrounded by her ladies, often compared to a goddess among her nymphs, the *libellistes* soon set to work against the woman they now called *l'Autruchienne* – playing on *autruche*, 'ostrich', and *chienne*, 'bitch'. Her sentimental attachments to the Princesse de Lamballe and later Yolande, Duchesse de Polignac were transformed in their scurrilous tracts into highly sexual lesbian affairs. The queen was also supposedly carrying on an incestuous liaison with her brother-in-law, the Comte d'Artois, who had shown himself much more adept at fathering children than his elder brother.

In fact, compared to many aristocratic women in France, Marie Antoinette was a model of chastity, her only possible deviation from the straight and narrow being on account of a handsome Swede, Count Fersen, with whom she might have had a physical affair. Ironically, he was one of the few men in court circles whom the *libellistes* did not mention in relation to the queen's allegedly insatiable lusts.

In addition to her carnality, Marie Antoinette was accused of outrageous extravagance. This charge was nearer the mark, although she was not as profligate as some suggested, despite the innumerable lavish court dresses, the three-foot-high hairdos and the lashings of rouge. In fact, others criticized her for not being showy enough, after she began to favour simple white muslin dresses and straw hats. This was part of the then fashionable cult of sensibility and simplicity, inspired by Jean-Jacques Rousseau (whose grave she visited). It was this fashion that inspired her to build her *hameau*, her model village at the Petit Trianon at Versailles, with its deliberately 'distressed' peasant cottages, its milk pails full of flowers and its cows with names such as Blanchette and Brunette. This was Marie Antoinette's tame Arcadia. She may not have known it, but when she visited, most of the produce on display came from a less picturesque working farm nearby.

The *hameau* at the Petit Trianon represented the chasm the French court had created between themselves and the lives of ordinary people. The deluded discourse of sentiment and sensibility coexisted with a desperate determination by the *noblesse* to hang on to every last vestige of inherited privilege. This sense of alienation among Louis' subjects was epitomized in the two best-known, albeit apocryphal, stories that circulated about the queen. The first was that she and her ladies liked to play at milkmaids at her *hameau*; she never did, although she took the part of shepherdesses in the amateur theatricals of which she was so fond (another mark of frivolity in the eyes of stern-minded republicans). The second story has her responding to reports that the people were starving with the dismissive 'Let them eat cake!' While Marie Antoinette had a more tender heart than the latter tale suggests, and cared for the sufferings of those with whom she came into contact, the trouble was that neither she nor her husband, largely isolated in Versailles, saw anything of the impoverishment of the ordinary people of France, nor of their growing discontent.

> When the last king is hanged with the bowels of the last priest, the human race can hope for happiness.
>
> *La Bouche de fer* ('the iron mouth'), a revolutionary journal, 11 July 1791

Blunder upon blunder

It was this narrowness of vision, this inability to adapt, that led to the extinction of the French monarchy. By July 1790 Lord Gower, the new British ambassador in France, was writing:

> If this country ceases to be a monarchy it will be entirely the fault of Louis XVI. Blunder upon blunder, inconsequence upon inconsequence, a total want of energy of mind accompanied by personal cowardice, have been the destruction of the reign.

In October of the preceding year, the king and queen had been forcibly removed from Versailles and installed in the Tuilleries Palace in Paris, to make them physically closer to the people to whom they were now accountable. Louis was outraged at the lack of privacy and the sense of confinement, with revolutionary soldiers guarding the queen in her bedroom as she slept. The 'want of energy of mind' that Gower perceived may well have been due to depression, perhaps sparked off by the death of his eldest son in June 1789. As the revolution became more radicalized, Louis entered into secret negotiations with more moderate politicians in the hope of restoring some of his power, but these came to nothing. Louis was too lethargic of mind, too obsessed with his royal dignity, to reconcile himself to the role of constitutional monarch: when in August 1789 the National Assembly, in its decree abolishing feudalism, had declared him to be the 'Restorer of French Liberty' it was largely a matter of wishful thinking. In June 1791 the king made a poorly planned attempt to flee from France with his family, but was intercepted at Varennes and taken back to Paris.

It was at this point that the other crowned heads of Europe began to demonstrate their solidarity with Louis XVI, a solidarity that overrode national boundaries, but which to the French revolutionaries began to make Louis look

'**The war it is forced to wage is not a war of nation against nation, but the just defence of a free people against the unjust aggression of a king.**'

The French Legislative Assembly declares revolutionary war against Austria, 20 April 1792

The execution of Louis XVI on 21 January 1793. According to his executioner, Charles-Henri Sanson, his last words were: 'I wish that my blood may be able to cement the happiness of the French.'

like a traitor. On 27 August 1791 Leopold II of Austria and the king of Prussia jointly declared 'that they regard the present situation of the king of France as a subject of common interest to all the sovereigns of Europe … They will not refuse to employ … the most effective means relative to their strength to assist the king of France.' They did not rule out the use of force. By December, Louis himself was writing to Leopold, Catherine the Great of Russia and the kings of Prussia, Spain and Sweden, suggesting 'a congress of the great powers of Europe, supported by an armed force, as the best means of putting a stop to the factions here'.

In August 1792 a joint Prussian and Austrian force crossed the frontier into France, with the stated intent of restoring Louis to his full powers, and of putting to death all who opposed them. If any harm was to come to any member of the royal family, the invaders stated, they would 'exact exemplary and eternally memorable revenge, handing over the city of Paris to military execution and overthrow'. This blustering came to nothing: the invaders were comprehensively defeated at Valmy on 20 September. In the aftermath, the new National Convention in Paris voted to abolish the monarchy and declared a republic, while French revolutionary armies penetrated into Germany and the Austrian Netherlands.

'Louis must die'

It looked to many – with some justification – as if the king had been colluding with foreign powers against his own country. The royal family were now confined in the Tower, a dark, forbidding medieval structure attached to the palace of the Temple in the Marais district of Paris. No place could have been further removed in spirit

than the faux-pastoral of the Petit Trianon, and when the royal party first arrived the guards had chanted:

Madame goes up into the Tower –
When will she come down again?

The radicals in the National Convention were baying for blood. 'No one can be a king and not do harm,' declared Louis de Saint-Just in his maiden speech to the Convention on 13 November, while on 3 December Maximilien Robespierre asserted – despite having demanded the abolition of the death penalty – that 'Louis must die that the country may live'. In this fevered atmosphere, on 11 December Louis was brought before the Convention and charged with high treason and crimes against the state. The revolutionaries named the ex-king 'Citizen Louis Capet', the French monarchs having traced their descent from Hugh Capet, king of France in the 10th century. On the day of his indictment, Louis merely commented that 'Capet' was inaccurate.

The trial began two weeks later, on the day after Christmas, which Louis had spent writing his will. The vote on Louis' guilt came on 15 January 1793: 691 returned a guilty verdict; no one voted for innocence; a handful abstained. The Convention was more evenly divided the following day when it came to deciding Louis' sentence. Many were in favour of exile, so that the king might decline into obscurity rather than shine brightly as a martyr in the imaginations of hot-headed monarchists. This was the argument of Thomas Paine, recently elected to the Convention, who felt a debt of gratitude to 'the man who helped my much loved America to burst her fetters'. But others were determined on death: 'The tree of liberty does not flourish unless moistened with the blood of kings,' argued the lawyer Bertrand Barère, a follower of Robespierre. In the end, the majority in favour of immediate death was just one. The

'Certainly none of us will ever suggest that France should keep its disastrous race of kings; we know too well that all dynasties are nothing but rapacious cannibals ... Those who love freedom may rest assured: this talisman will be destroyed, its magical properties will dazzle men no longer.'

Abbé Henri Grégoire, during the debate in the National Convention on the abolition of the monarchy, 21 September 1792

unkindest cut for Louis was the fact that among those who had voted in favour of his execution was his cousin, the Duke of Orléans, who now called himself Philippe Egalité.

A motion the following day to grant Louis a reprieve was voted down. The former king was informed of his fate on 20 January, and asked for three days to prepare himself for death. This was denied, although he was allowed to spend his last evening with his family. The following morning, mounting the scaffold in the Place de la Révolution (now the Place de la Concorde), he began to declare his innocence to the crowd when he was silenced by a drum roll. This was swiftly followed by cheers and yells as the guillotine delivered his head into the waiting basket.

Within a matter of months Marie Antoinette – now known as 'Widow Capet' – was to follow her husband to the scaffold. In August she was separated from Louis-Charles, her only surviving boy, and incarcerated in the Conciergerie as Prisoner No. 280, and on 14 October, having been given no time to prepare a defence, she was tried before a revolutionary tribunal. Although she had played a key role in persuading Louis to cling to a reactionary path following the revolution, and had conducted secret negotiations with the Austrians, the charges faced by the ex-queen were largely fabricated, many of them inspired by the *libellistes*. She had siphoned off French state funds and sent them to Austria; she had organized orgies at Versailles; she had plotted the murder of the Duke of Orléans; most bizarre and cruel of all, she was accused of sexually abusing Louis-Charles. The intent, presumably, was to eliminate any public sympathy for her, and to blacken her name in perpetuity. It took just two days to find her guilty of treason, and within hours of the verdict the blade of the guillotine in the Place du Carrousel had descended. She was, according to one eyewitness, 'audacious and insolent to the end'.

> 'Fame, let thy trumpet sound,
> Tell all the world around
> How Capet fell.
> And when great George's poll
> Shall in the basket roll,
> Let mercy then control
> The Guillotine.'
>
> Joel Barlow, an American supporter of the French Revolution, suggests new words to 'God Save the King', the British national anthem; 'great George' is George III

Some felt sympathy for the royal couple. 'It would seem strange,' wrote an American observer in Paris to Thomas Jefferson, 'that the mildest monarch who ever filled the French throne … should be prosecuted as one of the most nefarious tyrants that ever disgraced the annals of human nature.' The Scottish poet Robert Burns was less sympathetic. 'What is there,' he wrote in 1795, 'in the delivering over a perjured Blockhead & an unprincipled Prostitute to the hands of the hangman?' But, in the end, it was not so much for what they had done that Louis and his queen ended up on the scaffold, but rather for who they were and what they represented. As Saint-Just had thundered to the Convention on 13 November 1792, 'Louis cannot be judged, he is already judged … He is condemned, or if he is not, the sovereignty of the republic is not absolute.' In short, as Robespierre had stated, the king and queen had to die that the revolution might live.

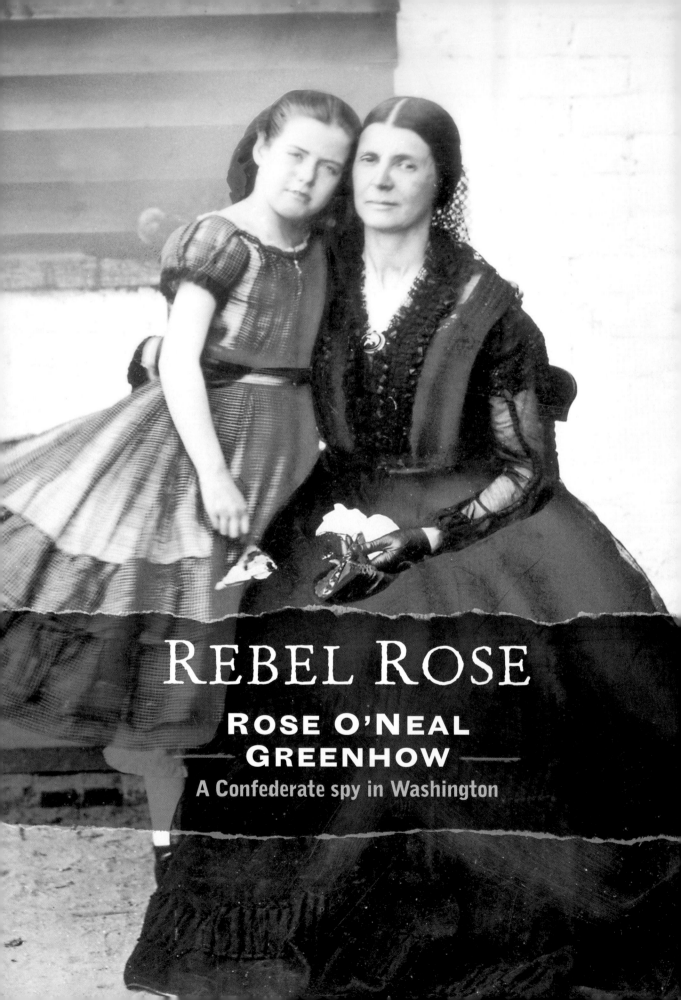

REBEL ROSE

ROSE O'NEAL GREENHOW

A Confederate spy in Washington

The question of what constitutes treason in the context of a civil war is impossible to ascertain with any degree of objectivity: it all depends which side one is on, and which side wins. In 1649, during the English Civil Wars, the king himself was charged with high treason and 'other offences against the kingdom'. He had, his accusers averred, raised an army against Parliament, the elected representatives of the people, and should lose his head for it. In his defence, Charles I argued that all he had done was for 'the freedom and liberty of the people of England', and maintained on the scaffold that he died 'the martyr of the people'.

With the Restoration of the monarchy in 1660, those involved in the trial, together with the 59 commissioners who had condemned Charles to the block by signing his death warrant, were deemed regicides. Although some were now dead and some were pardoned, others were sentenced to life imprisonment, or worse. One man was hanged, while twelve more suffered the traditional traitor's death: hanging, drawing and quartering. The body of Oliver Cromwell was dug up from its grave and hanged in chains at Tyburn, while his severed head was, for a quarter of a century, displayed on a pole outside Westminster Abbey.

> ROSE O'NEAL GREENHOW, NÉE MARIA ROSATTA O'NEAL
>
> *Born* c. 1815, in Montgomery County, Maryland, USA
> *Died* drowned 1 October 1864, near the mouth of the Cape Fear River, North Carolina, USA

Questions of loyalty during the American Civil War – as bitter and bloody a conflict as that in England two centuries before – were equally fraught. Now the quandary that many Southerners faced was whether they owed their allegiance to their native state or to the Union. Many were never in any doubt, and adhered defiantly to their caste, the slave-owning plantation owners of the secessionist South. One such was Rose O'Neal Greenhow, who used her position in Washington society, her charm and her guile, to pass military secrets to the Confederacy.

Washington hostess

'I have no sympathy for John Brown,' Rose Greenhow pronounced as she hosted a dinner party in Washington towards the close of 1859. One of her guests had just expressed support for the radical abolitionist who had led a raid on the Federal arsenal at Harpers Ferry in the hope of inciting a slave rebellion. On 2 December Brown had been hanged for treason against the state of Virginia, and Greenhow was

OPPOSITE **Rose Greenhow and her daughter Little Rose** in Federal custody, 1862. The incarceration of mother and daughter proved a propaganda coup for the Confederacy.

> **I am a Southern woman, born with revolutionary blood in my veins ...**
>
> Rose O'Neal Greenhow

in no doubt as to Brown's crime: 'He was a traitor,' she declared, 'and met a traitor's doom.' Greenhow later regretted this breach of decorum on her part, but never concealed her powerful pro-Southern sympathies.

Greenhow was born Maria Rosatta O'Neal into a planter family in Montgomery County, Maryland. After her father was murdered by one of his slaves in 1817, her mother struggled to keep the plantation going, and in her mid-teens Greenhow was sent to stay in Washington with an aunt who ran the upmarket Congressional Boarding House in the Old Capitol building. Greenhow grew up into something of a beauty, earning her the sobriquet 'Wild Rose'. She was also refined, intelligent, well-educated and well-connected, ideally suiting her to the role of society hostess. This role she duly took up after her marriage in 1835 to Dr Robert Greenhow, an official in the State Department. She now mixed in the highest circles, her friends including Daniel Webster, Dolley Madison, James Buchanan, Jefferson Davis and John C. Calhoun, the intellectual champion of states' rights – particularly when it came to the right of each state to decide whether it wished to maintain the institution of slavery. Calhoun died in 1850, and later Greenhow was to describe him as 'the best and wisest man of this century'.

Confederate agent

Greenhow was in her mid-40s and a widow by the time the Civil War broke out in April 1861. The year before, an officer from Virginia, Thomas Jordan, had started a pro-Southern espionage network in Washington, and had recognized that Greenhow's sympathies and her position in Washington society fitted her perfectly for the role of spy in the service of the rebel cause. He had thus sought the authority of General P.G.T. Beauregard to propose to her that she undertake such work. She responded enthusiastically, and ended up taking over Jordan's network. By July 1861 she was demonstrating her worth. With the assistance of pro-Confederate members of Congress and certain Union officers upon whom she practised her charms, she came into the possession of various crucial pieces of military intelligence – particularly the information that in mid-July Union forces would be advancing on Manassas, Virginia. Greenhow encrypted the information, then sewed the message into a small packet of silk, which she entrusted to her courier, a young woman named Betty Duvall.

On 16 July Miss Duvall made her way to the courthouse of Fairfax County, Virginia, where she met Confederate General Milledge L. Bonham, and announced that she had a message for General Beauregard. Bonham subsequently wrote about the encounter:

> Upon my announcing that I would have it faithfully forwarded at once, she took out her tucking comb and let fall the longest and most beautiful roll of hair I have ever seen. She took then from the back of her head, where it had been safely tied, a small package, not larger than a silver dollar, sewed up in silk.

Shortly afterwards Greenhow received a reply from Thomas Jordan: 'Yours was received at eight o'clock at night. Let them come: we are ready for them. We rely upon you for precise information. Be particular as to description and destination of forces, quantity of artillery, &c.' Greenhow quickly responded, as she recalled in her memoir, *My Imprisonment and the First Year of Abolition Rule at Washington* (published in London in 1863):

> On the 17th I despatched another missive to Manassas, for I had learned of the intention of the enemy to cut the Winchester railroad, so as to intercept Johnson, and prevent his reinforcing Beauregard, who had comparatively but a small force under his command at Manassas.

Confederate President Jefferson Davis later said that the information Greenhow supplied had a critical impact on the Confederate victory near Manassas on 21 July – the First Battle of Bull Run – which Greenhow herself considered a battle as 'memorable in history as that of Culloden or Waterloo'. Jordan wrote in gratitude: 'Our President and our General direct me to thank you. We rely upon you for further information. The Confederacy owes you a debt.'

More was to come. In her memoir Greenhow describes how she and other fifth columnists within Washington planned to disrupt communications in the event of a Confederate attack, for example by cutting the telegraph wires linking the War Department with the various military positions around the city. On 11 August she sent a detailed report on these defences, describing each fort, the number and calibre of its guns, the strengths and state origins of the regiment manning each fort, the number and political sympathies of the officers, the morale and state of equipment of the men, the quantities and condition of stores, mules, wagons, and so on. It was intelligence of a quality that most spymasters can only dream of.

> 'Upon no class of the community did this total abnegation of all the laws, both human and divine, tell with such saddening effect as upon the free coloured population, especially the women, whose sober industrious habits of former days had given place, under the influence of the new order of things, to the most unbridled licentiousness, and who were to be seen at all public places bedecked in gorgeous attire, sharing the smiles of the volunteer officers and soldiers with the republican dames and demoiselles.
>
> I have frequently received the answer, when I have sent to demand the services of a negro serving-woman, 'that she would not come, for the reason that she had an engagement to drive or walk with a Yankee officer'.

Rose O'Neal Greenhow shows her true colours in her memoir, *My Imprisonment and the First Year of Abolition Rule at Washington* (1863)

Imprisonment and release

Given her known sympathies, Greenhow was not above suspicion, and she did little to conceal her activities. She gleefully recalls in her memoir the state of paranoia in Washington after Bull Run:

> The capital … had been made one of the strongest fortified cities of the world – every avenue to it being guarded by works believed to be impregnable. Thirty-three fortifications surrounded it. But this alone was not deemed sufficient. Extraordinary vigilance was exercised; market-carts and news boys were overhauled, to look for treasonable correspondence – every box was either a masked battery, or infernal machine – but, alas! without success, until a sudden inspiration seized them. The Southern women of Washington are the cause of the defeat of the grand army! They are entitled to the laurels won by the brave defenders of our soil and institutions! They have told Beauregard when to strike! They, with their siren arts, have possessed themselves of the plans and schemes of the Lincoln Cabinet, and warned Jeff Davis of them.
>
> The most skilful detectives were summoned from far and near, to trace the steps of maids and matrons. For several weeks I had been followed, and my house watched, by those emissaries of the State Department, the detective police …

The 'detective police' were in fact members of the newly formed Union Intelligence Service, headed up by Allan Pinkerton. On 23 August Pinkerton placed Greenhow under house arrest, and he and his men found further incriminating evidence in her home, including plans of the fortifications around the capital and notes of troop movements.

On 17 November, after nearly three months of captivity, Greenhow wrote in indignant terms to Secretary of State William Seward 'that all my private letters, and my papers of a life time, were read and examined by them; that every law of decency was violated in the search of my house and person, and the surveillance over me'. Her home had by this time been used to house more female prisoners, and in her letter to Seward she proceeded to compare herself with another woman suspected of treason by her captors:

> 'She has not used her powers in vain among the officers of the Army, not a few of whom she has robbed of patriotic hearts and transformed them into sympathizers with the enemies of the country which made them all they were … With her as with other traitors she has been most unscrupulous in the use of means. Nothing has been too sacred for her appropriation so as by its use she might hope to accomplish her treasonable ends.'
>
> Allan Pinkerton, head of the Union's counter-espionage operation, who arrested Greenhow on 23 August 1861

We read in history, that the poor Maria Antoinette had a paper torn from her bosom by lawless hands, and that even a change of linen had to be effected in sight of her brutal captors. It is my sad experience to record even more revolting outrages than that, for during the first days of my imprisonment, whatever necessity forced me to seek my chamber, a detective stood sentinel at the open door. And thus for a period of seven days, I, with my little child, was placed absolutely at the mercy of men without character or responsibility; that during the first evening, a portion of these men became brutally drunk, and boasted in my hearing of the 'nice times' they expected to have with the female prisoners …

Greenhow then justifies her espionage in terms of her constitutional rights:

In the careful analysis of my papers I deny the existence of a line I had not a perfect right to have written, or to have received. Freedom of speech and of opinion is the birthright of Americans, guaranteed to us by our Charter of Liberty, the Constitution of the United States. I have exercised my perogative, and have openly avowed my sentiments.

Early in 1862 Greenhow, along with her eight-year-old daughter Little Rose, was transferred to the Old Capitol, which had now been converted into a prison. In March she was charged with espionage, but defied her accusers: 'If I gave the information

Union soldiers pose in front of the Old Capitol in Washington DC, where Greenhow lived with her aunt prior to her marriage. During the Civil War it was to become her prison.

you say I have,' she told the hearing, 'I must have got it from sources that were in the confidence of the government … If Mr Lincoln's friends will pour into my ear such important information, am I to be held responsible for all that?' The authorities decided that only bad publicity would follow a trial – the Confederacy had already achieved a propaganda coup by pointing out how these ungallant Northerners locked up gentlewomen and their delicate young daughters in filthy, barbarous prisons. It was decided, therefore, to exile Greenhow from Washington, on condition that she gave her word not to return so long as the war continued.

> 'You may prostrate the physical strength, by confinement in close rooms and insufficient food – you may subject me to harsher, ruder treatment than I have already received, but you cannot imprison the soul. Every cause worthy of success has had its martyrs … My sufferings will afford a significant lesson to the women of the South, that sex or condition is no bulwark against the surging billows of the "irrepressible conflict".'
>
> Rose O'Neal Greenhow, letter written while under house arrest to Secretary of State William Seward, 17 November 1861

Mission to Europe

On her arrival in Richmond, the Confederate capital, Greenhow was welcomed as a heroine of the rebel cause. She was not one to sit on her laurels, however, and in 1863 Jefferson Davis sent her as his informal ambassador to Europe. On 16 July, before she embarked from Charleston, she wrote a long letter to the Confederate president reporting on the local military situation and on the broader strategic picture, something of which she gleaned from a European journalist:

> Vizitelli of the *London News* … thinks that the tighter we are pressed the better our chance of recognition – He says that the European world will never allow the reconstruction of the American Union – that their sympathies are naturally with the Anglo-Saxon race who are represented in the South[,] that they will say let them alone they can accomplish their destiny with[out] us – but the moment they found that the chances are that we are likely to be overcome by that Northern race – that moment will they rise up to prevent it.

While in Britain, Greenhow worked tirelessly as a propagandist for the Confederacy – 'carrying out my mischief' as she described it in a letter to a friend, Colonel Alexander Boteler. She was received at court, and found herself feted by many among the aristocracy who felt an affinity with the Southern land-owning elite in their vast mansions, an elite whose leisurely way of life was threatened by the puritanically minded industrialists of the North. 'I believe,' she wrote to Boteler from London on 10 December, 'that all classes here except the Abolitionists sympathize with us and are only held back from recognizing us for fear of war with the United

States.' She also travelled to France, where she had an audience with the Emperor Napoleon III. On 17 February 1864 she reported to Boteler on her visit:

> I was treated with great distinction, great kindness, and my audience in Court Circles was pronounced 'une grande success' – and altho the Emperor was lavish of expressions of admiration of our President and cause there was nothing upon which to hang the least hope of aid unless England acted simultaneously – the French people are brutal ignorant and depraved to a degree beyond description and have no appreciation of our struggle – they believe it is to free the slaves and all their sympathies are really on the Yankee side.

In the same letter she continued: 'My belief is that from England alone are we to expect material aid. The better classes here are universally in our favour …'

As it turned out, the European powers never did intervene, and in September 1864 Greenhow embarked for home on board a British ship, the *Condor*. Nearing the American coast the *Condor* found itself pursued by a Union gunboat, the USS *Niphon*, and on 30 September ran aground on a sandbar as it tried to escape up the Cape Fear River in North Carolina. Fearing capture and a return to a Federal prison, Greenhow demanded that she be taken ashore, but the lifeboat in which she fled capsized in the stormy waters and she herself sank below the surface, weighed down by the gold she had received as royalties from sales of her memoir. Her body was later washed up on the shore, and the following day Rose O'Neal Greenhow was buried with full military honours at the Oakdale Cemetery in Wilmington, North Carolina, her coffin draped by the Confederate flag. A squad of Confederate soldiers fired a volley above her grave, answered by a salute from the guns at Fort Fisher. Her burial place is marked by a white stone surmounted by a cross, inscribed with the following words:

> 'The "iron heel of power" may keep down, but it cannot crush out, the spirit of resistance in a people armed for the defence of their rights; and I tell you now, sir, that you are standing over a crater, whose smothered fires in a moment may burst forth.'
>
> Rose O'Neal Greenhow, letter to Secretary of State William Seward, 17 November 1861

Mrs ROSE O'N. GREENHOW
A BEARER
OF DISPATCHES
TO THE CONFEDERATE GOVERNMENT
DROWNED OFF
FORT FISHER,
FROM THE STEAMER CONDOR,
WHILE ATTEMPTING TO
RUN THE BLOCKADE
SEP. 30, 1864.

The stone was erected by the Ladies' Memorial Association, and rebel flags and red roses are still sometimes left by her grave.

THIS
MOST GALLANT
GENTLEMAN

ROGER CASEMENT

The British diplomat who died for Ireland

Irish poets and songwriters have long celebrated the 'Sixteen Dead Men', the martyred leaders of the 1916 Easter Rising, and their ghosts have hovered over the politics of a divided Ireland ever since. The fifteen Republican leaders taken after the fighting in Dublin – including Pádraic Pearse, James Connolly, Thomas MacDonagh and John MacBride – were court-martialled by the British army and shot. The sixteenth, Roger Casement, had not been in Dublin. He had been put ashore from a German U-boat in the remote south-west of Ireland on the Good Friday before the rising started. But the 20,000 rifles that were to have come with him from Germany were nowhere to be seen.

Confined in the Tower of London, Casement faced a civilian, not a military, trial. After he was found guilty of high treason he addressed the court, seeking to justify his actions as a rebel against the British Crown:

> SIR ROGER DAVID CASEMENT
>
> *Born* 1 September 1864, in Sandycove, near Dublin, Ireland
> *Died* hanged 3 August 1916, at Pentonville Prison, London, England

> Where all your rights become only an accumulated wrong; where men must beg with bated breath for leave to subsist in their own land, to think their own thoughts, to sing their own songs, to garner the fruits of their own labours ... then surely it is a braver, saner and truer thing, to be a rebel in act and deed against such circumstances as these than tamely to accept it as the natural lot of men.

His appeal fell on deaf ears. The death sentence was handed down, and Casement – whom the poet Yeats described as 'this most gallant gentleman' – was hanged at Pentonville Prison on 3 August 1916, and buried in quicklime in the prison cemetery.

Into the heart of darkness

Casement was an unlikely rebel. Although his mother was a Catholic, his father was a Protestant and an army officer, and brought up his children as Protestants. Of course, not all Irish Protestants were Unionists – figures such as Wolfe Tone, Robert Emmet, John Mitchel and Charles Stewart Parnell had all struggled for Irish freedom. But Casement was brought up in Ulster, where the Protestants were almost all Unionists, and their children learnt nothing of Ireland's history or culture at their

OPPOSITE **Roger Casement as a younger man.** 'When he entered a room,' his cousin Gertrude remembered, 'he seemed to make the other people in it commonplace.'

'Come speak your bit in public
That some amends be made
To this most gallant gentleman
That is in quicklime laid.'

W.B. Yeats, 'Roger Casement', from *New Poems* (1938)

schools. (After the deaths of his parents when he was still a boy, Casement had gone to live with relatives in Ulster.) Casement's family did not conform to the norm, however. His father had sympathized with the Fenian rebels of 1867, and his uncle in Antrim had a library full of books on all things Irish. With his sister accompanying him on the piano, young Roddie would sing old Irish airs in a fine baritone voice.

But his career was to take Casement far from Ireland. Having left school in 1880, he went to live with his mother's sister in Liverpool, where he started work as a shipping clerk. His younger cousin Gertrude ('Gee') remembered him from this time:

> In appearance Roddie was strikingly handsome. He was over six feet when he was seventeen; his eyes were grey and deep-set, his face rather thin; and his hair nearly black and curly. He had good teeth, and a very clear skin. ... His speaking voice was beautiful – he never lost a very slight Irish accent, but his English was that of a cultured gentleman. His demeanour in society, or in public, was always quiet and unobtrusive – he hated publicity and loathed being 'shown off'. When he entered a room, he seemed to make the other people in it commonplace.

Casement fretted against the desk-bound life, and at the age of nineteen persuaded his employers to send him to the Congo as purser on one of their ships. He spent much of the next twenty years in Africa, working in a variety of capacities and eventually joining the British consular service. In 1903 he was commissioned by the Foreign Office to investigate reports of appalling misrule and inhumanity in the Congo Free State, which the novelist Joseph Conrad had famously depicted in his novella *Heart of Darkness*. At that time the Congo, with its vast natural resources, was the private fiefdom of Leopold II, king of the Belgians, whom Casement described as 'an autocrat whose chief preoccupation is that autocracy should be profitable'. In Leopold's Congo, millions of local people had been forced to work as

'Wild beasts – the leopards – killed some of us while we were working away in the forest and others got lost or died from exposure or starvation and we begged the white men to leave us alone, saying we could get no more rubber, but the white men and their soldiers said: 'Go. You are only beasts yourselves. You are only Nyama [meat] ... Many [of us] were shot, some had their ears cut off; others were tied up with ropes round their necks and bodies and taken away.'

Testimony included in Casement's *Congo Report*, presented to the British foreign secretary in December 1903

rubber tappers, and if they did not produce enough they were likely to have a hand or a foot or an ear amputated, or be killed and have their head stuck on a pole. Casement's report helped to stimulate international pressure on the Belgian government, which in 1908 took over the administration of the Congo from King Leopold. In 1910–11 Casement went on to investigate similar atrocities in South America, committed against the Putumayo Indians by the Peruvian Amazon Company.

This beloved country

In 1911 Casement was knighted by King George V in recognition of his humanitarian work, but by this time his Irish nationalism was becoming increasingly fervent. He had been a strong supporter of the British during the Boer War of 1899–1902, but his experiences in the Congo and Peru had focused his mind on the evils of colonialism – and he began to see Ireland for what it was: Britain's oldest, most maltreated colony. Already by 1904 Casement had been seeing his future in terms of Ireland: 'I should like to stay in

> 'Figure and face, he seemed to me to be one of the finest-looking creatures I had ever seen; and his countenance had charm, distinction and a high chivalry. Knight-errant he was; clear-sighted, cool-headed, knowing as well as any that ever lived how to strengthen his case by temperate statement, yet always charged with passion.'
>
> The Ulster writer Stephen Gwynn recalls Casement, whom he met in 1904

this beloved country till I die,' he said. He set himself to learn Irish, 'a lovely, glorious language', and, from his study of Irish history, came to the conclusion that Ireland would be better off, both materially and spiritually, without the Union. He rejected the constitutionalism of the old Irish Party, the party once led by Parnell, and became an avid supporter of the newly formed radical alternative, Sinn Féin.

It began to look to Casement as if Irish freedom could not be achieved without a fight. In 1912 Protestants in the north of Ireland formed the Ulster Volunteer Force to oppose – by force – the Westminster government's proposals for Irish home rule. That same year Casement resigned from the consular service, and in 1913 helped to found the Irish Volunteers – the Nationalist equivalent of the UVF. 'Rise, men of Ireland,' Casement wrote, 'and arm, too. Arm yourselves to defend your land, your homes, and assert your freedom as men.' Tensions continued to rise, and in April 1914 the UVF brought in 25,000 rifles from Germany; in response Casement went to the United States to raise money for weapons, and in July 1,500 rifles were landed at Howth, near Dublin, for distribution among the Volunteers.

The British government's plans to grant home rule were put on hold by the outbreak of the First World War in August, but a minority among the Nationalist community were not prepared to wait. In October, following the principle that 'England's difficulty is Ireland's opportunity', Casement sailed for neutral Norway, from where he made his way to Germany. There he assumed the role of ambassador of as-yet unliberated Ireland, and in November he negotiated a statement by the German government to the effect that it had no intention of conquering Ireland, and that it was 'inspired by goodwill towards a country and people for whom Germany desires only national prosperity and national freedom'. Casement's main purpose in Germany was to recruit an Irish Brigade among Irish prisoners-of-war to fight, not for the Germans, but for Irish freedom. But he had little success: there was no conscription in Ireland, so all the Irish who had fought for the British had done so voluntarily. Casement met with nothing but mistrust, and was even threatened with violence.

Countdown to Easter

It was not until March 1916 that Casement learnt that there were plans for a rising in Ireland at Easter. What he did not realize was that Eoin MacNeill, chief of staff of the Volunteers, knew nothing of it; MacNeill judged that any such rising against the might of the British Empire would be futile. But elements within the Irish Republican Brotherhood – a small, extreme faction – were planning to go ahead all the same, in the belief that their bloody sacrifice would radicalize the Irish. The revolutionary socialist James Connolly and his Irish Citizen Army had also agreed to participate.

The Germans offered to supply arms, but not officers, and Casement realized that the Germans were only interested in the rising in so far as it would distract the British; they did not care whether it succeeded or failed. Casement was thoroughly disillusioned with the German government by this stage, calling them 'swine and cads of the first order'. Although he intended to accompany the arms to Ireland in readiness for some future use, he believed that the rising was doomed to failure, and determined to try to persuade MacNeill to call it off – not realizing that MacNeill was only informed of the plan on the Thursday before Easter, and was only reluctantly persuaded to issue a mobilization order on hearing that arms were en route from Germany.

The German trawler *Aud*, disguised as a Norwegian vessel, had sailed from Lübeck on 9 April with 20,000 rifles and ammunition aboard. A few days later Casement, together with two other Irish Nationalists, Robert Monteith and David Julian Bailey, embarked by U-boat. They were to rendezvous with the *Aud* in Tralee Bay, in the southwest of Ireland. However, due to poor communications and poor navigation, the two vessels failed to meet up. The *Aud* was intercepted by the Royal Navy on Good Friday, 21 April, but the crew scuttled the ship before it could be taken to port. Meanwhile, Casement and his two companions had been landed on Banna Strand, a long stretch of beach in Tralee Bay. Monteith described them as 'the smallest invading party known to history'.

Before he had left Germany – where he had teetered on the edge of a nervous breakdown – Casement had written that he 'must be sacrificed'. He was in poor shape when he landed on Banna Strand – sick with a bout of malaria, contracted during his many years in the tropics – but he was euphoric. 'Although I knew that this fate waited on me,' he wrote to his sister on the eve of his execution, 'I was for one brief spell happy and smiling once more.' While the others walked on to Tralee, Casement rested at McKenna's Fort, an ancient ring fort, where he was discovered by a member of the Royal Irish Constabulary. At first the RIC man did not recognize him, Casement having shaved off his beard, but his possession of a German train ticket and a cipher aroused the constable's suspicions. Casement was taken to Tralee police barracks where he asked for a priest, whom he urged to go to Dublin to press for the rising to be cancelled. When MacNeill heard that the arms had been seized, he countermanded his mobilization order. So when the rising started on Easter Monday, the only rebels to come out were around a thousand men and women in Dublin. Pádraic Pearse and the others proclaimed the Republic, and during the course of the week they were joined by perhaps eight hundred more fighters, but they faced a British force eight times as large, and by Saturday 29 April British artillery had forced the rebels to agree to an unconditional surrender.

The Dublin populace did not think much of the rebels and the havoc they were causing in their city. But the British went on to display their complete lack of understanding of Ireland when they proceeded to shoot the captured rebel leaders one by one, between 3 May and 12 May. The last of the fifteen to die was James Connolly, so badly wounded that he had to be strapped to a chair before he could be put in front

The RIC were hunting for Sir Roger high and low,
They found him at McKenna's Fort, said they: 'You are our foe.'
Said he: 'I'm Roger Casement, here upon my native land,
I meant to free my countrymen on lonely Banna Strand.'

They took Sir Roger prisoner and they sailed for London town,
Where in the Tow'r they laid him, as a traitor to the Crown.
Said he, 'I am no traitor,' but his trial he had to stand,
For bringing German rifles to lonely Banna Strand.

'Twas in an English prison that they led him to his death.
'I'm dying for my country dear,' he said with his last breath.
He's buried in a prison yard, far from his native land
And the wild waves sing his Requiem on lonely Banna Strand.

Verses from 'Lonely Banna Strand', an anonymous ballad popular with Irish Republicans. After Casement's remains were returned to Ireland in 1965, Derek Warfield of the Wolfe Tones added a final verse:

They took Sir Roger home again in the year of sixty-five
And with his comrades of Sixteen in peace and tranquil lies,
His last fond wish it is fulfilled for to lie in his native land,
And the waves will roll in peace again on the lonely Banna Strand.

of the firing squad. Pearse had got the blood sacrifice he'd wanted, and it had the desired effect. As Yeats wrote,

> All changed, changed utterly:
> A terrible beauty is born.

There was an immediate outpouring of revulsion at the vengefulness of the British, and more and more of the Irish swung behind the radical Republicans. In the 1918 election Sinn Féin swept the board, and, refusing to sit in Westminster, set up a parliament in Dublin. The Anglo-Irish War – and independence – were to follow.

The right to love our kind

But all that was in the future. Casement avoided the summary 'justice' meted out to the Dublin rebels. He was taken to London, where he was initially held in the Tower – where so many charged with treason had been held in the past. His trial at the Old Bailey began on 26 June, and the prosecution was led by the attorney general, F.E. Smith, a fervent Unionist who had aligned himself with the UVF before the war in its threat of armed opposition to home rule.

Casement initially felt confident that the revulsion in Ireland – and America – at the shootings of the rebel leaders would dissuade the authorities from hanging him. Elements within the government had different ideas, and in early May had begun to circulate Casement's so-called Black Diaries, which recounted his numerous homosexual encounters – hitherto unsuspected by the public at large. The intention, in those less enlightened times, was to turn Casement from heroic martyr into repellent monster, so no one would care whether he hanged. (For many years, Irish Republicans argued that the Black Diaries were forgeries concocted by the British intelligence services, but today they are accepted as genuine, just as today Casement's homosexuality is accepted without condemnation.)

Casement was found guilty on 29 June. In his speech from the dock he stated his right as an Irishman to be tried in Ireland, before an Irish court and by an Irish jury. How could an Irishman be guilty of treason against England?

> We are told that if Irishmen go by the thousand to die, not for Ireland, but for Flanders, for Belgium, for a patch of sand on the deserts of Mesopotamia, or a rocky trench on the heights of Gallipoli, they are winning self-government for Ireland. But if they dare to lay down their lives on their native soil, if they dare to dream even that freedom can be won only at home by men resolved to fight for it there, then they are traitors to their country, and their dream and their deaths alike are phases of a dishonourable fantasy.

Towards the end, he proclaimed:

> Self-government is our right, a thing born in us at birth, a thing no more to be doled out to us, or withheld from us, by another people than the right to life itself – than the right to feel the sun, or smell the flowers, or to love our kind.

Casement in the dock of the Old Bailey, London, June 1916. His plea to be tried in an Irish court by an Irish jury was rejected.

All this fine oratory, of course, made no difference. Nor did calls for clemency from the likes of Sir Arthur Conan Doyle, W.B. Yeats and George Bernard Shaw. While waiting for his appeal to be heard, Casement, confined in Pentonville Prison, seems to have resigned himself to his fate: 'I have a happier mind than I had for a long time,' he wrote to his old friend Alice Green.

The bravest man

As expected, the appeal was dismissed, and Casement set about writing farewell letters to those who had worked with him and supported him through his career – although many of these letters were censored on the grounds that they contravened Defence Regulations. On the eve of his execution, Casement converted to Catholicism – something made easier by the fact that as a small boy his mother had had him secretly baptized. The Church gave him something he had long been looking for. 'In Protestant coldness I could not find it,' he wrote, 'but I saw it in the

In 1965 Casement's remains were taken back to Ireland. Half a million people filed past his coffin, which was then buried with full military honours in Glasnevin Cemetery, Dublin.

faces of the Irish. Now I know what it was I loved in them. The chivalry of Christ speaking through human eyes.' Roger Casement, now stripped of his knighthood, marched out to the scaffold the next day, 3 August 1916. The hangman, John Ellis, recalled that he was 'the bravest man it fell to my unhappy lot to execute'.

A few days earlier, Casement had received one last visit from his beloved cousin Gertrude. 'Don't let me lie here in this dreadful place,' he begged her. 'Take my body back with you and let it lie in the old churchyard in Murlough Bay.' But he knew the fate of executed men: burial in quicklime in the prison cemetery. And for nearly fifty years he lay in Pentonville, until, in 1965, his remains

> 'Hark! in the still night. Who goes there? *'Fifteen dead men.'* Why do they wait? *'Hasten, comrade, death is so fair.'* Now comes their Captain through the dim gate.'

Dora Sigerson Shorter, 'Sixteen Dead Men' (1919). Pious, sentimental poems such as these helped to create the iconography of sacrifice that was to become the mainstay of certain strands of Irish Republicanism for the rest of the 20th century.

were repatriated to Ireland, where he was given a state funeral. Casement was buried in the Republican plot in Dublin's Glasnevin Cemetery – not, as he had wished, at Murlough Bay on the north coast of Antrim, the land of his boyhood. The British prime minister, Harold Wilson, had only agreed to release the remains so long as they were not taken to Northern Ireland, the province that the Ulster Unionists had successfully kept a part of the United Kingdom, and where the memory of Casement was held in execration by the majority Protestant population. The ghost of Roger Casement still had the power that Yeats had written of many years before:

> Draw round, beloved and bitter men,
> Draw round and raise a shout;
> *The ghost of Roger Casement*
> *Is beating on the door.*

HARLOT, YES. TRAITOR, NEVER!

MATA HARI

The exotic dancer accused of spying for the Germans

So many myths have accumulated around Margaretha Geertruida MacLeod, née Zelle – better known to the world as the exotic dancer Mata Hari – that it is almost impossible to penetrate the veils of fantasy that have wrapped themselves around her. One thing, though, is certain: she was shot by the French on 15 October 1917, found guilty of spying for the Germans. But the story that she blew a kiss to the firing squad before she died, or the rumour that she flung open her coat to reveal her naked body in an effort to distract her executioners, are entirely unsubstantiated. Similarly without foundation, but fitting the legend, is the story that her last words were 'Harlot, yes. Traitor, never!'

MARGARETHA GEERTRUIDA MACLEOD, NÉE ZELLE

Born 7 August 1876, at Leeuwarden, Netherlands

Died executed by firing squad 15 October 1917, at Vincennes, near Paris, France

---

The mythologizing of Margaretha Zelle began during her own lifetime, in which she passed herself off as a mysterious princess from the East Indies, an acceptable guise in which to perform sensual dances wearing a bare minimum of clothing. During the First World War, when suspected of espionage, she claimed to be acting as a double agent – although this failed to save her. The truth about her activities remains murky: the official documents regarding her case were sealed for a hundred years and will not be opened until 2017

With little regard to the known facts of her life, Mata Hari was recreated by film-makers as the arche-typical femme fatale, first appearing on screen in 1920, portrayed by Asta Nielsen. The role was subsequently taken by many others, most notably Greta Garbo in 1931. *Mata Hari* was Garbo's most successful venture commercially (*Variety* called it 'an important grosser'), and, despite risible lines such as 'What's the matter, Mata?', this classic melodrama did much to turn Mata Hari into an icon of popular culture.

An orchid among buttercups

Dark-haired, olive-skinned Margaretha Zelle – known as 'Grietje' to her family – was the daughter of a prosperous Dutch businessman who owned a hat shop in Leeuwarden in the Netherlands. Even from an early age,

> 'Men worshipped her like a goddess, only to be betrayed by a kiss!'
>
> Slogan for the 1931 film *Mata Hari*, starring Greta Garbo in the title role

---

OPPOSITE **Mata Hari in her stage role** as an oriental temple dancer and devotee of Siva. For a decade her performances caused a sensation across Europe.

Margaretha had a penchant for self-dramatization, favouring flamboyant costumes and telling her friends she was born in a castle. She had three brothers, but she was her father's favourite, 'an orchid among buttercups' as she later put it, and was sent to the best schools until, in 1889, her father went bankrupt following some unwise investments. The family split up, and her mother became ill, dying when Margaretha was fifteen. She lived for a while with her godfather, then sought to make her own way, beginning to train as a kindergarten teacher. She was obliged to leave the school after the headmaster, an older man, began to press his attentions on her.

For a while Margaretha lived with her uncle in the Hague, then at the age of eighteen answered a newspaper advertisement placed by a colonial army officer on home leave from the Dutch East Indies who was looking for a wife. The man concerned, Captain Rudolf John MacLeod (or Campbell MacLeod in some sources), was of Scottish descent, wore fine whiskers and a row of medals attesting to past glories, but otherwise had little to recommend him: he was 38, diabetic, rheumatic, alcoholic and, it turned out, prone to domestic violence. But perhaps Margaretha was not hopeful of her marital prospects: although she had an undoubtedly pretty face, at 5 ft 10 in she towered over most men – and she was so conscious of the modest dimensions of her breasts that she stuffed extra padding into her corsetry.

> **'My husband won't get me any dresses because he's afraid that I will be too beautiful. It's intolerable. Meanwhile the young lieutenants pursue me and are in love with me ...'**
>
> Mata Hari, when plain Mrs Margaretha MacLeod, a colonial wife in the Dutch East Indies

The couple married in 1895, and in due course settled in Java, in the Dutch East Indies. Margaretha became absorbed in her new surroundings, and was fascinated by the local culture, especially the dances. However, despite the birth of a girl, soon followed by a boy, Margaretha's relations with her husband were poor. He took a local woman as his concubine, but was violently jealous if any man even looked at his wife.

Relations between the two deteriorated further after both children fell horribly ill one night in 1899. The parents said the children had been poisoned by a disaffected servant. Whatever the cause, the boy died. The family returned to Europe in 1902, and Rudolf and Margaretha divorced the following year, Rudolf keeping custody of their daughter.

Birth of a princess

Margaretha moved to Paris, where she found work riding a circus horse under the name Lady MacLeod. To make ends meet, she also posed as an artist's model. In 1905, adopting the persona of a Javanese princess and the name Mata Hari (which she claimed was Malay for 'eye of the day', i.e. the sun), she launched her career as a scantily clad performer of sensual, quasi-oriental dances. Aware that people in Europe were largely ignorant of the range of cultures and religions in Asia, she

The execution of Mata Hari – almost certainly a reconstruction for the 1920 film, with Asta Nielsen in the title role.

claimed that she had been born in India of a Brahmin family, and that her mother, a temple dancer, had died giving birth to her; she had subsequently been brought up in a temple, and had dedicated her life to Siva.

Mata Hari's highly eroticized dancing took Europe by storm. She found men falling at her feet, and became one of the most celebrated *grandes horizontales* of the era, conducting affairs with industrialists, senior army officers, politicians and even, it was said, the crown prince of Germany. Nevertheless, she reputedly continued to pad out her bust, and it was rumoured that she would never let her lovers see her breasts – explaining that her violent ex-husband had bitten off her nipples.

> 'The diaphanous shawls she wore as the dance began were cast away to tempt the god until finally, as the candelabras were capped and only the flickering oil light gleamed on Siva's features, the sarong was abandoned and her silhouette, with her back to the audience, writhed with desire toward her supernatural lover …'
>
> Russell Warren Howe, *Mata Hari: The True Story* (1986), describing Mata Hari's debut at the Musée Guimet in Paris, 13 March 1905. For her part, Mata Hari claimed: 'My dance is a sacred poem.'

Siren, spy or scapegoat?

During the First World War, Mata Hari's status as a neutral Dutch citizen enabled her to travel relatively freely round Europe: she had been performing in Germany just before the outbreak of hostilities, and thereafter spent time in the Netherlands, France and – possibly – German-occupied Belgium. Perhaps inevitably, a woman of such a 'loose' character came under suspicion, especially as the war dragged on and anti-German hysteria mounted in France, together with vitriolic attacks against anyone who spoke out in favour of peace negotiations. Such people were immediately suspected of being in German pay – and in the first half of 1918 several were executed following a series of sensational treason trials. In this atmosphere, with the public baying for blood, the authorities might well have deemed that Mata Hari, a woman who had pursued a far from respectable profession, was a useful scapegoat. It has even been suggested that the French counter-espionage service framed her, anticipating that the enormous publicity that the trial of such a notorious woman would generate might help to justify their demands for increased funding.

Mata Hari was arrested in her room at the Hotel Plaza Athénée in Paris on 13 February 1917. The evidence produced against her is unclear. One account suggests that while in the Hague in 1916, the German consul had offered her money to supply any valuable intelligence she could glean the next time she was in France. She herself, after her arrest, admitted that she had passed on some outdated information, and at the same time claimed that she had been recruited by the French to spy for them in German-occupied Belgium. She had not, however, informed the French of her previous arrangement with the Germans.

It is possible that the Germans themselves had found out that Mata Hari was working as a double agent. According to another account, in January 1917 the German military attaché in Madrid transmitted a coded radio message to Berlin mentioning the activities of a German agent known as H-21. The message was intercepted by the French, who from circumstantial evidence were able to identify H-21 as Mata Hari. The fact that the Germans transmitted this key message using a code that they already knew the French had broken suggests that they now wished to dispense with H-21's services.

> 'Mata Hari ... performed useful services for the Germans in the First World War but was an awful spy ... I would not have kept her on my payroll.'
> Markus Wolf, *Man Without a Face* (1997). From 1952 to 1986 Wolf was the highly successful head of the HVA, the East German foreign intelligence agency (see p.178).

Mata Hari was tried before a military court on 24–25 July 1917, accused of spying for Germany and causing the deaths of tens of thousands of French soldiers. Found guilty, she was sentenced to death, and on 15 October, her plea for clemency having failed, she was woken at daybreak in her cell by a priest, Father Arbaux, accompanied by two Sisters of Charity, together

'She did not die as actors and moving picture stars would have us believe that people die when they are shot. She did not throw up her hands nor did she plunge straight forward or straight back. Instead she seemed to collapse. Slowly, inertly, she settled to her knees, her head up always, and without the slightest change of expression on her face. For the fraction of a second it seemed she tottered there, on her knees, gazing directly at those who had taken her life. Then she fell backward, bending at the waist, with her legs doubled up beneath her.'

An eyewitness account by Henry Wales, International News Service, 19 October 1917

with Captain Bouchardon and Maître Clunet, her lawyer. Dressed in a long, black, fur-lined cloak, and wearing a large black hat and black kid gloves, she was driven at speed across Paris in the early morning light to the fort at Vincennes. Met by a squad of twelve Zouaves, rifles at the ready, she was offered a blindfold, but declined. Her hands were left untied as she stared at her executioners. An eyewitness described how the officer in command let his sword drop, the signal to fire. A volley rang out. Mata Hari fell to her knees, then collapsed backwards. An NCO then marched over to where she lay, put his pistol close to her left temple, and fired.

Mata Hari's bullet-ridden corpse was taken to the Museum of Anatomy in Paris, no family members having claimed it for burial. At the museum her head was severed from her body and preserved, to join a collection of heads of other executed criminals. More than eighty years later, in July 2000, it was discovered that her remains had disappeared. Perhaps, when the museum moved premises in 1954, Mata Hari's head had been spirited away by one of her many old admirers.

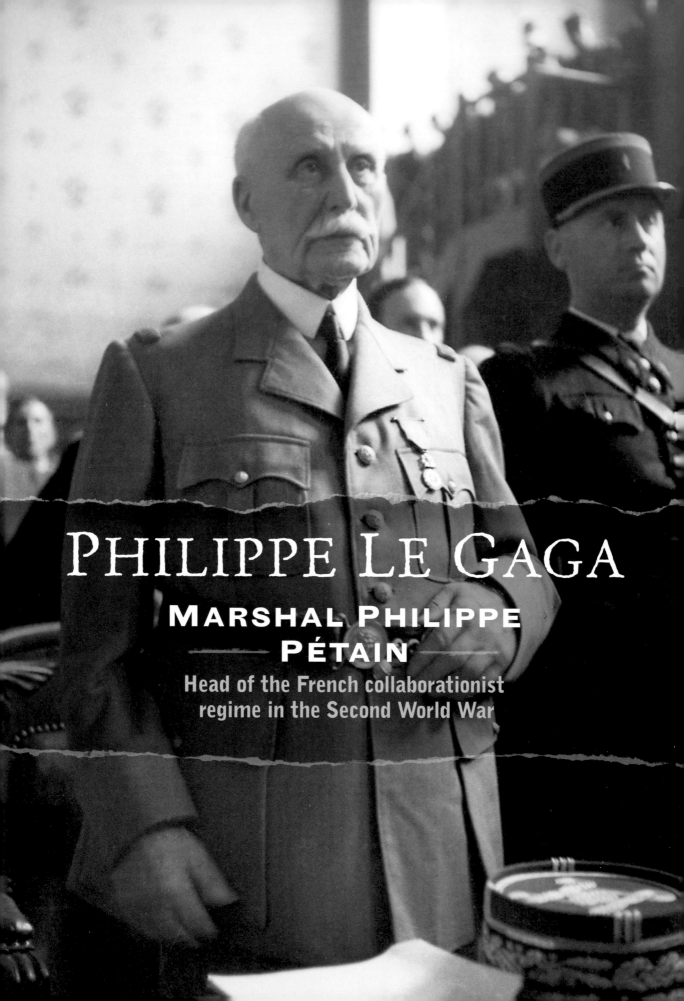

PHILIPPE LE GAGA

MARSHAL PHILIPPE PÉTAIN

Head of the French collaborationist
regime in the Second World War

Of all the European countries occupied by the Nazis during the Second World War, France has the most shadowed record. Although the doings of *le Maquis* – the French Resistance – have long been celebrated in memorials, memoirs and films, the fact that so many of the French population actively or passively collaborated with their occupiers was for many years skimmed over. Something of a covenant of collective amnesia reigned, like a scab over a raw wound; those who swung like weather-cocks between defeatism in 1940 to postures of defiance in 1944 would later claim they had never truly bowed the head.

Once the war had turned definitively against the Germans, these *girouettes*, as they were known in France, would turn out to cheer the Allied armies as they entered town after town following the Normandy landings; they would point the finger at the uniformed thugs of the Milice who had served the foreign occupier; they were only too keen to shave the heads of the *collabos horizontales*, those young and not so young women who had slept with the enemy. And those who had once hailed Marshal Philippe Pétain as the hero who had twice saved France – once at Verdun in 1916, and once again in 1940 when he had made peace with the Germans – called for retribution against the man they now called the greatest traitor of them all.

> ### HENRI-PHILIPPE PÉTAIN
>
> *Born* 24 April 1856, at Cauchy-à-la-Tour, France
> *Died* of natural causes, 23 July 1951, on Île d'Yeu, France

THE ORIGINAL QUISLING

OTHER COUNTRIES OCCUPIED BY THE NAZIS also had their collaborators. When the Germans invaded Norway on 9 April 1940 Vidkun Quisling, the leader of National Unity, the tiny Norwegian Nazi party, stormed into the radio station in Oslo, seized the microphone, declared himself prime minister and ordered all resistance to stop. He later formed a puppet government under the Nazis. 'To writers, the word *Quisling* is a gift from the gods,' declared an editorial in the London *Times* on 15 April 1940. 'If they had been ordered to invent a new word for traitor ... they could hardly have hit upon a more brilliant combination of letters. Actually it contrives to suggest something at once slippery and tortuous.' At the end of the war Quisling was arrested, found guilty of treason and executed by firing squad. His infamy lives on in the word 'quisling', which, in a number of European countries, continues to this day to be used as a word for 'traitor'.

OPPOSITE **Marshal Philippe Pétain**, aged 89, on trial for treason, 30 July 1945. His death sentence was commuted to life imprisonment.

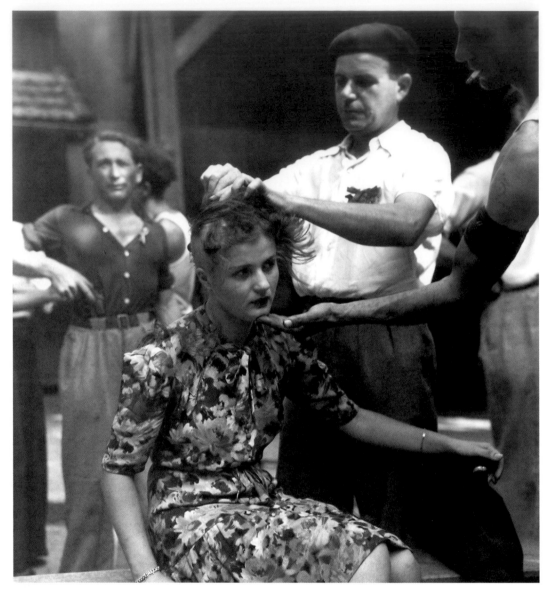

At the end of the Occupation, French women who had had affairs with German soldiers were humiliated by having their heads shaved in public.

The victor of Verdun

Colonel Philippe Pétain was already 58 years old in 1914 and planning for his retirement – the son of peasants, he had in anticipation bought himself a plot of land in the Pas de Calais. His military career thus far had been unremarkable: as an officer-cadet at St Cyr, he had been ranked 229 out of 386; he had never seen action, having only served in mainland France, never in any of the colonies; and he had whiled away his leisure hours in a number of provincial garrison towns practising his charms on the wives of local dignitaries. His one claim to fame was the unfashionable doctrine he had propounded while lecturing at the École de Guerre, where he had argued against the conventional all-out infantry attack, which he saw as a waste of men and resources unless preceded by intensive artillery and machinegun fire. 'Firepower kills' was one of his maxims. 'One does not fight with men against *matériel*.'

With the outbreak of war with Germany in August 1914, Pétain put aside all thoughts of retirement. After the first few months of fighting, he found himself in command of an army corps, and through the battles of Artois and the Champagne he began to develop new tactics, emphasizing the importance of a strong second line of defence from which to mount a counterattack. But the Germans too learnt this lesson, while the French commander-in-chief, Marshal Joseph Joffre, continued to order all-out attacks, dismissing Pétain as *'trop negatif, trop timide'*. Joffre packed Pétain off to the rear, near Paris, to train up reservists for an anticipated offensive in the spring of 1916.

The Germans pre-empted this plan by launching a major offensive of their own, when on 21 February 1916 they began a massive artillery bombardment of the French forts round Verdun, which since 1914 had formed the heart of a great salient bulging into German-occupied territory. The German intention was to 'bleed the French army white': they knew the iconic value the French placed on Verdun, and knew that they would expend huge numbers of men defending it. Five days after the beginning of the onslaught, Pétain, in the midst of one of his regular assignations with his mistress in the Hôtel Terminus in Paris, was summoned by Joffre . He was to take command of the defence of Verdun, and to hold it at all costs. *'Ils ne passeront pas,'* Pétain famously promised, 'They shall not pass.'

Unlike many French generals of the time, Pétain positioned his headquarters close to the front, lived in Spartan simplicity, as befitted the son of a peasant, and made regular tours of inspection, keeping in touch with his men and caring for their morale. His common touch earned him the sobriquet *le médecin de l'Armée* – the doctor of the army – while his organization of the defence saved the situation and prepared the ground for a counterattack, albeit after the sacrifice of hundreds of thousands of French lives. A quasi-religious iconography grew up around the killing fields of Verdun, an iconography in which regiment after regiment marched to their deaths along the *Voie Sacrée*, the 'sacred road' that took them to the front and sacrificial slaughter.

In May, displeased that Pétain had requested permission to withdraw, Joffre kicked him upstairs to command Army Group Centre, and replaced him in the field with General Robert Nivelle, who took not only the credit for the final attack in October, but also the job of commander-in-chief when Joffre was dismissed in December. Pétain had been leapfrogged.

Nivelle's policy was 'attack at all costs', but with the disastrous spring offensive in 1917 and the subsequent mutinies in the French army, Nivelle fell from grace, and Pétain took the top job. The mutinies had been a shock, and Pétain, while dealing harshly with the ringleaders (some fifty of whom were shot), set about improving conditions for the *poilus*, the ordinary French soldiers, ensuring they got regular leave, increasing their rations and generally looking after their welfare. But in April 1918, as the Germans mounted their final onslaught, Pétain was again leapfrogged, when Marshal Foch was appointed Allied supreme commander over his head. Perhaps Pétain had been tainted with the whiff of retreat and defeatism – the British commander-in-chief, General Haig, said that during the German spring offensive Pétain 'was in a funk and had lost his nerve'. Perhaps he had become infected with what the French call *le crise de tristesse sombre* ('attack of dark gloom') that haunted so many of the men who had returned from the 'meat grinder' of Verdun. Pétain himself had described these men, their faces frozen by terror, their bodies betraying an utter dejection, bent under the burden of the horrors they had witnessed.

Victory, when it came, with millions of Frenchmen dead, must have seemed to many a hollow one, more like a defeat. Pétain himself wept when he heard the news of the armistice – he had been planning an offensive that would take the French into the enemy's own territory, outflanking the German army and forcing it to surrender. In December 1918 he was awarded the marshal's baton, and during the victory parade in Paris in 1919, wearing a sky-blue uniform to match his piercing blue eyes and riding his white horse through the Arc de Triomphe, Pétain was the darling of the crowds, *le vainqueur de Verdun*.

'Business-like, knowledgeable, and brief of speech.'

Field Marshal Earl Haig, commander of British forces on the Western Front, on Pétain

Between the wars

Pétain's prestige was at a peak after the First World War. He continued in active service for some years, commanding French forces in the suppression of the Rif rebellion in Morocco in 1925, and going on to become vice president of the Supreme War Council and inspector general of the army. Having bitterly learnt at Verdun the cost of neglecting frontier forts, he was an ardent supporter of the Maginot Line, the system of fortifications built by the French in the early 1930s along their border with Germany. In so doing, Pétain made the mistake of so many generals in assuming the next war would be a rerun of the last: investment in the Maginot Line was at the expense of investment in armour and aircraft (favoured by the likes of Charles de Gaulle, who had served under Pétain before the First World War); and the line itself did not extend along the border with neutral Belgium.

The French did not want another war, and it was almost inconceivable to them that there should be one. The war of 1914–18 was meant to be *le der des ders* ('the last of the last'), and the punitive terms that the French insisted upon at Versailles had been intended to prevent Germany from waging offensive war ever again. But, as can be seen in hindsight, the very harshness of the terms of the peace sowed the seeds of future conflict.

MARSHAL PHILIPPE PÉTAIN II7

In the mood for defeat

When war came it was at first on the other side of Europe, in Poland. The French sat snugly behind their Maginot Line during the Phoney War, the period the French call *le drôle de guerre*. 'There is nothing more to do,' declared General Weygand, the future commander-in-chief. 'Everything is in place.'

But when the German *Sichelschnitt* ('sickle cut') came on 10 May 1940, the French found once again that their enemy refused to play by the rules. As in the First World War, the Germans ignored Belgian neutrality and poured their panzer columns through the rugged Ardennes and over the River Meuse, bypassing the Maginot Line. The French military suffered a collective *crise de tristesse sombre*, a general paralysis of will. Maurice Gamelin, the gloomy and defeatist 68-year-old commander-in-chief, found it impossible to adapt his pre-planned static deployments to deal with the fast-moving nature of the German *Blitzkrieg*, before which the French army, with a few notable exceptions, simply crumbled. On 19 May Gamelin was replaced, too late, by the even gloomier and older Maxime Weygand, a 73-year-old Catholic right-winger, who promptly informed Prime Minister Paul Reynaud that there was no hope of beating back the Germans.

The appointment of Weygand came the day after another appointment that Reynaud was to regret even more. On 18 May he made the 84-year-old Philippe Pétain his deputy, largely on account of his reputation as the defender of Verdun a quarter of a century before. Pétain was, Reynaud asserted, 'the man who knows how a French victory can come out of a cataclysm'. But Pétain, like Weygand, was a Catholic right-winger and deeply mistrustful of the Third Republic, which he believed to have had a corrupting effect on French national life; his previous post, as ambassador to Franco's Spain after the conclusion of the Civil War, had brought him into close proximity with the Spanish far right, who espoused a heady mix of religiosity, traditionalism and authoritarianism.

Pétain had never concealed his belief that France should not have gone to war with Nazi Germany in the first place, and that it should now sue for peace. This was fundamentally at odds with Reynaud's position, and when Reynaud expressed his support for Churchill's proposal that the nations of France and Britain should enter a formal union to combat Hitler, Pétain declared that such a union would be like a union with a corpse: 'Better to be a Nazi province,' he said. 'At least we know what that means.' Reynaud's cabinet was split: the prime minister, General de Gaulle and others favoured continuing the war alongside Britain from France's territories in North Africa, but Pétain and the other 'defeatists' managed to force Reynaud's resignation on 16 June. President Albert Lebrun, a largely ceremonial figure, then invited Pétain to take over the premiership, and on 22 June the new prime minister signed an armistice with Germany. It was, Pétain said, 'the necessary condition for the survival of eternal France'. In the view of many, the old marshal had once more become the saviour of the nation.

'Better to be a Nazi province'

By the terms of the armistice, Pétain and his government – which set up shop in the resort town of Vichy – were left in control of around two-fifths of the country, in the centre and south, while German forces occupied the remainder, including the whole of the Atlantic coast. In July, the 70-year-old Third Republic was abolished, and Pétain assumed near-absolute power as head of state, replacing the republican slogan, '*Liberté, égalité, fraternité*', with a new one: '*Travail, famille, patrie*' ('work, family, fatherland'). The new motto heralded a 'National Revolution', in which the liberal, secular values of French republicanism were to be replaced by devotion to conservatism, Catholicism and discipline.

The French were stunned with the ease with which they had been defeated, and looked for scapegoats. Rumour and paranoia abounded. '*Qui nous a trahi?*' people asked. 'Who has betrayed us?' Pétain's government supplied the answer, pandering to the French bourgeoisie's dislike of Jews, Freemasons, secularists, socialists and other pillars of the rickety republic. 'Better Hitler than Blum,' was a common sentiment, referring to the leader of France's 1936 Popular Front government, a socialist with a Jewish name. Pétain and his many followers also blamed the British – for sending too few divisions to France, for running away at Dunkirk, and, most treacherously of all, for sinking the French fleet at Mers-el-Kébir, at the cost of some 1,300 French lives, to prevent it from falling into the hands of the Germans. To many in France the ruthlessness of their one-time allies confirmed them in their opinion of *la perfide Albion*.

The Germans themselves proved surprisingly civilized guests – at least to begin with (mass shootings of hostages in reprisal for Resistance attacks was to come later). In 1940 there was little sign of the ravening blond beasts conjured up by the propagandists of 1914; instead, small groups of soldiers could be seen sightseeing round Paris, taking photographs of each other before the Eiffel Tower, behaving more like tourists than conquerors. The French capital had been left as an 'open city', and had suffered little in the way of damage, although the middle classes had deserted the place en masse. 'It would have pained me greatly if I'd had to destroy Paris,' Hitler later remarked. With hundreds of thousands of young Frenchmen taken captive by the Germans, at least some of the hundreds of thousands of young Frenchwomen left behind took consolation, and cigarettes and chocolate, in the arms of these powerful, well-behaved, smiling strangers.

There was no reason, Pétain's many followers argued, why the two countries should not be friends, or at least not outright enemies; at the very least, the French should be realistic, and grasp the best bargain they could out of defeat. This stance they called *collaboration à raison*. On 30 October Pétain himself made a broadcast in his unmistakable high-pitched, reedy voice:

> It is in the spirit of honour and in order to preserve the unity of France – a
> unity that has lasted for ten centuries – within the New European Order which
> is being built, that I today embark on the path of collaboration.

He had just met Hitler at Montoire, and 'the New European Order' was a useful euphemism for those who did not wish to recognize the reality of a continent crushed under the Nazi jackboot.

The cult of Pétain

It is unlikely that Pétain had any very clear idea what 'collaboration' might actually entail. He was not a natural politician, and his wits were not what they had been. He was becoming increasingly deaf, tended to wander away from the point during discussions, and was known to nod off in public. As the experience of occupation dragged on, the man once known simply and admiringly as *le Maréchal* became to many a figure of derision, *Philippe le Gaga*, the senile old man who would be king.

But that was still to come. When he took over the government in 1940 he was still a revered figurehead, telling his radio audience: 'I give myself to France as a gift to ease her misfortune.' The rhetoric of sacrifice, long associated with the salvation of national honour at Verdun, continued to be his strongest suit: 'I have suffered for you, with you,' he was to tell his audience in his last broadcast.

> 'Before you, saviour of France,
> We, your boys, swear to follow in your steps ...
> For Pétain is France, France is Pétain.'
>
> André Montagnard, *'Maréchal, Nous Voilà!'*, a song composed in 1941 as part of the cult of Pétain

Pétain was the perfect subject for a cult of personality: war hero, saviour of France, father of the nation. All public buildings had to display his portrait; all oaths of loyalty were sworn to him personally rather than to the state; the youth of the nation, singing the Vichy anthem *'Maréchal, Nous Voilà'*, dedicated itself to his service, 'For Pétain is France, France is Pétain'. The Vichy administrator Charles Donati, on his installation as prefect of Angers in August 1943, left no superlative unuttered, describing Pétain as 'indisputably the greatest Frenchman by virtue of his military past, the glory that he evokes, his perfect success in all domains and the heroism that he demonstrates on a daily basis, even though he is in his 88th year'. May Day, the day on which organized labour traditionally celebrated its solidarity, was reclaimed from the communists and syndicalists and turned into a muted celebration of the sanctity of work – the first element in *Travail, Famille, Patrie*; 1 May also conveniently coincided with the feast of St Philip, Pétain's name day. In reverence to the second element, *Famille*, married women were barred from public service, and encouraged to stay at home and breed – and if a mother proved particularly fecund, her fifteenth child would be honoured by having *le Maréchal* as godfather.

When it came to actually running the government, Pétain relied on more cunning operators as his deputies, among them Admiral Darlan (a trimmer who collaborated with the Nazis while keeping his options open with the Allies) and, most infamously, Pierre Laval. Laval had had a chequered political career of wandering political allegiances, earning him the nickname *le Maquignon* (the 'horse trader' or

As part of the cult of *le Maréchal*, busts of Pétain were mass-produced for distribution to town halls and prefectures.

'shady dealer'), and had served both as prime minister and foreign minister several times during the 1930s. When someone complained to him that Pétain did no work, he riposted: 'Who's talking about work? We need a flag. A flag doesn't do any work. You stand in its shade.' For his part, Pétain was suspicious of Laval's pro-German enthusiasms – the latter had proposed a Franco-German union to Hitler – and dismissed him in December 1940; it was only following pressure by the Germans that Pétain recalled him sixteen months later.

It is a measure of the complexity of the times that many people stayed loyal to Pétain even while they expressed their loathing of Laval, and looked forward to de Gaulle, exiled in London since 1940, taking over the reins of power. The crowds were still cheering for Pétain at Easter 1944 when he attended Mass at Notre Dame de Paris; only a few months later they turned out to cheer de Gaulle as he strode through the liberated capital.

The varied fate of French collaborators

IT IS ESTIMATED THAT SOME 10,000 suspected collaborators were executed without trial before and after the liberation. Between 1944 and 1951, official French courts condemned 6,783 people to death for treason and related offences, although only 791 of these sentences were actually carried out. The more common punishment, meted out to some 50,000 people, was *dégradation nationale*, by which those found guilty were stripped of their civil rights for a specified period.

Many prominent figures escaped trial until the 1980s or 1990s. For example, it was not until 1998 that Maurice Papon, head of the Paris police in the 1950s and 1960s, was convicted of crimes against humanity for his part in the deportation of 1,690 Jews from Bordeaux to the Drancy concentration camp between 1942 and 1944. Sentenced to ten years in prison, he was released in 2002 on the grounds of ill health, and died on 17 February 2007. There was outrage when he was permitted to be buried with the insignia of the Order of the Legion of Honour, despite having been stripped of the decoration after his conviction.

To this day in France there is still a minority who, in private at least, remain admirers of Pétain, seeing him as a bulwark against rule by German Gauleiters and the 'banditry' of the communist *voyous* (hooligans) who 'took to the Maquis to pillage and steal'. As for that 'troublemaker' de Gaulle, his going into exile in Britain amounted to desertion; and in any case he and the Maquisards were nothing but tools of Moscow.

Collaboration and resistance

The armistice signed by Pétain in June 1940, although it allowed the French to keep their government, their empire and their navy, only gave an illusion of national sovereignty. Some of its terms echoed those imposed on Germany at Versailles 21 years earlier: the French army was restricted to 100,000 men, put on leave for the duration of hostilities; reparations were imposed in terms of a daily charge to cover the cost of the German occupation; the two-fifths of the country left to Vichy comprised the poorest and least productive areas of France. Although France gave up all its German POWs, French POWs remained incarcerated in Germany.

Vichy did manage to remain technically neutral; no non-colonial French forces fought with the Germans against the Allies – with the exception of some far-right French volunteers who served with the SS Charlemagne Division and similar units. But within France, the Germans managed to get the French themselves – civil servants, gendarmes – to do much of their dirty work, including the arrest and deportation of French Jews. The Vichy government had begun introducing anti-Jewish measures as early as July 1940, steadily increasing restrictions on both foreign-born

'Collaboration means: give me your wristwatch and I will tell you the time.'
Popular saying in occupied France

The Trial and Execution of Pierre Laval

PIERRE LAVAL, VICHY PRIME MINISTER from 1942, had been taken along with Pétain to the castle of Sigmaringen by the Germans in August 1944. In May 1945, as Germany collapsed, he made his way to Spain, but the Spanish authorities deported him. He eventually found his way to Austria, where he was taken into custody by the Allies.

At his trial, which took place in Paris that October, his lawyers objected that they had not had time to prepare a defence and pulled out. Laval was left to defend himself, which he did – vigorously. When the procurator general told him he was being tried 'for public acts of which the evidence was the laws promulgated over his signature', Laval retorted 'If I signed them you executed them' – referring to the role the French judiciary had played in carrying out the policies of Vichy. Laval claimed the right to answer the procurator, but the judge denied him this right, then started to shout at Laval to be quiet, even though Laval had not, for once, said a word. Eventually, after accusing the judge of 'formulating both question and answer', and claiming to be the victim of a 'judicial crime', Laval declared his intention of remaining silent, and withdrew to his cell. The rest of the proceedings took place without the presence of either the accused or a defence – a state of affairs that many observers found scandalous. The death sentence was handed down on 9 October.

Prior to his execution, while being held in Fresnes prison, Laval attempted to take his own life by swigging from a bottle of potassium cyanide that he had managed to conceal in his cell. He left the following note:

> To my advocates – for their information: to my executioners – for their shame. I refuse to be killed by French bullets. I will not make French soldiers accomplices in judicial murder. I have chosen my death – the poison of the Romans, which I have carried with me through my long wanderings and which has escaped the searchings of my guards.
>
> I wish to be buried with the Tricolour scarf round my neck. I die because I loved my country too much. My last thought is for France.

The suicide attempt was unsuccessful, however: he had not shaken the bottle nor did he succeed in draining it, and immediate medical attention restored him to the degree of consciousness required by French law for a man to be executed.

Accounts of his execution on 15 October vary. According to some he wore one of his customary white ties and a Tricolour round his neck, and, refusing a blindfold, he addressed the soldiers who were to shoot him in the following terms: 'I pity you for having to execute this crime. Aim at my heart. Long live France!' Others report that he was vomiting and only half-conscious when he was dragged before the firing squad and shot.

and French-born Jews. It seems no pressure was required from the Germans; the French right had vaunted its virulent anti-Semitism since at least the Dreyfus Affair of the 1890s. Meanwhile, the collaborationist militia, the Milice, crushed any suspicion of resistance by the French themselves with a vigour that even Pétain found excessive.

Conditions for the ordinary French citizen grew steadily worse. Food shortages were the most obvious source of complaint, and it was not uncommon to see a respectable bourgeois matron wringing the neck of a pigeon in the park. During the war, only Italy had a smaller average daily intake of calories. Vichy blamed *la cupidité paysanne* – the greed of the peasant farmers whom they accused of hoarding produce. Just as much to blame was the fact that much of France's agricultural production was going to Germany, and that many who had worked on the land before the war were now prisoners of war.

Grumblings increased after November 1942, when the Germans occupied the Vichy zone following the Allied landings in Vichy-controlled Morocco and Algeria. Pétain had issued public protestations regarding the Allied action, although he had secretly instructed Admiral Darlan, then in Algiers, to order Vichy forces in North Africa to join the Allies. More and more, passive resentment became active resistance, especially when the Germans stepped up the recruitment of French workers to go to work in Germany; to avoid this, many ran off to join the Maquis.

> **Where on earth are we heading if we can't trust our traitors any more?**
>
> René Lefèvre, on hearing that Admiral Darlan had abandoned Vichy and declared for the Allies in November 1942

Downfall

With the German occupation of the whole of France, the Vichy government continued to exist, but with even less of a semblance of the government of a sovereign power. The actively collaborationist Laval – who had proposed a Franco-German union to Hitler in October 1940 – had been recalled by Pétain as prime minister in April 1942, and *le Maréchal* now became not just a cipher, but the shadow of a cipher.

Armed resistance escalated in 1944 during the run-up to D-Day, and after the Allied landings in Normandy the Pétain–Laval government was forcibly moved by the Germans from Vichy to Belfort, and then at the end of August to Sigmaringen in Germany, where they were installed in a castle high above the Danube. Pétain, who had refused to leave France in 1940, and who after the liberation of Paris had secretly contacted de Gaulle suggesting a peaceful handover of power, now regarded himself as a prisoner, and refused any dealings either with those Vichyites who jockeyed to succeed him, or with the Germans. On 24 April 1945, as the Red Army hammered at the doors of Berlin, Pétain made his way over the border into Switzerland, and thence to the French frontier. There he was met by General Koenig, representing de Gaulle's Free French. Koenig refused to shake Pétain's proffered hand. Instead, he put him under arrest.

Pétain had returned to France largely to justify his actions. Many – including de Gaulle – would have preferred it if he had stayed away, for the case of Pétain, coloured in various shades of grey, epitomized the cases of so many Frenchmen in the years after 1940. The Vichy prefect Charles Donati, giving evidence at Pétain's trial in August, stated that 'millions and millions of French people think that this trial is an immense political mistake'. Unlike the blatantly pro-Nazi schemer Laval, Pétain was cherished to varying degrees by a broad spectrum of French society, even by some on the left (including François Mitterand, the future socialist president), who remembered Pétain's care for his men in the First World War, and his efforts to secure the return of POWs in the Second.

Le Maréchal est un grand homme ... qui est mort en 1925. [The Marshal is a great man ... who died in 1925.]

Charles de Gaulle on Pétain, whose last active command had been in the Rif War in Morocco in 1925

In his opening statement at his trial, Pétain repeated the declaration he had made in a broadcast years before: 'I give myself to France as a gift to ease her misfortune.' He also repeated the image he had offered in his last broadcast before being taken to Sigmaringen: 'If I could no longer be your sword, I wanted to be your shield.' After this he said little, apart from asking for a question to be repeated a little louder. When the verdict and sentence came, no one was surprised: military degradation (which stripped him of his rank), and death by firing squad. However, the judges put in an appeal for clemency, and de Gaulle, now president of the provisional government, commuted the sentence to life imprisonment, on the grounds of *le Maréchal's* advanced age and his actions during the First World War. Pétain spent his remaining days confined alone, declining deeper into senility, on the rocky Île d'Yeu, off the coast of the Vendée. He died in 1951, aged 95, and is buried on the island.

Pétain had expressed his wish to be laid to rest among his men in the vast cemetery at Verdun, but repeated requests for his remains to be transferred there have always been rejected. Nevertheless, in honour of his role in the First World War, successive French presidents from de Gaulle onwards have laid wreaths on his grave on the Île d'Yeu every 11 November, the date of the 1918 armistice.

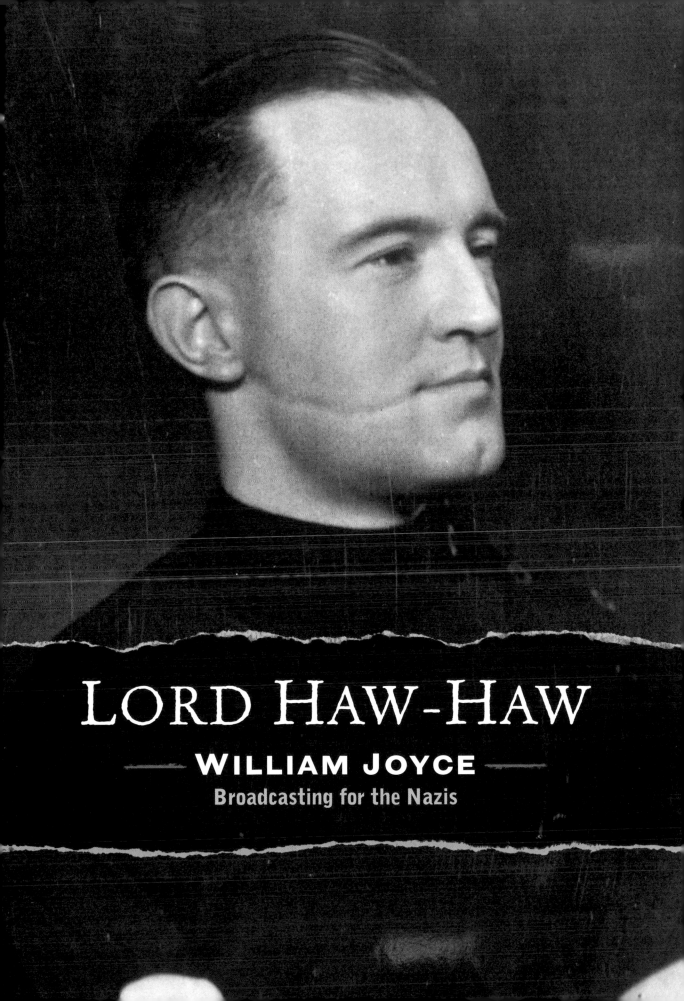

LORD HAW-HAW

WILLIAM JOYCE

Broadcasting for the Nazis

On 14 September 1939, just a fortnight after the Nazis had marched into Poland, a journalist writing the 'Jonah Barrington' column in the *Daily Express* described one of the voices that had begun to make propaganda broadcasts to Britain from Germany: 'He speaks English of the haw, haw, damn-it-get-out-of-my-way variety, and his strong suit is gentlemanly indignation.' Within a week, the same journalist was referring to this anonymous broadcaster as 'Lord Haw-Haw'. In fact, more than one pro-Nazi Briton broadcast on behalf of the Germans during the Second World War, but the most familiar of these men, who was soon attracting a regular audience of some 6 million people, was William Joyce, and it was he who has ever since been known disparagingly as Lord Haw-Haw.

WILLIAM JOYCE

Born 24 April 1906, in New York City, New York, USA

Died hanged 3 January 1946, at Wandsworth Prison, London, England

---

On 28 May 1945, shortly after the end of the war in Europe, Joyce was captured by British soldiers in Germany, near the Danish border. Brought back to Britain, he was charged with high treason, on the grounds that, 'being a person owing allegiance to our Lord the King', he 'adhered to the King's enemies' by broadcasting propaganda. Found guilty, he was hanged on 3 January 1946 – the last man to be executed for treason in the United Kingdom. At the time – and since – questions have been raised about the verdict, given that, technically speaking, Joyce had never been a British citizen.

The making of a Nazi

William Brooke Joyce was born in Brooklyn, New York City, on 24 April 1906, the son of a Catholic Irish father and a Protestant English mother, both of whom had become naturalized American citizens. The family left the USA for Ireland in 1909. His parents' marriage was not a happy one, partly owing to religious differences, but both were ardent Unionists, opposing the aspirations of Irish nationalism, and William himself, a precocious adolescent, adopted a hatred of all things Irish: one of his former schoolmates later wrote of his 'sneering venom when speaking of anything Irish', while another observed that the young Joyce 'bubbled over with self-importance', adding that he was 'heartily detested' even by many loyalists. Joyce himself later claimed that during the Anglo-Irish War of 1919–21, having abandoned his schooling, he served on an irregular basis with the Auxiliaries, the infamous

---

PREVIOUS PAGE **A photo of William Joyce** taken in Germany in March 1940. He acquired the prominent scar in a brawl at a political meeting in 1924.

'Black and Tans', although he would only have been a young teenager at the time.

With the creation of the Irish Free State the Joyces felt they were no longer welcome in Ireland, and moved to England. William Joyce made an unsuccessful attempt to join the British army, then enrolled at Birkbeck College, part of the University of London. In 1927 he gained a first-class degree in English and History, those who knew him at the time commenting that he was 'as fanatical in his studies as he is in other directions'. These 'other directions' largely comprised his involvement in far-right politics, which gave Joyce an opportunity to indulge his enthusiasm for intemperate patriotism and extreme violence. During an election meeting in 1924, while he and other members of the British Fascisti were stewarding a Conservative Party meeting, he

> His friends prophesied a great career for him, but I am afraid he had a queer streak in him.
>
> Hazel Kathleen Barr, Joyce's first wife, quoted in the *Sunday Pictorial*, 17 December 1939

was slashed across the face with a razor, an attack he blamed on 'Jewish communists'. Thereafter he bore a scar extending from the corner of his mouth to his earlobe, a scar that gave character to an otherwise bland, pudding-like face.

After his graduation, Joyce taught languages, married Hazel Kathleen Barr, fathered two daughters and joined the Junior Imperial League, the youth wing of the Conservative Party. However, by 1933 his increasingly virulent anti-Semitism, anti-Catholicism and anti-communism had propelled him into Sir Oswald Mosley's British Union of Fascists, with whom, having abandoned a proposed doctorate in psychology, he took up a full-time paid post as director of propaganda. Joyce became one of the BUF's most effective speakers, basing his vitriolic oratorical style on the wild rants of his idol, Adolf Hitler. He relished his blackshirt uniform (until such uniforms were

> He is a rare combination of dreamer and man of action.
>
> Charles Maxwell Knight, an undercover MI5 agent within the British Union of Fascists, describing Joyce in a note dated 28 January 1935. Maxwell Knight was one of the models for Ian Fleming's fictional character, James Bond.

banned by the Public Order Act of 1936), and grew a Hitler-style toothbrush moustache to go with his ferocious short-back-and-sides. His colleagues admired his leadership qualities but found him aloof, over-fond of intrigue, and fanatical almost to the point of insanity.

Joyce didn't confine his penchant for violence to his political opponents, as his first wife found to her cost. Nor did he follow in the ascetic steps of his hero, Hitler, preferring rather to indulge his fondness for cigarettes, alcohol and women. His affairs and his physical abuse led to the breakdown of his first marriage, and in 1937 he married Margaret Cairns White, a fellow fascist activist, who (mostly) put up with his infidelities and his angry fists.

The road to Berlin

In 1937 the BUF suffered a financial crisis, and Mosley laid off most of his full-time staff. Many returned to work for him on a voluntary basis, but Joyce was not a man to cross, and would never again have anything to do with Mosley – whom he considered too soft on the Jews. It is likely that Mosley had, in fact, engineered Joyce's removal from the movement, fearing a potential rival, and there is an inkling of this in the assessment of Joyce by Charles Maxwell Knight, an MI5 agent working undercover within the BUF:

> Joyce knows what he wants in life, and is out to get it. I feel somehow … that in him there is someone who might one day make history. With all his faults he remains … one of the most compelling personalities of the whole movement.

Joyce went on to found a new party, with himself as leader: the National Socialist League. Now he was not just aligning himself with fascist ideology in general, but specifically calling for Britain to unite with Hitler's Nazi Germany against the 'twin Jewish manifestations' of Bolshevism and international finance. 'If there is a war with Germany,' he told a German acquaintance, 'I will be shot rather than take any part in it on behalf of Britain.'

As the 1930s drew to a close and the clouds of war gathered, Joyce became increasingly involved with a number of German agents in Britain. By July 1939 MI5 were recommending that in the event of war Joyce should be detained, but their man proved to be one step ahead. On 26 August Joyce and his wife sailed for the Continent, and the same day reached Berlin, where, in due course, he obtained a job with the Reichsrundfunk – the Nazi broadcasting organization. Soon his voice would be heard over the airwaves announcing 'Germany calling, Germany calling [with 'Germany' pronounced *Jairmany*]. Here is the news and views on the news …'

Germany calling

When Britain declared war on Nazi Germany on 3 September 1939, the government immediately introduced strict censorship. As far as broadcasting was concerned, that meant the BBC, so many people began to twiddle the dials on their wireless sets to see whether they could get a better idea of what was going on from other stations,

THE OTHER HAW-HAWS

BY THE TIME WILLIAM JOYCE ARRIVED IN BERLIN two other Britons were already working at the Reichsrundfunk in Berlin: Norman Baillie-Stewart, a former army officer who had been imprisoned in the Tower of London in 1933 for selling secrets to the Germans; and John Amery, the fascist son of the British Conservative cabinet minister Leo Amery. It was in fact Baillie-Stewart's 'haw-haw' way of speaking that 'Jonah Barrington' had heard when he wrote his column on 14 September 1939. At the end of the war Baillie-Stewart escaped a treason charge, and was sentenced to five years for 'committing an act likely to assist an enemy'. He died in a Dublin bar in 1966. Amery was a more sinister figure: as well as making propaganda broadcasts, he also proposed the establishment of what was to become the British Free Corps, a unit of the Waffen-SS, and actively recruited for it among British and Dominion POWs. He was executed for treason on 19 December 1945.

broadcasting from Europe. Among the babble of voices was one from Berlin who spoke in a fake upper-class English accent and told the most preposterous stories: the Royal Navy aircraft carrier *Ark Royal* had been sunk, the towns of England's south coast had been flattened by the Luftwaffe. This was the period of the Phoney War, long before the Blitz, so people in Britain found the bluster and absurdity of Lord Haw-Haw – as he quickly became known – highly amusing, and Haw-Haw himself became a figure of fun and entertainment: there

> 'When the warmongers of Downing Street intimated that there could be no terms of peace with the present German government, we knew that the war must be fought out to the bitter end. Britain appealed from negotiation to force. Force then it had to be, and force it shall be until German victory is total.'
>
> William Joyce, *Germany Calling*, 16 May 1940

was, for example, a popular song entitled 'Lord Haw-Haw, the Humbug of Hamburg' and a musical review starring Max Miller. The British government was less amused, especially when research in December 1939 revealed that 6 million people listened to Lord Haw-Haw regularly, and a further 18 million tuned in every now and again. Together, this amounted to two-thirds of the British public. Further research in March 1940 found that the main reason that people listened to him was that 'his version of the news is so fantastic that it is funny', while others were 'amused by his voice and manner'; perhaps more alarmingly, nearly a third of listeners wanted 'to hear the German point of view'.

In the late spring of 1940, with the beginning of the German offensive in the west, attitudes began to change. With the fighting in France, then the desperate withdrawal at Dunkirk, the Battle of Britain and the Blitz, the war was coming home. Lord Haw-Haw continued to inveigh against Jews, communists, capitalists and the British press, but now he also began to gloat over the sufferings of the British people as their homes were reduced to rubble. Accompanying this were sinister threats that much worse was to come unless the British got rid of the 'warmonger' Churchill, the prime minister who refused to make peace. As British paranoia about fifth columnists grew, rumours circulated that Lord Haw-Haw (who had been unmasked as Joyce) was running a network of agents in Britain, and that his broadcasts included code words predicting where the next air raids would come.

The intention of Haw-Haw's broadcasts was, of course, to weaken morale, to destroy the British will to resist. In some broadcasts, he tried to sow division between the classes in Britain:

> We have learned with horror and disgust that while London was suffering all the nightmares of aerial bombardment a few nights ago, there was a contrast between the situation of the rich and the poor which we hardly know how to describe. There were two Londons that night. Down by the docks and in the poor districts and the suburbs, people lay dead, or dying in agony from their

wounds; but, while their counterparts were suffering only a little distance away, the plutocrats and the favoured lords of creation were making the raid an excuse for their drunken orgies and debaucheries in the saloons of Piccadilly and in the Café de Paris. Spending on champagne in one night what they would consider enough for a soldier's wife for a month these moneyed fools shouted and sang in the streets, crying, as the son of a profiteer baron put it, 'They won't bomb this part of the town! They want the docks! Fill up boys!' (29 August 1940)

Following the Nazi invasion of the Soviet Union in June 1941, Haw-Haw also attempted to alienate Britain from its new communist ally:

Communism is based on the lowest tendencies of rapacity ... In England I have seen crowds of sub-anthropoid creatures using razor blades and pieces of lead piping against disabled ex-servicemen who happened to belong to patriotic movements or to the Conservative Party. In almost every case, they were led from behind by Jews. It is with creatures of the same kind that Churchill has made his pact. (13 June 1941)

The level of misinformation was staggering. On 16 January 1943, as the German 6th Army faced annihilation at Stalingrad, Haw-Haw was bragging:

The extent of the enemy's sacrifices has been colossal and cannot be maintained. In the Stalingrad sector, above all, the Soviets have been employing heavy forces and their losses have been proportionately high. Day after day, more Soviet tank losses have been reported and at the same time, the ratio between the German and Soviet air losses is incomparably in favour of the Luftwaffe.

Even on 3 February 1943, the day after the German surrender in this, the most decisive battle of the war, Haw-Haw was questioning whether Stalingrad was truly a defeat:

Whatever individuals have lost, whatever they may have sacrificed, there is nothing in the position as a whole to controvert the view that the main objectives of the enemy offensives have been frustrated. Stalingrad was a part of the price which had to be paid for the salvation of Europe from the Bolshevik hordes.

'Had it not been for his hysteria about Jews he might easily have become a Communist agitator. Strange as it may seem he thinks the Nazi movement is a proletarian one which will free the world from the bonds of 'plutocratic capitalists'. He sees himself primarily as a liberator of the working class. ... [But] Any mind which sees Hitler's cold-blooded trampling down of the free peoples of Europe as a sacred struggle speaks for itself.'

Walter Shirer, 'I meet Haw-Haw', *Sunday Chronicle*, 14 September 1941

Axis Sally

MILDRED GILLARS WAS BORN IN MAINE IN 1900, and grew up in New York City, dreaming of becoming an actress. But she dropped out of drama college, and went to Dresden to study music. By 1935 she was teaching English for the Berlitz School in Berlin, and subsequently achieved her ambition when Radio Berlin offered her a job as an announcer and actress. She continued to broadcast – in English – after America's entry into the Second World War, introducing herself as 'Midge at the mike'. In her sultry voice she murmured to homesick GIs that Germany was unbeatable, death almost certain, and that at that very moment their wives and girlfriends were being comforted in the arms of others. To Allied servicemen she became known as 'Axis Sally' – or 'the Bitch of Berlin'.

After the war Gillars became the first woman in US history to be convicted of treason, and on 8 March 1949 she was sentenced to ten to thirty years' imprisonment. Having converted to Catholicism, she taught in a convent school after her release in 1961. She died in 1988.

The venom directed at Bolsheviks and Jews was relentless, and even after D-Day, with the tide turning fatally against Germany, Haw-Haw gloated over the devastation caused by the new V-1 flying bombs in England, and looked forward to an unimaginable orgy of violence in which Germany's foes would perish:

> It can reasonably be assumed that the battle in the East against the Bolshevik foes of civilization will be hard and fierce and there is every reason to believe that the battle in the west against the capitalist agents of Jewish international finance will attain a climax of violence possibly without precedence. But in the closing rounds of this war it will be seen that Germany has conserved her strength to a degree that will confound her enemies. **(29 June 1944)**

Decline and fall

The Nazis were pleased with their renegade Englishman. Promotions, pay rises, a luxurious Berlin flat and the War Merit Cross First Class (awarded by Hitler in 1944) all followed. His boss at Reichsrundfunk later recalled that Joyce 'did nothing for personal ambition but always because of inner convictions'. Joyce's other duties included touring prisoner-of-war camps to try to bring over British POWs to the Nazi cause; on one occasion he was 'surprised and annoyed' when informed that people in

Britain listened to him because they found him 'very amusing'. He also worked for various black propaganda stations; these purported to be broadcasting from within Britain, and attempted to sow the seeds of discord, for example between British and American soldiers. Joyce's wife Margaret also pursued a successful career in radio, broadcasting as 'Lady Haw-Haw'.

Well-supplied by his hosts, Joyce drank more and more heavily. By now he was also a chain-smoker, and increasingly violent towards his frequently unfaithful wife. On one occasion she noted in her diary that Joyce beat her so badly that she 'could hardly stand'; they then went out to dinner at the International Club. It was a bizarre relationship, mutually destructive and mutually devoted in equal measure: they divorced in August 1941 (she citing cruelty, he adultery), but, seemingly incapable of living without each other, they remarried on 11 February 1942.

By 1943 Berlin was coming under almost constant attack from the air, and the Joyces were moved to Luxembourg, from where they continued to broadcast. But as the Allied armies approached in the autumn of 1944 they returned to Berlin, until, in March 1945, the advancing Red Army made Berlin doubly dangerous, and they left for the town of Apen, near Hamburg. Joyce was deeply despondent: 'I fear that I am spent now,' he confided in his journal at the end of March. 'Damn it! I wish I could go out like a man – with plenty to drink and good cigars.' A month later he was looking his fate squarely in the face:

> 'I still love England and hate to think that I am to be regarded as a traitor to her, which in my opinion I am not.'
> William Joyce, Journal, 29 March 1945

The future does not look promising. We have several plans, but I doubt if any of them will work. However, I am not worried, if I cannot dodge the bill, I must pay it.

On 30 April, as the Battle of Berlin approached its climax, Joyce made his last, defiant, drunken broadcast:

No coercion, no oppression, no measures of tyranny that any foreign foe can introduce will shatter Germany. Germany will live because the people of Germany have in them the secret of life, endurance and will of purpose. And therefore I ask you in these last words – you will not hear from me again for a few months, I say *Es lebe Deutschland*. Heil Hitler and farewell.

That same day, Hitler committed suicide.

Arrest and trial

On 1 May 1945 two SS officers drove Joyce and Margaret from Hamburg to the small town of Flensburg, near the Danish border. 'Too little to drink,' Joyce noted in his journal, although he did manage some wine for breakfast. Top of the list of their 'several plans' was an escape via Denmark to neutral Sweden, but everything was in chaos, including the trains. There was nothing to be done.

On 28 May, three weeks after the German surrender, two British officers, Captain Lickerish and Lieutenant Perry, encountered Joyce quite by chance in some woods outside Flensburg. It was his voice that gave him away. 'You wouldn't happen to be William Joyce, would you?' Perry asked. As Joyce put his hand in his pocket the lieutenant opened fire, fearing he was going for a gun. Joyce fell to the ground, wounded in the leg, protesting that he was not armed. In fact he had been reaching for his pass, which gave his name as Wilhelm Hansen. Unfortunately, Lickerish found another pass on him, bearing the name William Joyce.

Joyce was taken back to London, where at Bow Street police station he was formally charged with high treason. His trial began on 17 September 1945 in the Old Bailey, surrounded by the ruins of the blitzed city. The prosecution realized that they faced a major difficulty: how could Joyce be guilty of treason against Britain if he had never been a British citizen, especially as the offences concerned were carried out abroad? Joyce *had* had a British passport, which he had applied for on 4 July 1933, and renewed on 24 August 1939 – two days before he left Britain for Berlin. However, to get a British passport in the first place he had lied, asserting that he had been born in Ireland (part of the United Kingdom at the time of his birth), not the United States. Furthermore, Joyce had become a naturalized German citizen on 2 July 1940, a year and a half before the USA entered the war – so the Americans could not try him for treason. Thus the prosecution, which at the trial was led by the attorney general, Sir Hartley Shawcross, narrowed down the period of the charges to less than a year: from 18 September 1939, when Joyce had made his first broadcast, to 2 July 1940. That still left the difficulty of whether, as an American citizen, he owed allegiance to the British Crown. Based on a number of learned opinions, the judge, Sir Frederick Tucker, directed the jury that in applying for, and receiving, a British passport, Joyce asked for, and received, the protection of the Crown, to which he therefore owed his allegiance. The judge thus ruled that all the jury had to determine was 'whether or not at the relevant dates he [the accused] adhered to

> '**As by reasons** of my opinions I was not conscientiously disposed to fight for Britain [against] Germany, I decided to leave the country since I did not wish to play the part of a conscientious objector and since I supposed that in Germany I should have the opportunity to express and propagate views the expression of which would be forbidden in Britain during time of war.'
>
> William Joyce, statement to Captain Skardon of MI5, 30 May 1945

the King's enemies with intent to assist the King's enemies'. The prosecution, and the government, must have given a huge sigh of relief. They knew that the British public – who for seven long years had listened to Lord Haw-Haw's poisonous diatribes, his bullying and gloating and threats – would not stand for an acquittal.

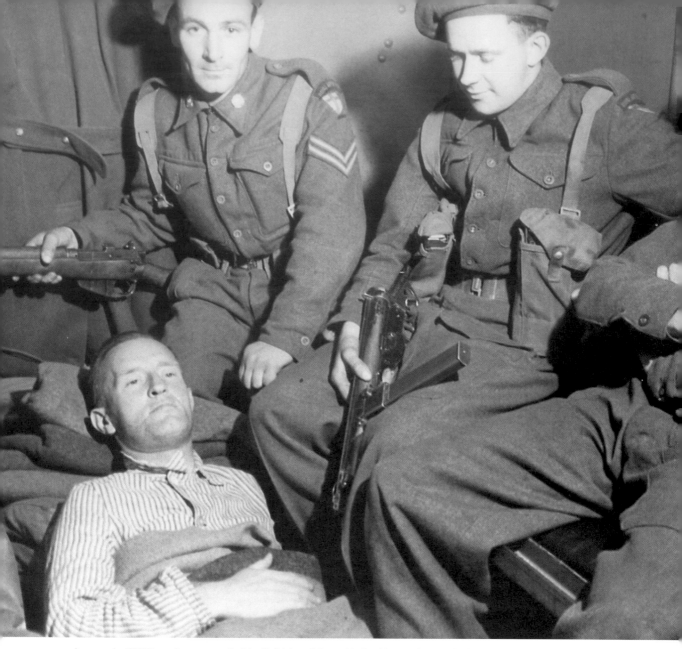

A wounded **William Joyce** guarded by British soldiers. He had been shot in the leg in the course of his arrest by two British officers on 28 May 1945.

With the judge's ruling, Joyce's fate was sealed. MI5 had been assembling transcripts and recordings of his broadcasts for years. Virtually the whole country had heard them; Joyce himself had told the world he was Lord Haw-Haw. The inevitable verdict came on 19 September. The judge had no choice about the sentence: death was mandatory in cases of high treason. The defence appealed, but both the Court of Appeal and the House of Lords upheld the original verdict. Throughout all the proceedings, apart from pleading 'Not guilty', Joyce said not a word.

A cold grey morning

In *Twilight over England*, a book Joyce wrote in 1940, he imagined a Nazi future for Britain, a future in which the arch-criminal Churchill would one day be led out to his execution by the governor of a British prison 'on that last cheerless walk on a cold grey morning just before eight …' In the end it was Joyce himself who, within the walls of Wandsworth Prison, found himself taking that last grim walk. It was 3 January 1946: a cold grey morning indeed. At 9 o'clock precisely the hangman, Albert Pierrepoint, pulled the lever and Joyce dropped through the trapdoor to his death. Outside the walls a small crowd had gathered: there were the usual opponents of capital punishment, singing and saying their prayers, but there were also some of Joyce's old comrades from the BUF and the National Socialist League. Joyce's family were at church; Margaret Joyce remained in her cell in Holloway Prison.

Eventually the authorities decided not to prosecute Margaret; she moved to Ireland and died in 1972. Joyce himself was buried, as was customary, in unconsecrated ground within the prison. Forty years later, in 1986, his remains were re-interred in Galway, Ireland, while a Catholic requiem Mass was said: a bizarre irony, given the hatred Joyce had so long expressed for Catholics and all things Irish. But perhaps it was a suitable finale for this angry, paradoxical man with his warped but brilliant mind, this Anglo-American-Irish-German who professed his love for England while giving aid and comfort to those who would destroy it.

TOKYO ROSE

'TOKYO ROSE' WAS THE NICKNAME given to a number of women who broadcast propaganda in English on behalf of the Japanese, including the American Ruth Hayakawa and the Canadian June Suyama (known as 'the Nightingale of Nanking'). It was even rumoured that one of the voices belonged to the American aviator, Amelia Earhart, whose plane had disappeared in the Pacific in 1937. Rumours persisted that she had been captured by the Japanese, and after the war the US government even asked her husband, George Putnam, to listen to recordings of these broadcasts, to see if any of the voices belonged to her. They didn't.

The woman most commonly identified as 'Tokyo Rose', however, was a Japanese-American called Iva Toguri D'Aquino (1916–2006), who was visiting a sick relative in Japan when Pearl Harbor was attacked. She refused to renounce her American citizenship, but was eventually persuaded to work as an English-language radio announcer, having been assured that she would not be required to broadcast any propaganda against the Allies. She used some of her meagre earnings to help feed Allied prisoners of war in a nearby camp, and in April 1945 married a Japanese-Portuguese called Felipe D'Aquino. After the Japanese surrender she was arrested by the US authorities, but no evidence of anti-American activity could be found, and she was released after a year. However, a press campaign was mounted in the USA against her, and in 1948 she was taken back to California to face treason charges. She had just lost her first baby, and was forcibly separated from her husband, whom she never saw again. Toguri was convicted of treason in July 1949, on the grounds that on one occasion she had mentioned the loss of American ships. Sentenced to ten years, she was released on parole in 1956. Irregularities during her trial, and the discovery that certain key witnesses had lied, led to a presidential pardon being issued in 1977.

WE ARE YOUR
BAD CONSCIENCE

SOPHIE SCHOLL

The White Rose and the German resistance

For Johann Reichhart, whose family had been executioners for eight generations, it was just another beheading. He took a pride in his work, always dressing correctly for the occasion in black coat, white shirt, white gloves and top hat. Since embarking on his career in 1924, Reichhart had been responsible for some 2,000 executions. This was an unusual one, though. Young Sophie Scholl, just 21, was little more than a girl – but a convicted traitor nevertheless.

It was 5 p.m. on 22 February 1943. Just a few hours earlier Sophie, together with her brother Hans and their friend Christoph Probst, had been found guilty of treason in the People's Court presided over by the notorious Nazi judge, Roland Freisler. And now they were to die. The three were at the heart of *die Weisse Rose*, the White Rose, a group of Munich students devoted to non-violent resistance to Hitler. They had done no more than hand out pamphlets, but in so doing they knew they faced almost certain death.

> SOPHIE MAGDALENA SCHOLL
>
> *Born* 9 May 1921, at Forchtenberg, Württemberg, Germany
> *Died* guillotined 22 February 1943, in Stadelheim Prison, Munich, Bavaria, Germany

A fractured resistance

During the 1930s and through the early military successes of the Second World War, the vast majority of Germans broadly supported Hitler, even if they were not active Nazis. Had not Hitler restored national pride after the humiliations forced on Germany after the First World War? And had not the Nazis 'cured' unemployment (albeit largely through conscription and rearmament)?

There were some dissenting voices, but opposition to Hitler was fragmented and disorganized, and largely confined to small, disconnected groups within the professional classes, the officer corps, the civil service and the churches. The left had been brutally emasculated after 1933, and those social democrats and communists who were not held prisoner in concentration camps were forced to go into exile or underground. Their efforts were largely devoted to survival, to maintaining their networks, rather than to active resistance.

At the other end of the political spectrum, the officer corps – many of whom came from aristocratic Prussian families – disliked the fact that the Nazis relied on support from the masses and the middle classes, and that their leader, a former corporal, interfered so much in military affairs. Although they were often fiercely

OPPOSITE **Sophie Scholl,** the 21-year-old German student of biology and philosophy guillotined for defying Hitler.

nationalistic, anti-communist and eager to reverse the terms of the Versailles treaty, they feared that Hitler's recklessness would lead Germany to disaster. Senior generals – with the backing of elements within the German Foreign Office and the Abwehr (military intelligence) – had seriously considered mounting coups against Hitler in 1938 and 1939, the first time to prevent a war with Britain and France over Czechoslovakia, the second time to stop Hitler mounting his onslaught on Western Europe (which was in fact postponed until the following spring). As a whole, however, the officer corps supported the war against Poland, which they saw as restoring Germany's historic borders. The success of the Blitzkrieg campaigns in both east and west in 1939–41 boosted army morale and decreased opposition to Hitler, and it was only after the tide turned at Stalingrad that conspiracies began to emerge again, as senior army officers feared that the Führer's disastrous direction of strategy would lead to a Soviet invasion of Germany itself. The result was a series of failed assassination attempts against Hitler, most famously the 1944 July Bomb Plot. The failure of the latter resulted in vicious bouts of reprisals against anyone even vaguely associated with the plotters. Some 5,000 people were arrested; many of them were tortured, and 200 were executed – many of them dying slow deaths, hanged by piano wire from a meat hook. Hitler had ordered that they should be 'hung like cattle'.

Another strand of resistance came from the churches – or at least from some elements within them. After Hitler's rise to power the main Evangelical Church became increasingly dominated by the Nazi supporters known as German Christians, while the Roman Catholic Church discouraged opposition to the regime. However, many Catholics, notably Bishop Clemens Galen, took a firm (and eventually successful) stand against the Nazis' compulsory euthanasia programme aimed at people with severe mental or physical disabilities. There were dissenters too among the Evangelicals, such as Dietrich Bonhoeffer and Martin Niemöller, both of whom helped to found the breakaway Confessing Church (*Bekennende Kirche*). Niemöller spent seven years in concentration camps; Bonhoeffer was arrested in 1943 and murdered by the Gestapo in 1945.

> 'In Germany, they came first for the communists, but I didn't speak up because I wasn't a communist. Then they came for the social democrats, but I didn't speak up because I wasn't a social democrat. And then they came for the trade unionists, but I didn't speak up because I wasn't a trade unionist. And then they came for the Jews, but I didn't speak up because I wasn't a Jew. And then they came for me ... and by that time there was no one left to speak up.'
>
> Martin Niemöller, the Protestant pastor and former U-boat captain who spent seven years in Sachsenhausen and Dachau concentration camps for his criticism of the Nazis. During his tour of the USA in 1946 he would finish his lectures with variations on the above words.

'Hitler's compulsion, it
      makes us small,
Still we're bound in chains.
But one day we'll be
      free again,
We'll smash through
      the chains.

For our fists they are hard,
Yes, and the knives hang
      loose.
For the freedom of youth
Navajos are struggling.'

The song of the Cologne-based Navajos, one of
the informal anti-Nazi youth groups known as the
Edelweiss Pirates

Young people, indoctrinated for much of
their lives and corralled into the Hitler Youth,
tended to be the most avid upholders of Nazi
beliefs. There were exceptions. From the late
1930s small numbers of disaffected working-
class youths in the Rhineland and the Ruhr
formed themselves into groups known as
'Edelweiss Pirates', from the metal edelweiss
badges they wore. The nonconformist Pirates
– who loved hiking and singing and camping
in the countryside – loathed the enforced
regimentation of the militaristic Hitler Youth,
whose members they would beat up if they got
the chance. The authorities dealt with them
harshly: after disturbances in bomb-shattered
Cologne in October 1944, six teenage
Edelweiss Pirates were hanged.

Among middle-class youth, some
demonstrated their rebellion by attending
clubs to listen to jazz and swing – 'degenerate'
forms of music condemned by the Nazis. Even such apparently harmless activities
could lead to severe penalties, and some so-called *Swingjugend* found themselves
in concentration camps. The universities – in other places and at other times so often
centres of radical dissent – were in Germany centres of enthusiastic support for the
Nazi regime. There was an honourable exception, and that was the group of students
who made up the White Rose.

We will not be silent

The father of Sophie and Hans Scholl was a respectable Lutheran burger, the mayor
of Forchtenberg am Kocher in southwest Germany. As was required by law under
the Nazis, Hans joined the Hitler Youth while Sophie went into the female equivalent,
the League of German Girls, but it was not long before both became disillusioned.
In 1942 Sophie followed her brother to the
University of Munich, where he was studying
medicine; her subjects were biology and
philosophy. She joined his circle of friends,
including Alexander Schmorell, Willi Graf,
Christoph Probst and an older man, Kurt
Huber, who was a professor of philosophy and
musicology. The circle shared a passion for art,
music, literature, philosophy and theology – but
they did not turn their backs to the horrors of the

'We will not be silent.
We are your bad
conscience. The
White Rose will not
leave you in peace!'

The motto of the White Rose, ending the
fourth of the 'Leaflets of the White Rose'

Three of the central figures of the White Rose: Sophie Scholl (centre) and her brother Hans (right) say goodbye to their friend Christoph Probst (left), as he departs from Munich's Ostbahnhof for the Eastern Front, 1942.

world around them, and their ethical concerns (for many of them were religiously inspired) soon focused on the need for political action. Several of them had witnessed atrocities while undertaking military service on the Eastern Front; Graf had seen the realities of the ghettos in Warsaw and Łódź.

The 'Leaflets of the White Rose', as they were entitled, started to appear in the summer of 1942. Hans initially kept Sophie in the dark about what he and his friends were up to, but it was not long before she too became involved. The first leaflet, written in the lofty style of the serious-minded young student, and making free with quotations from Schiller and Goethe, nevertheless pulled no punches. 'Adopt passive resistance,' it adjured its readers:

Adopt passive resistance – *resistance* – wherever you are, and block the functioning of this atheistic war machine before it is too late, before the last city is a heap of rubble, like Cologne, and before the last youth of our nation bleeds to death on some battlefield because of the hubris of a sub-human.

The authors, Hans Scholl and Alexander Schmorell, ended with a plea: 'Please make as many copies of this leaflet as possible and pass them on!'

> **It is unbelievable to what extent one must betray a people in order to rule it.**
> Adolf Hitler, quoted in the second of the 'Leaflets of the White Rose' (1942)

The second leaflet attacked National Socialism, reported the murder of 300,000 Polish Jews, and stated that it was 'the holiest duty of every German' to destroy 'this brown horde'. The third leaflet gave more practical advice on what form passive resistance should take: readers were asked to sabotage the armament industries, to sabotage every aspect of the war machine, to sabotage every institution associated with National Socialism. The fourth leaflet identified Hitler with Satan, and asserted that 'His mouth is the foul-smelling maw of Hell.'

The White Rose embarked on their second series of leaflets, the 'Leaflets of the Resistance', in November 1942. The fifth leaflet foresaw the imminent defeat of Germany and looked to a new post-war order, with a federal Europe and a 'reasonable form of socialism'. The sixth leaflet was written by Kurt Huber in February 1943 in the aftermath of the overwhelming German defeat at Stalingrad, and was addressed to the students of Germany:

Women students! Men students! The German people look to us! Just as in 1813 when the people expected us to shake off the Napoleonic yoke, so in 1943 they look to us to overthrow the National Socialist terror through the power of the spirit. Beresina and Stalingrad are aflame in the East; the dead of Stalingrad beseech us!

'Up, up, my people, let smoke and flame be our sign!'

Our people stand ready to rebel against the National Socialist enslavement of Europe in an impassioned uprising of freedom and honour.

Holy fools

The leaflets, reproduced on a hand-cranked mimeograph machine, were distributed to many cities throughout Germany and Austria, provoking the Gestapo into a frenzied search for those responsible. Their exasperation was increased when on several nights in February 1943 the slogans 'Freedom' and 'Down with Hitler' began to appear on walls throughout Munich.

On 18 February, in Berlin, Goebbels addressed a massive rally to urge the German people to embrace total war in the wake of Stalingrad. 'Do you agree,' he demanded of the crowd, 'that everyone who goes against the war effort in any way should pay for it with his head?' The crowd roared its assent. On the same unseasonably mild day in Munich, Hans and Sophie Scholl took a suitcase full of leaflets – the sixth leaflet, the one authored by Huber – to the university. Marching along the corridors, they left piles outside the lecture theatres so that the students would find them when they emerged. Hans and Sophie then climbed the stairs to the gallery at the top of the central covered courtyard, and threw the remaining leaflets down into the space below. It was an extraordinarily foolhardy thing to do. They were spotted by a janitor, who pursued them and took them to the office of the rector. The Gestapo were summoned, and the brother and sister were taken away in handcuffs. Hans had tried to swallow the draft of a seventh leaflet that he had in his pocket, but the Gestapo managed to retrieve the torn pieces and put them together. 'Hitler and his regime must fall,' the draft read in part, 'so that Germany may live.' Hans claimed that the paper had been handed to him by a stranger.

> 'Somebody, after all, had to make a start. What we wrote and said is also believed by many others. They just do not dare express themselves as we did.'
>
> Sophie Scholl, at her trial, 22 February 1943

Hans and Sophie were subjected to lengthy, separate interrogations. Searching their apartment, the Gestapo found a letter to Hans from Christoph Probst. The handwriting was the same as that in the draft leaflet Hans had tried to swallow. Hans and Sophie remained calm, but eventually confessed. They insisted that no one apart from them was involved. But further arrests followed, and between February and October 1943 some thirty people associated with the White Rose were brought to trial. The Scholls, Probst, Graf, Schmorell and Huber all received death sentences.

'I have to go'

'I am dying without any hate,' Probst wrote to his wife, the mother of his three young children, the evening before he was to be tried, alongside the Scholls. Hans wrote a line from Goethe on the wall of his cell: '*Allen Gewalten zum Trotz sich erhalten*' – 'Despite all the powers closing in, hold yourself up.' In her cell, on the copy of her indictment, Sophie scrawled a single word: 'Freedom'.

The trial took place on 22 February. The charges were high treason and aiding and abetting the enemy. The proceedings were perfunctory, the outcome fore-ordained; it was no more than a piece of theatre, giving the vicious Judge Freisler the opportunity to harangue and vilify the three in the dock. The horrific drama was intensified by the sudden appearance of Hans and Sophie's parents, who had belatedly been informed of their children's arrest. Robert Scholl requested to be allowed to defend his son and daughter. The request was dismissed, and Freisler ordered that the parents be removed from the courtroom. As he was bundled out, Robert Scholl bellowed: 'There is a higher justice! They will go down in history!'

Back in Berlin, Reichsführer-SS Heinrich Himmler, the second most powerful man in Germany, had already decided that the three should die. Such a measure would discourage other students from indulging in dissent. When he heard the death sentence, Hans shouted to Freisler, 'You will soon stand where we stand now!'

The three condemned were immediately taken to Stadelheim Prison, their place of execution. Just before 5 p.m. Sophie Scholl was led across a courtyard to a small building, inside which was the *Fallbeil*, the smaller, heavier German version of the guillotine (the word literally means 'drop hatchet'). The executioner, Herr Reichhart, in his black coat and *zylinder* hat, instructed his assistants to hold her

The black granite memorial to the White Rose resistance fighters in the Hofgarten, Munich. On it is inscribed an extract from their fifth leaflet, calling for a new Europe built on freedom.

down. This was one of his humanitarian innovations. It was quicker than fastening leather straps around the body of the condemned. Shortly afterwards Hans Scholl followed his sister across the courtyard. His last words, yelled at the top his voice, were 'Long live freedom!' Last to go was Christoph Probst. 'I didn't know death could be so easy,' he said.

> 'Good, splendid young people! You shall not have died in vain; you shall not be forgotten.'
>
> Thomas Mann, the exiled German novelist and Nobel laureate, broadcasting in the radio series *German Listeners*, 27 June 1943

Shortly before her death, Sophie Scholl confided in her cellmate, a political prisoner called Else Gebel. 'How can we expect righteousness to prevail when there is hardly anyone willing to give himself up individually to a righteous cause?' she said. Then, looking through the bars of the cell window, she continued: 'Such a fine, sunny day, and I have to go. But how many have to die on the battlefield in these days, how many young, promising lives? What does my death matter, if through us thousands of people are awakened and stirred to action? The students will definitely rise up.'

Such was Sophie's boundless optimism – unfortunately in this case unfounded. Shortly after her death, hundreds of students gathered at the university to express their horror at the traitors found in their midst, and to acclaim the janitor who had apprehended them. But the work of the White Rose was not forgotten. The sixth leaflet was smuggled out of the country, and a few months later millions of copies were dropped over Germany by the RAF.

As for Johannes Reichhart, he carried on with his work, achieving, according to his own records, a career total of 3,165 executions. By a strange irony, after the German defeat he was employed by the Allied occupying forces to assist in the hanging of Nazis convicted of war crimes. Judge Roland Freisler never did get to stand in the dock, as Hans Scholl had defiantly predicted. On 3 February 1945 he was killed by an American bomb dropped directly on his courthouse in Berlin. When his body was taken to the local hospital, a worker was heard to comment: 'It is God's verdict.' No one contradicted him.

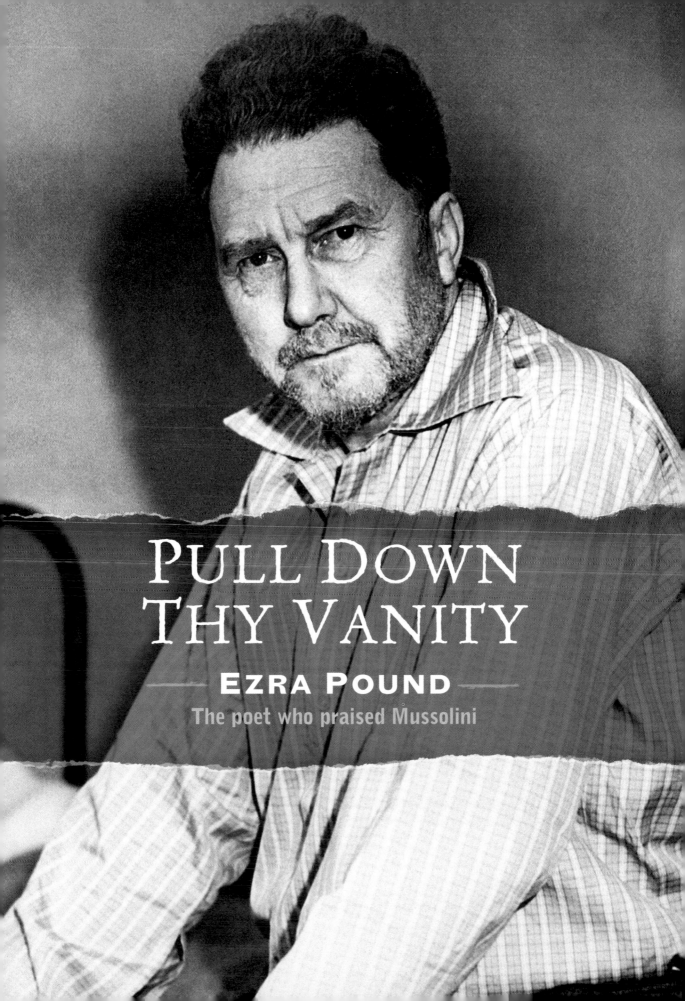

PULL DOWN THY VANITY

EZRA POUND

The poet who praised Mussolini

In April 1945, as Nazi resistance collapsed across the north of Italy, two partisans armed with a tommy gun arrested the American poet Ezra Pound at his home above Rapallo on the Italian Riviera. Handed over to the Allies, Pound told a journalist Hitler was a martyr, like Joan of Arc. Confined to the US Army Disciplinary Training Centre near Pisa, he was put in a cage 10 feet square by 7 feet high, open to the elements, and told if he tried to escape he would be shot. There were fourteen guard towers round the perimeter, each armed with a machine gun.

EZRA WESTON
LOOMIS POUND

Born 30 October 1885, at Hailey, Idaho, USA
Died of natural causes, 1 November 1972, in Venice, Italy

It was a bitter time for Pound, a time of great physical and mental suffering. By day a hot wind blew in from the marshes, at night a death-chill from the mountains. The dust burnt at his eyes. At first there was no bed, just the concrete floor of the cage. Later, he remembered the smell of mint, especially after rain. He began to write, once he was given access to a typewriter. This was the beginning of the *Pisan Cantos*, a polyvocal, multilingual, omnicultural poem-sequence, shot through with broken images: shards of lute music, wreaths of incense for Apollo, the peach-blossom fountain beloved of Ho-Kien, snow on the marble of Carrara. Such strains intermingle with darker shades of war: Stalin, Winston P.M., Berlin 1945. And then there is the tolling refrain, sounded again and again: 'Pull down thy vanity, I say pull down ...'

The *Pisan Cantos* went on to win the prestigious Bollingen Prize, awarded by a jury of Fellows in American Letters of the Library of Congress. The poet himself was not so honoured: in November 1945 he found himself in a Washington courtroom, facing charges that he had 'knowingly, intentionally, willfully, unlawfully, feloniously, traitorously and treasonably' adhered and given aid and comfort to the enemies of the United States of America.

Make it new

Although born in Idaho, Ezra Weston Loomis Pound was brought up a middle-class Presbyterian Easterner, an experience he later felt had torn him from his roots in American's Western heartlands. The fact that he was no more than three or four when his family moved East suggests that the process of mythologizing himself

PREVIOUS PAGE **Ezra Pound photographed in Rome** in March 1941, before the **USA** was at war with Italy.

started early. After studying at the University of Pennsylvania – where he befriended the poets William Carlos Williams and Hilda Doolittle and acquired a knowledge of many European languages,

> 'Literature is news that STAYS news.'
>
> Ezra Pound, *The ABC of Reading* (1934)

both ancient and modern – he took up a teaching position at a Presbyterian college in Indiana. But his bohemian ways (the man wrote *poetry*, for God's sake) quickly led to his dismissal. In February 1908, carrying with him little apart from the unpublished manuscript of his first collection of poems, he set sail for Europe, which was to be his home for the next four decades.

It was in London that Pound – as poet and cultural entrepreneur – was to help give birth to the modernist movement in English literature, with his injunction to 'Make it new'. Anticipating William Carlos Williams' motto 'No ideas but in things', with Hilda Doolittle, T.E. Hulme and others he founded the Imagist school of poetry, devoted to concision and the concrete. Pound was a great midwife of talent, championing the likes of James Joyce and T.S. Eliot (*The Waste Land* bears the stamp of Pound's editing and advice) and, along with Wyndham Lewis and Henri Gaudier-Brzeska, he became a key figure in the aggressive literary and artistic movement known as Vorticism. Their journal, *Blast*, sought to sweep away the sentimental, decorative, decorous complacencies of late-Victorian painting and poetry, and replace it with rule-breaking boldness and energy. Plain-speaking and directness was now the thing: it was through Pound's prompting that the already well-established Irish poet W.B. Yeats abandoned the Celtic-twilit lusciousness of his early verse for a mature poetry that was leaner, harder and more engaged with the modern world.

The lost generation

The First World War knocked the stuffing out of the vigorous, optimistic young men and women who had created the pre-war avant-garde. Hulme and Gaudier-Brzeska were dead and buried, along with millions of other victims of the slaughter. They had died, Pound wrote in *Hugh Selwyn Mauberley*,

> For an old bitch gone in the teeth,
> For a botched civilization.

He found post-war London a gloomy place, and in 1920, with his wife Dorothy Shakespear, he moved to Paris. He had published his first three Cantos in 1917, and his poetry was now becoming wider-ranging in its cultural references, looser, more elusive. The writing of the long sequence of Cantos – of which the *Pisan Cantos* are but a part – was to take the rest of his life.

In Paris Pound moved in the circle of American ex-pat writers that included Ernest Hemingway and Gertrude Stein – the latter somewhat resenting Pound's challenge to her assumed role as queen bee of American modernism. In 1924, to escape the distractions of metropolitan life and concentrate on the Cantos, Pound moved with Dorothy to Italy, to the small, picturesque seaside town of Rapallo. Pound also brought his mistress, the violinist Olga Rudge, who the following year gave birth to a daughter, Maria. Pound – ever the organizer of everyone else, particularly when it came to ensuring his own convenience – had the baby bundled off to be fostered by a peasant couple in the Southern Tyrol. Dorothy gave birth to a son, Omar, in 1926; he was dispatched to London, where he was cared for by Dorothy's mother for the next twenty years.

> 'with usura, sin against nature, is thy bread ever more of stale rags'
>
> Ezra Pound, Canto XLV. Pound's obsession with the 'evils' of usury converged with his anti-Semitism and his support for fascism.

A wasp's nest in the brain

Italy had been a fascist state since 1922, when Mussolini had taken power. Pound was – as can be seen by the way he treated his family – a totalitarian by nature, and found himself in complete sympathy with Il Duce, whom he referred to as 'the Boss'. During the 1920s he became increasingly obsessed with history, economics and monetary reform, and blamed the international banking system – which he claimed was dominated by Jews – for the succession of depressions and wars that the West had suffered over the centuries. Although friendly with individual Jews, Pound had never bothered to conceal his anti-Semitism; already in 1914, in 'Salutation the Third', he was writing:

> Let us be done with Jews and Jobbery,
> Let us SPIT upon those who fawn on the JEWS for their money.

(His attitudes were not unusual for the time: T.S. Eliot's 1920 poem 'Gerontion' contains the following lines: 'the Jew squats on the window-sill, the owner, / Spawned in some estaminet in Antwerp'.)

Pound's meeting in London in 1918 with Clifford Douglas, the founder of the Social Credit movement, only served to increase his hatred of 'usury'. Mussolini's corporatist state appeared to Pound an admirable alternative to international capitalism, and when the poet was eventually presented to Mussolini in 1933, he gave the dictator a copy of *A Draft of XXX Cantos*, which the recipient described as '*divertente*'. Pound praised the 'men of order' in charge in Italy, who, he believed, recognized the importance to society of an artistic elite. (In fact, it's likely that if Mussolini had attempted to read Pound's gift, he would have thrown it across the room.)

As the 1930s progressed, Pound was firing off hundreds of articles on all nature of subjects to periodicals on both sides of the Atlantic. His restless, butterfly mind could not settle on poetry of the disciplined, crafted kind that had previously been his metier. Instead, the Cantos became a battleground for his social, political and economic ideas, a battlefield littered with snatches of personal experience,

Benito Mussolini, to whom Pound presented a volume of his poems in 1933 in the belief that the dictator was the saviour of high art. The slogan on the poster translates as 'Believe, obey, fight'.

Pound composing one of his pro-fascist wartime radio talks. The paper on which he types is emblazoned with Mussolini's motto: 'Liberty is a duty, not a right.'

> **The man is sunk, in my opinion, unless he can shake the fog of Fascism out of his brain during the next few years.**
>
> William Carlos Williams, letter to James Loughlin,
> after Pound's visit to the USA in 1939

remembered echoes of other men's words. More often than not it was the poetry that lay dead on the field; in 1936 Yeats wrote that Pound's oeuvre had become 'constantly interrupted, broken, twisted into nothing by … nervous obsession, nightmare, stammering confusion'.

This confusion reflected an inner turmoil, and the poet often looked, according to his daughter, to be 'fighting a wasp's nest in his brain'. Pound's poetic personae had been so diverse the man had got lost behind the masks, the self swallowed up by the monstrous ego that would hector and lecture and not listen for hours. When Pound briefly visited the USA in 1939, he alienated many, including his old friend William Carlos Williams, the latter remarking: 'The man is sunk, in my opinion, unless he can shake the fog of Fascism out of his brain during the next few years.'

The Axis side of the line

For two years after the outbreak of war in Europe, the USA remained neutral, although favouring Britain against Germany and Italy. Pound favoured the Axis powers, and contributed rabid articles to magazines in Germany and Japan as well as Italy, blaming the war on the Jews, and (following up his monetary obsessions) their supposed determination to control nickel production. 'Democracy,' he wrote in the *Japan Times* on 12 August 1940, 'is now currently defined in Europe as "a country governed by Jews".' A year later he was writing to William Carlos Williams complaining that America was cut off from all contemporary thought, especially that 'on the Axis side of the line'. It may have been this that led Pound to accept an offer from the Italian government to broadcast on its English-language service in January 1941; now at last he could get over to America 'thought on the Axis side of the line' – particularly *his* thought. Besides, he needed the money.

Then, in December 1941, came Pearl Harbor, and America was now at war not only with Japan, but also Germany – and Italy. For a while Pound stopped broadcasting on Rome Radio. It seems that he contemplated returning to America at this stage, but either the State Department would not sanction his return, or Pound himself, for one reason or another, decided to remain in Italy – perhaps to stay close to his elderly parents, who had moved to Rapallo many years before. On 29 January 1942 Pound resumed his broadcasts, the first of which was introduced by an announcer thus:

> 'You are not going to win this war ... You have never had a chance in this war.'
>
> Ezra Pound, broadcast on Rome Radio, 28 June 1942

> Rome Radio, acting in accordance with the Fascist policy of intellectual freedom and free expression of opinion by those who are qualified to hold it, has offered to Dr Ezra Pound the use of the microphone twice a week. It is understood that he will not be asked to say anything whatsoever that goes against his conscience, or anything incompatible with his duties as a citizen of the United States of America.

Pound's broadcasts covered a whole range of topics, and were delivered in an idiosyncratic array of voices, from mock-Confucian to folksy Mid-Western, drawling and squeaking and bellowing. He talked about his friends and fellow writers such as Eliot, Lewis and Joyce, he read from the Cantos, he discoursed on modern art, he lectured on the achievements of Japanese civilization, and, above all, he banged on about monetary reform, usury and the Jews. By now his hatred of 'kikes' was taking a more sinister turn, and on 30 April 1942 he was advising his listeners:

Don't start a pogrom. That is, not an old style killing of small Jews. That system is no good. Of course … if some man had a stroke of genius, and could start a pogrom up at the top, there might be something to say for it. But on the whole, legal measures are preferable. The sixty kikes who started this war might be sent to St Helena, as a measure of world prophylaxis, and some hyper-kikes or non-Jewish kikes along with them.

'Prophylaxis' has an unpleasant ring of the Nazi eugenicists' ideas of 'racial hygiene' – with which Pound expressed his agreement on 18 May 1942. A year later, on 4 May 1943, Pound was resuscitating the anti-Jewish libels of the medieval Church, explaining that Christ 'was crucified for trying to bust a racket'.

Loathsome though all this was, it was not treasonous. But other pronouncements were to prove more dangerous. 'For the United States to be making war on Italy and Europe is just plain nonsense …' (16 April 1942). 'Mussolini and Hitler … are your leaders, however much you think you are conducted by Roosevelt or told by Churchill' (26 May 1942). 'You are not going to win this war … You have never had a chance in this war' (28 June 1942). Pound wrote all his own scripts, and would not allow a comma to be changed. The Italian authorities couldn't quite believe that he was not a spy, using some kind of cipher.

The US authorities knew better. On 26 July 1943, the day after the fall of Mussolini, a federal grand jury in the United States District Court, District of Columbia, indicted Ezra Weston Loomis Pound for treason.

> **I do not believe that the simple fact of speaking over the radio, wherever placed, can in itself constitute treason. I think that must depend on what is said, and on the motives for speaking.**
>
> Ezra Pound, letter to the US attorney general, 4 August 1943, after his indictment for treason

The cage

On hearing of his indictment, on 4 August 1943 Pound wrote a long letter to the US attorney general, in which he claimed he had not addressed his remarks to America's fighting men with the intent of inciting revolt, had 'not spoken with regard to *this* war', and had merely exercised his right to free speech, which could not constitute treason.

Pound's disingenuous letter failed to deflect the slow wheels of justice. On 3 September 1943 the Allied armies invaded mainland Italy; on 5 June 1944 they entered Rome; and in April 1945 they swept across northern Italy, ending German resistance. Once Pound was in custody, the Allied commander, Field Marshal Alexander, wired the US War Office to ask what he should do with this hot potato. The reply came back: Pound was to be taken to the DTC at Pisa, a prison camp for the toughest criminals in the US army. 'Exercise utmost security measures to prevent escape or suicide. No press interviews authorized. Accord no preferential treatment.'

The less dangerous prisoners at the DTC slept in pup tents, while the harder cases were kept in solitary confinement in the cages – the 'death cells'. What these tough men must have thought of Pound when they saw his cage being reinforced with heavy airstrip steel is unrecorded.

> # 'I found the poor devil in a rather desperate condition. He is very wobbly in his mind ...'
>
> Julien Cornell, Pound's lawyer, describing a visit to Pound in jail on 19 November 1945, in a letter to James Laughlin

Pound, deprived of belt and shoelaces, paced his cage, which gave no shelter from rain, sun or dust. After some three weeks of solitary confinement he suffered a breakdown and was transferred to the medical compound, where he was given a pup tent with an army cot and a packing case for a table. Gradually his isolation was reduced, and he was allowed the use of the typewriter in the dispensary, translating Confucius into English and beginning the *Pisan Cantos*, poems that stand testament to the confusion of his mind at this time, though shot through with glimmers of unsurpassed beauty. It was said he also typed letters home for condemned men. 'No man who has spent a month in the death cells,' he wrote, 'believes in cages for beasts.'

St Elizabeth's and after

In November Pound was taken to Rome, from where he was flown to Washington. Here he was visited in the District of Columbia jail by his court-appointed lawyer, Julien Cornell, who found 'the poor devil in a rather desperate condition. He is very wobbly in his mind and while his talk is entirely rational, he flits from one idea to another ...' On 4 December Pound was admitted to Gallinger Hospital. Two days later, when he was due to appear in court, Cornell again visited him and asked whether he wanted to stand mute or to enter a plea. 'His mouth opened once or twice as if to speak,' Cornell wrote, 'but no words came out. He looked up at the ceiling and his face began to twitch.' That afternoon Cornell asked Chief Judge Bolitha J. Laws to enter a plea of not guilty on his client's behalf. Over the next week Pound was examined by four psychiatrists, who reported to Judge Laws that he was 'insane and mentally unfit for trial'. This view was contested by the government's lawyers, who suggested Pound was faking it, but on 13 February 1946 the jury returned a verdict of 'unsound mind'. Pound was then committed to St Elizabeth's Hospital, where he was confined in a ward for the criminally insane.

Pound spent twelve long years in St Elizabeth's. He ignored the other patients, browbeat his doctors, fidgeted and blustered in the presence of his many visitors, who included T.S. Eliot, William Carlos Williams, e.e. cummings, Robert Lowell and – most frequently and most devotedly – his wife Dorothy. His political, economic and anti-Semitic bees buzzed incessantly in his bonnet, and he became convinced that he was the victim, or target, of an international conspiracy. At the same time, he continued to write and publish poetry, and as his literary reputation grew, there was increasing pressure from around the world for his release. The trouble was, if he was discharged from St Elizabeth's he would legally be judged sane, and thus the government could revive the treason charges. There was considerable behind-the-scenes lobbying, and eventually, on 18 April 1958, the attorney general dropped all charges against Pound. In June he and his wife set sail once more for Italy.

> At seventy I realized that instead of being a lunatic, I was a moron.
>
> Ezra Pound, interview with Alan Ginsberg, 1968

His last years were hardly happy ones. He resumed his relationship with Olga Rudge, and relations with Dorothy became increasingly strained. The two eventually separated. Pound was broken in spirit, convinced his creativity had deserted him. In 1928 he had written of himself as 'a man hurling himself at an indomitable chaos, and yanking and hauling as much of it as possible into some sort of order (or beauty)'. In old age he felt he had failed. In 1968, talking to the poet Alan Ginsberg, and no doubt aware that the latter was Jewish, he said: 'Any good I've done has been spoiled by bad intentions – the preoccupation with irrelevant and stupid things. But the worst

> The lunatic, the lover and the poet Are of imagination all compact.
>
> William Shakespeare, *A Midsummer Night's Dream*, V.i

mistake I made was that stupid, suburban prejudice of anti-Semitism.' Around the same time the critic Donald Cory put a blunt question to Pound about the Cantos as a whole: 'Do you or do you not consider the poem a botch – that it didn't come off as you had hoped it would?' Pound picked his nails for a moment, thinking about his life's work, and then answered: 'Yop. I botched it.'

Don't Kill my Mommy and Daddy

Julius and Ethel Rosenberg

Electrocuted for espionage

'You sat the Rosenbergs in the electric chair for nothing. We got nothing from the Rosenbergs.' So Boris V. Brokhovich, the man in charge of developing the Soviet atom bomb, told the *New York Times* in 1989. Thirty-six years previously, Julius and Ethel Rosenberg had become the first American civilians to be executed for espionage, and the first convicted spies to be put to death in peacetime. They had been found guilty of passing military secrets – including details of America's atom bomb – to the Soviet Union. The only reason that they were not charged with treason was that the USA and the USSR were not technically at war.

JULIUS ROSENBERG;
ETHEL ROSENBERG
NÉE GREENGLASS

Born 12 May 1918 (Julius),
28 September 1915 (Ethel),
both in New York City, USA
Died both executed on the electric
chair 19 June 1953, in Sing-Sing
Prison, Ossining, New York, USA

For many years there was doubt expressed as to the soundness of the convictions. With the Cold War turning hot in Korea, the early 1950s was the peak of the 'red scare' in America, a time of anti-communist hysteria, and the FBI pursuit of the Rosenbergs and the conduct of the trial judge bear all the hallmarks of the witch-hunt. Although it has since become clear that Julius Rosenberg was indeed working for the Soviets, he seems not to have provided them with any particularly valuable information. For her part, Ethel was only guilty by association. The fact that the others involved in the spy ring merely received jail sentences suggested to some that the Rosenbergs were condemned to death because they were Jewish. 'My husband and I must be vindicated by history,' Ethel Rosenberg declared before her execution. 'We are the first victims of American fascism.' Ironically, while the Rosenbergs were sent to the chair, the US government was happily employing ex-Nazi scientists to help develop their missile programme.

The Rosenberg ring

Ethel Greenglass met Julius Rosenberg in 1936 at the Young Communist League in New York, and the two married in 1939. She worked as a secretary in a shipping company, while he was an electrical engineer, the son of a Polish garment worker who hoped his son might become a rabbi. In 1940 he started work with the Army Signal Corps as a civilian employee, and in 1942 – by which time the USA and the USSR had become allies in the war against Nazi Germany – he was recruited by the NKVD, the

PREVIOUS PAGE **Julius and Ethel Rosenberg**, handcuffed, embrace outside the Federal Court following their arraignment on espionage charges, before being taken to separate cells.

predecessor of the KGB. His role was to pass over classified documents, via a courier called Harry Gold, to the Soviet vice-consul in New York. He was also told to recruit other agents – among them Ethel's brother, Sergeant David Greenglass, a machinist with the Manhattan Project, the programme that was developing the US atomic bomb at Los Alamos. As Julius was a convinced communist – and as even such right-wing figures as Winston Churchill and General Douglas MacArthur were praising their Soviet ally's heroic struggle against Nazi tyranny – the prospect of passing over atomic secrets cannot have troubled his conscience overmuch.

In 1945 Julius Rosenberg was discharged from the army when it was found he had lied about his membership of the US Communist Party. Five years later his spy ring began to unravel following the arrest of the nuclear scientist Klaus Fuchs, a German communist who had fled Hitler's Germany and who had worked on the Manhattan Project. Fuchs had also used Gold as a middleman for passing atomic secrets to the Soviet Union, which detonated its first nuclear weapon in 1949. The arrest of Fuchs led to the arrest of Gold, who in turn incriminated Greenglass. The latter confessed that he too had leaked secrets, and named Julius Rosenberg as his contact.

A legal lynching

On the evening of 17 July 1950 two FBI agents turned up at the Rosenbergs' apartment and handcuffed Julius in front of his two young sons. Rosenberg refused to supply the FBI with names, so the Bureau director, J. Edgar Hoover, concluded

EMANUEL BLOCH (THE ROSENBERGS' COUNSEL): Would you fight for this country?

JULIUS ROSENBERG: Yes, I will.

BLOCH: If it were engaged in a war with –

ROSENBERG: Yes, I will, and in discussing the merits of other forms of governments, I discussed that with my friends on the basis of the performance of what they accomplished, and I felt that the Soviet government has improved the lot of the underdog there, has made a lot of progress in eliminating illiteracy, has done a lot of reconstruction work and built up a lot of resources, and at the same time I felt that they contributed a major share in destroying the Hitler beast who killed six million of my co-religionists and I feel emotional about that thing.

BLOCH: Did you feel that way in 1943?

ROSENBERG: Yes, I felt that way in 1945 –

BLOCH: Do you feel that way today?

ROSENBERG: I still feel that way.

Extract of transcript of Julius Rosenberg's testimony at his trial, March 1951

that 'proceeding against his wife might serve as a lever in this matter'. Thus on 11 August the FBI came for Ethel, arresting her as she walked to catch a subway. She was given no opportunity to return home to arrange care for her sons. Still Rosenberg refused to talk, and Ethel similarly declined to name names. Their trial began on 6 March 1951, and the chief witness for the prosecution was David Greenglass, who testified that it was his sister Ethel who had typed up notes containing US nuclear secrets. The Rosenbergs pleaded the Fifth Amendment, and refused to talk about their connections with the US Communist Party. Apart from that, they denied all the evidence brought against them: to nearly all the questions put to him regarding his activities, Julius replied: 'I did not.' He also asserted his patriotism: 'I am in favour, heartily in favour, of our Constitution and Bill of Rights,' he said, 'and I owe my allegiance to my country at all times.' At the same time, he was frank about his admiration for the Soviet Union. The jury was clearly hostile – already whipped into a mood of anti-communist paranoia by the witch-hunting activities of Senator Joe McCarthy – and returned a guilty verdict on 29 March.

On 5 April Judge Irving Kaufman passed sentence, and justified the first death sentences handed down for espionage in the United States since the Civil War in the following terms:

> Your conduct in putting into the hands of the Russians the A-bomb years before our best scientists predicted Russia would perfect the bomb has already caused, in my opinion, the Communist aggression in Korea, with the resultant casualties exceeding 50,000 and who knows but that millions more of innocent people may pay the price of your treason. Indeed, by your betrayal you undoubtedly have altered the course of history to the disadvantage of our country. No one can say that we do not live in a constant state of tension. We have evidence of your treachery all around us every day for the civilian defence activities throughout the nation are aimed at preparing us for an atom bomb attack … I feel that I must pass such sentence upon the principals in this diabolical conspiracy to destroy a God-fearing nation, which will demonstrate with finality that this nation's security must remain inviolate; that traffic in military secrets, whether promoted by slavish devotion to a foreign ideology or by a desire for monetary gains must cease.

It had become clear that this was a political trial: the claim that the Rosenbergs were to blame for the Korean War was patently absurd, and the information Julius had supplied about nuclear secrets was negligible compared to the detailed high-grade information supplied by Fuchs – who was only sentenced to fourteen years (and released early for good behaviour). When the FBI had arrested the Rosenbergs they had expected them to be 'just next in a row of falling dominoes'. Their sin was that they had refused to topple.

A national and international campaign was mounted to save the Rosenbergs, as appeal followed appeal through the US courts. Even those not on the left protested, including Pope Pius XII, but on 11 February 1953 President Eisenhower turned down

The Rosenbergs' two young sons, Robert, 6 (right), and Michael, 10 (holding the hand of his grandmother, Sophie Rosenberg), take part in a protest march on 15 June 1953.

the pontiff's plea for clemency. In his memoir *My Silent War*, the Soviet double agent Kim Philby (see p. 162) wrote that 'Eisenhower explained his refusal to reprieve Ethel Rosenberg on the grounds that, if he did, the Russians in future would use only women as spies. It was an attitude worthy of the most pedestrian of United States presidents.'

The couple were executed on the electric chair in Sing Sing prison, New York, just before sunset on 19 June, so that they would not die on the Jewish Sabbath. There were reports that Ethel was so small – she had suffered from curvature of the spine since she was about thirteen – that the electrodes did not fit her properly. Thus it took her executioners three attempts to kill her. On the last attempt, one eyewitness reported, smoke was seen rising from her head. Ethel Rosenberg was the first woman to be executed by the United States government since Mary Surratt was hanged for her role in the assassination of Abraham Lincoln.

'Don't Kill my Mommy and Daddy.'

Slogan on placards carried by the Rosenbergs' children, Robert and Michael, while marching with other protestors

In the wake of the executions the French philosopher Jean-Paul Sartre called the killing of the Rosenbergs a 'legal lynching' and accused the Americans of trying 'to halt the progress of science by human sacrifice':

> Your country is sick with fear. You're afraid of everything: the Russians, the Chinese, the Europeans. You're afraid of each other. You're afraid of the shadow of your own bomb.

The Rosenbergs' two children, Robert and Michael, were adopted by Abel Meeropol, the real name of the songwriter Lewis Allan, best known for his anti-lynching song, 'Strange Fruit'. In 1975, in their book *We Are Your Sons*, Robert and Michael printed the last letter they received from their parents, written on the day of their execution. 'Dearest sweethearts, my most precious children,' Ethel began, and then went on to try to give them some kind of consolation:

> Eventually, too you must come to believe that life is worth the living. Be comforted that even now, with the end of ours slowly approaching, that we know this with a conviction that defeats the executioner!
> Your lives must teach you, too, that good cannot flourish in the midst of evil; that freedom and all the things that go to make up a truly satisfying and worthwhile life, must sometimes be purchased very dearly …

New revelations

In that last letter Ethel wrote 'Always remember that we were innocent …'. Many of the couple's sympathizers were apt to believe her. Although Ethel probably did no more than condone her husband's activities, revelations following the end of the Cold War made it clear that Julius had indeed been a Soviet spy. But a number of key Russians denied that the information he supplied to the Soviet Union had enabled it to develop its own weapon. 'He didn't understand anything about the atomic bomb, and he couldn't help us,' Aleksandr Feklisov, a retired KGB colonel and Julius Rosenberg's one-time handler, told the *New York Times* in 1997. 'And still they killed them. It was a contract murder.' As for Ethel Rosenberg: 'She had nothing to do with this – she was completely innocent,' he said. 'I think she knew, but for that you don't kill people.' In comparison Fuchs, who was only sentenced to fourteen years, 'told us everything about Los Alamos'.

> 'Indeed the defendants Julius and Ethel Rosenberg placed their devotion to their cause above their own personal safety and were conscious that they were sacrificing their own children, should their misdeeds be detected – all of which did not deter them from pursuing their course. Love for their cause dominated their lives – it was even greater than their love for their children.'
> Judge Irving Kaufman passing sentence, 5 April 1951

'I would not sacrifice
my wife and my children
for my sister.'

David Greenglass, Ethel Rosenberg's brother,
explaining in a television interview in 2001 why he
had perjured himself at the Rosenberg trial in 1951

It has also become clear that the FBI
had put pressure on at least one key witness to
perjure himself. In a 2001 television interview
David Greenglass contradicted his court
testimony that he'd seen his sister Ethel typing
up information on US atomic secrets. 'I don't
know who typed it, frankly, and to this day I
can't remember that the typing took place. I had no memory of that at all – none
whatsoever.' He gave false testimony, he said, to protect himself and his wife Ruth,
who thus escaped prosecution. 'I would not sacrifice my wife and my children for my
sister,' he said. Greenglass himself only served ten years, and now he and his wife
live under an assumed name. Asked whether he was still haunted by what he had
done, he said: 'Every time I am haunted by it, my wife says "Look, we are still alive."'
He showed no remorse. 'I sleep very well,' he said.

ALDRICH AMES: JUST IN IT FOR THE MONEY

JULIUS AND ETHEL ROSENBERG WERE INSPIRED to spy for the Soviet Union entirely
out of ideological conviction. As Ethel wrote in her last letter to her sons, she and her
husband realized that 'freedom and all the things that go to make up a truly satisfying
and worthwhile life, must sometimes be purchased very dearly'.

The CIA officer Aldrich Ames, convicted in 1994 of spying for the Soviet Union
and then the Russian Federation, had no such ideals. He betrayed his country purely
for the money – largely to fund the lavish lifestyle of his demanding second wife, a
Colombian woman called Rosario Dupuy, and his own heavy drinking. It was the
resultant financial difficulties he found himself in that led him in 1985 to walk into the
Soviet embassy in Washington DC and offer secrets for sale. He eventually supplied
the Soviets with the names of every US agent at work in the USSR, leading to at least
ten executions.

For this Ames was paid $4.6 million, at least half of which he and his wife
lavished on designer clothing, jewellery, a new Jaguar and a half-million-dollar house,
paid for in cash. Somewhat belatedly this aroused suspicion, and in 1994 Ames and his
wife were arrested as they were about to fly to Moscow, supposedly on CIA business.
At their subsequent trial Ames was sentenced to life, while his wife got five years,
followed by deportation.

In an interview with CNN in 1998, Ames confessed that 'The reasons that I did
what I did in April of 1985 were personal, banal, and amounted really to kind of greed
and folly.' Demonstrating the calculated coldness of the professional intelligence
officer, he insisted that his treason had done little damage: 'At the time that I handed
over the names and compromised so many CIA agents in the Soviet Union ... I had
come to the conclusion that the loss of these sources to the United States government,
or to the West as well, would not compromise significant national defence, political,
diplomatic interests.' He showed little regret about the fate of those individuals he had
effectively sentenced to death.

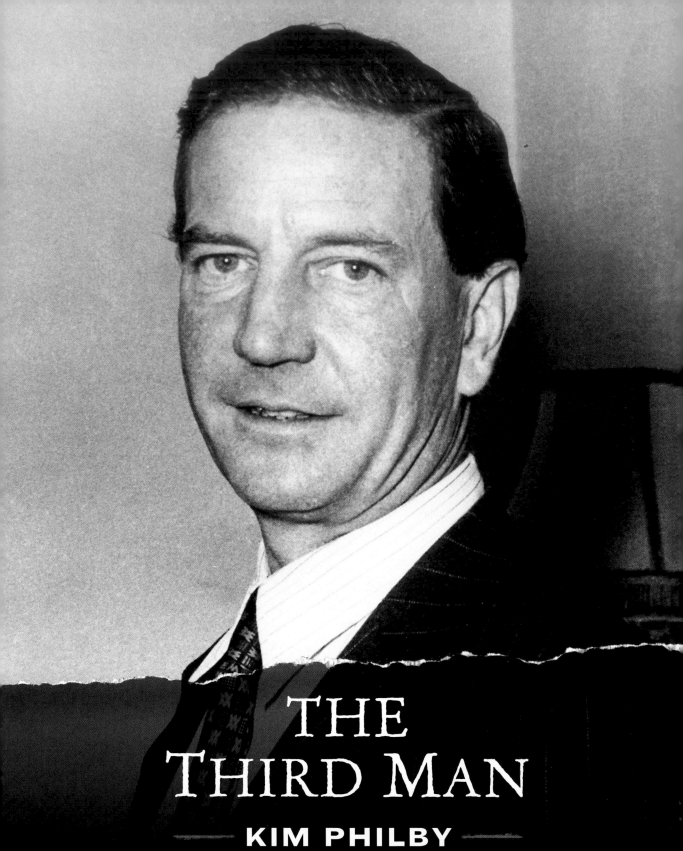

THE
THIRD MAN

KIM PHILBY

Double agent par excellence

Shortly before lunch on a day in late May a car drew up on a deserted stretch of road between Washington DC and Great Falls, Virginia. On one side of the highway was the mighty Potomac River, on the other a wood in which the undergrowth grew thick and rank. A distinguished-looking Englishman, about forty, of medium height and with suavely combed-back hair, emerged from the car. He carried with him a briefcase. For once his dark eyes did not twinkle; they were hard and focused. And his mouth, more used to beaming a seductive smile or a grin of bonhomie, was thin-lipped and intent.

The Englishman doubled back a couple of hundred yards through the bushes, then stopped. Out of his briefcase he took a trowel and started digging. It was hot, sweaty work. In the hole he placed some packages, then covered them with soil. As he emerged from the dark of the wood he made a show of doing up his fly, as if he had just relieved himself. In one sense he had: the buried packages contained a camera, a tripod and various accessories – items that if found in the basement of his Washington house on Nebraska Avenue could prove incriminating.

> HAROLD ADRIAN RUSSELL PHILBY
>
> *Born* 1 January 1912, at Ambala, India
> *Died* of natural causes, 11 May 1988, in Moscow, Russia

The year was 1951, and the Englishman was the representative in Washington of Britain's Secret Intelligence Service, known as SIS or MI6. His name was Harold Philby, but to those on first-name terms with him he was 'Kim'. Earlier that morning, when he had arrived as usual at the embassy for work, he had been greeted by Geoffrey Paterson, MI5's man in Washington. Having spent some hours de-encrypting a 'Most Immediate' telegram from London, Paterson had been grey-faced with shock and exhaustion. 'Kim,' he had said, half whispering, 'the bird has flown.' 'What bird?' Philby had asked, feigning surprise. 'Not Maclean?' 'Yes,' Paterson had answered. 'But there's worse than that … *Guy Burgess* has gone with him.' Now Philby did not have to feign surprise; he was genuinely shocked. Burgess going with Maclean had *not* been part of the plan.

The sort of fellow who smiles at breakfast

Charles Wheeler, the veteran BBC foreign correspondent, was once asked whether he was surprised at Philby's treachery. 'Not really,' he replied. 'I never really trusted him. He was the sort of fellow who smiled at breakfast, that sort of thing.'

OPPOSITE **Kim Philby in 1955,** the year he was publicly cleared of being the 'Third Man' by Foreign Secretary Harold Macmillan.

Dissembling was second nature to Philby, as it must be to any spy. But Philby was not just any spy: such was his mastery of his craft that for three decades, unbeknownst to everybody but his controllers, he worked as an undercover agent for the Soviet Union, while at the same time rising close to the very top of Britain's own espionage organization. Even after Burgess and Maclean fled to the Soviet Union in 1951, Philby successfully denied accusations that he was the 'Third Man' for another twelve years.

A certain degree of unconventionality might have been predicted for Philby. He was born in India, the son of Dora Johnston and the arrogant, brilliant scholar Harry St John Bridger Philby, a noted explorer, intelligence officer, Orientalist and administrator in the Indian Civil Service. Philby *père* later converted to Islam, settled in Saudi Arabia and took a number of additional wives, including a slave girl called Umferhad. Throughout his life, he was an unremitting hater of the British Establishment and all it stood for, and Philby *fils* later acknowledged (in his memoir, *My Silent War*) that his father's eccentricities enabled him to avoid 'some of the more outrageous prejudices of the English public-school system'.

Although christened Harold Adrian Russell, the young Philby was nicknamed Kim by his parents, after Kipling's fictional hero, the boy who becomes an undercover spy in the 'Great Game' between Russia and Britain in Central Asia. Philby's education at Westminster School and Trinity College, Cambridge was conventional enough, although his membership of the Cambridge University Socialist Club marked an increasingly fashionable departure from the upper-middle-class norm. The rout of the Labour Party in the 1931 general election was a turning point for Philby: 'The fact that a supposedly sophisticated electorate had been stampeded by the cynical propaganda of the day,' he later wrote, 'threw serious doubt on the validity of the assumptions underlying parliamentary democracy as a whole.'

His conversion from socialism to communism followed extensive reading and many heated discussions – not to mention the sight of long dole queues and the further impoverishment of the working classes as the Great Depression bit. Capitalism was collapsing; the promised revolution could not be far off. 'I left the university [in the summer of 1933] with a degree and with the conviction that my life must be devoted to Communism.'

'To this day I am convinced that he was not an ideologue. Spying was just his way of being above lesser mortals.'

Nigel West (pen name of Rupert Allason), former Conservative MP and writer on security and intelligence issues

From the sewers of Vienna to the war in Spain

It was at Cambridge that Philby first met Guy Burgess and Donald Maclean. Burgess, a flamboyant, brilliant, hard-drinking and promiscuously homosexual old Etonian, wore his Marxism on his sleeve; Maclean, tall and handsome, the son of a former Liberal cabinet minister, was a quieter figure. Quite how they all became Soviet agents isn't completely clear; in his memoir Philby would only say this: 'How, where and when I became a member of the Soviet intelligence service is a matter for myself and my comrades.' It has been suggested that Philby was the organizer; he almost certainly came into contact with officials of the Comintern (the Soviet-directed Communist International) during trips to the Continent in the summer vacations of 1931 and 1932. It was Philby who later asked Burgess to suggest recruits from their Cambridge set, among them Anthony Blunt and John Cairncross, who were subsequently revealed to be the 'Fourth Man' and the 'Fifth Man' respectively in the so-called Cambridge Spy Ring.

In the summer of 1933 Philby travelled to Austria, where he appears to have worked as a courier, carrying messages between the underground communists in Vienna and their Comintern backers in Prague. It was in Vienna that Philby met his first wife, a Jewish communist divorcée called Alice (Litzi) Friedman, née Kohlman; and it was in Vienna that he first saw the class war in all its bloody rawness. In February 1934 the far-right Austrian chancellor, Engelbert Dollfuss, mounted a putsch against the parties of the left, determined to replace parliamentary democracy with a one-party corporate state, on the model of Mussolini's Italy. The police, the army and the fascist paramilitary Heimwehr were ordered to attack the social democrats and communists, who had organized themselves into the Republican Defence League. Artillery was used against the workers' housing estates in the suburbs of Vienna, and many members of the Republican Defence League took to the sewers. Philby, who had been involved in the fighting in Heiligenstadt, joined one such unit under the streets of Florisdorf, where they attempted to continue resistance for a few more days, without either food or drinking water. In the end, it was Philby's British passport that saved him from arrest and imprisonment. After Dollfuss's victory Philby continued to assist the clandestine socialist underground, but eventually they rejected his help after it became clear to them that he was a tool of Moscow, which was seeking to control and then destroy social democratic movements across Europe. In May 1934 Philby left Vienna in a hurry, perhaps tipped off that his arrest was imminent. With him he brought Litzi, whom he had married on 24 February. It was she, it is thought, who persuaded him to become a Soviet agent.

Philby – the quiet, self-effacing, secretive Englishman – had first come to the attention of the NKVD, the Soviet intelligence and security service, during his time in Vienna. Back in London in June 1934, Philby was approached at a secret meeting in Regent's Park by Arnold Deutsch, a Soviet intelligence officer of Czech nationality. It was suggested to Philby that he could best serve the cause by penetrating the British Establishment, and to this end he was instructed to dissociate himself from his communist past by publicly performing a political volte-face. It was this that led him to join the Anglo-German Fellowship, an organization sympathetic to Hitler and the Nazis. Then in 1937, during the Spanish Civil War, he covered the fighting for *The Times* from the perspective of Franco's Nationalists – although under his pro-fascist cover he was reporting on the Nationalist war effort to Soviet contacts in

France. For urgent messages he had been supplied with a code on a tiny piece of paper, which on one occasion almost brought about his downfall, when he was apprehended and searched by members of Franco's Civil Guard. But he managed to distract them long enough to swallow the incriminating piece of paper unseen. It was a stark reminder of the high stakes he was now playing for.

A piquant situation

Philby slipped into the British intelligence community with extraordinary ease. At the outbreak of the Second World War he was still working as a foreign correspondent for *The Times*, but by the summer of 1940, having covered the

Philby was in Vienna in 1934 during the attempted crushing of the left by Chancellor Dollfuss. It was during this time that he first came to the attention of Soviet intelligence.

fall of France, he was letting it be known that he could be interested in 'war work'. His hints did not fall on deaf ears, and he soon found himself at St Ermine's Hotel in London's fashionable West End in conversation with an elderly lady called Miss Marjorie Maxse. She informed him that she could be in a position to recommend him for 'interesting' employment, and suggested they meet again a few days later. At this second meeting she was accompanied by a young man, whom Philby immediately recognized as his old Cambridge friend, Guy Burgess. Burgess had been a member of SIS since January 1939, and proposed that Philby come to work for him. The two spent the following weekend drinking together, and on Monday Philby reported for duty. MI5 looked into his past and concluded 'Nothing Recorded Against'.

The secret services expanded dramatically during the early years of the war. It was a time of innovation and improvisation, of long hours when there was something 'on', and drawn-out boozy lunches when there was not. For a while Philby found himself involved in Section D, dedicated to sabotage and subversion. In due course Section D evolved into the Special Operations Executive, concerned with supporting the resistance movements in Nazi-occupied Europe, but by 1941 Philby had worked his way into the counter-espionage branch of SIS, Section V, and, thanks to his earlier experience in the region, found himself in charge of the Iberian Peninsula. Fortified by pink gins and black-market pheasants, he achieved a number of coups against the Abwehr (German military intelligence) in neutral Spain and Portugal. One of his superiors,

'A rather altruistic left-winger, mixed-up and Byronic in outlook, eager to assist the left-wing cause without leaning as far as communism.'

Hugh Gaitskell, the future leader of the Labour Party, on Philby, with whom he worked at the Special Operations Executive during the Second World War

in his innocence, told him, 'You're not such a fool as I thought.' At this time Philby also had full access to SIS's agent files, including those of British agents at work in the Soviet Union, who, it is assumed, were duly liquidated.

Philby had had his doubts about Stalin's excesses in the later 1930s and about the Nazi-Soviet Pact of 1939, but with the German invasion of the USSR in 1941 his London and Moscow masters were now on the same side. As the war wore on, however, and defeat of Germany began to look certain, the British security services turned once more to what had been their principal area of interest through the 1930s: Soviet and 'Bolshevik' subversion. To this end, a new Section IX was proposed within SIS, to counter what was perceived as the resurgent communist threat. It seemed likely that Philby's boss at Section V, Felix Cowgill, would be made head of Section IX, but Philby's Soviet contact made it quite clear that he 'must do everything, but *everything*' to get the job himself. 'I liked and respected Cowgill,' Philby wrote in his memoir, 'and had much to thank him for. But he was a prickly obstacle in the course laid down for me, so he had to go.' Philby went on to demonstrate a chilling mastery of office politics, of the dagger-in-the-back variety. With a subtlety and indirectness that would have impressed Machiavelli, he briefed against his one-time mentor by suggesting meetings between those who would make the appointment and those in MI5 who saw Section V as a rival to their own counter-espionage activities, and who thus had no time for the notoriously proud and 'difficult' Cowgill.

Cowgill – whom Philby damningly described as 'a man too big for his talents' – was ousted, and Philby offered the job at Section IX. Graham Greene, the novelist, was then a member of SIS, and resigned in disgust at what he then thought was Philby's 'personal drive for power, the only characteristic in Philby which I thought disagreeable'. After the truth about Philby's motives came out, however, Greene wrote: 'I am glad now that I was wrong. He was serving a cause and not himself, and so my old liking for him comes back ...'

Making sure he covered all the bases, Philby insisted that his appointment be approved by the security people. The all-clear was personally supplied by Sir David Petrie, head of MI5. The 'Chief' of SIS, Major General Sir Stewart Menzies, then told Philby that he was to have no contact with the US intelligence agencies; Menzies was worried that the Americans were leaking to the Soviets. 'It was,' Philby wrote, relishing the irony, 'a piquant situation.'

Smoke and mirrors

Philby claimed in his memoir that 'What little secret intelligence we got was mostly fake'; Europe was full of people only too anxious to supply SIS with what they thought it wanted – for a generous financial consideration. Reading between the lines, it is clear that Philby was in an ideal position to suppress any genuine information. This did not always prove possible in the case of defectors from the Soviet intelligence service, and Philby could not cover up such windfalls that 'threw the

> "He betrayed his country" – yes, perhaps he did, but who among us has not committed treason to something or someone more important than a country? In Philby's eyes he was working for a shape of things to come from which his country would benefit.
>
> Graham Greene, introduction to Philby's memoir, *My Silent War* (1968). Greene worked under Philby in SIS during the Second World War.

stuff into our laps'. But with satisfaction he notes that some of these men who 'chose freedom', such as Walter Krivitsky and Victor Kravchenko, ended up as disillusioned suicides (although some suspected they were assassinated). It was Krivitsky who first let it be known that there was a Soviet mole in the British Foreign Office – probably Maclean.

In the years immediately after the Second World War, the countries of Eastern Europe came under Soviet control, while some of those in the West, such as France and Italy, teetered on the brink. Philby himself travelled to France, Germany, Italy and Greece, visiting local SIS stations. There is just one passage in his memoir that partly justifies Hugh Gaitskell's assessment of him as 'Byronic in outlook', and shows that somewhere in this secretive man there was a well of poetry that could bubble up through the thick crust of cynicism and deceit. 'In Larissa,' he writes, 'I watched one of the atmospheric marvels with which Greece is so generous: two separate and distinct thunderstorms, one over Ossa, the other over Olympus, while around us the plain of Thessaly rippled quietly under the clearest of blue skies.'

Philby's most significant overseas trip at this time was to Istanbul, where the Soviet vice consul, Konstantin Volkov, had approached his opposite number in the British consulate and asked for asylum. He said that he wasn't really a consular official; he was in fact an officer of the NKVD. He also said that there were two Soviet agents in the British Foreign Office – and one in charge of a counter-espionage organization. Naturally enough, it fell to Philby to assess the information that Volkov was supplying, and Philby knew that he would have to brazen it out: 'I told the Chief that we were on to something of the greatest importance.' Philby impressed upon his superiors that he needed to go to Istanbul in person, to assess whether Volkov was all he said he was. Needless to say, by the time Philby arrived in Istanbul, all attempts to contact Volkov at the Soviet consulate proved fruitless. At first his British counterpart was told that Volkov was in Moscow; and then he was told that no one in the consulate knew of anybody called Volkov. Philby was obliged to write a report outlining various theories on how Volkov might have been rumbled. He did not mention the possibility that the Soviets had been tipped off.

Turkey, Washington, Beirut, Moscow

In January 1947 Philby took up a permanent posting as SIS chief in Istanbul. In this role he undertook photographic surveillance of Turkey's frontier with the USSR – presumably as useful to his Soviet masters as to the West – and organized the penetration of agents into Georgia, then part of the Soviet Union. Of the first two to make it across the border, one was shot and the other was never heard of again.

In the summer of 1949 Philby was offered the position of SIS representative in the USA – what he called the 'lion's den' – with the brief of liaising with the CIA and the FBI. From his Washington base he was involved in an Anglo-American project to topple the communist regime in Albania, but – strangely enough – every force of anti-communist exiles sent to the small Balkan country was intercepted and annihilated. A similar fate met parties sent into the Ukraine to foment anti-Soviet rebellion there.

While in Washington, Philby learnt that in 1944–5 there had been leaks from the British Embassy regarding the Manhattan Project, the programme to build the first atomic bomb. The FBI, with considerable thoroughness and lack of flair, concentrated all their efforts on the non-diplomatic staff at the Embassy – despite the fact that both Krivitsky and Volkov had suggested a more senior figure, codenamed Homer, was responsible. The British Establishment shared the same mental block as the FBI: they could not conceive that a British diplomat could be guilty of such treachery. Philby, of course, knew that Homer was Maclean, now head of the American Department in the Foreign Office back in London. His anxieties that the net was closing in were increased when Guy Burgess – by now known as a loose cannon in the Foreign Office owing to his drinking and generally outrageous behaviour – was posted to Washington. Philby suggested that Burgess stay with him – in the hope of keeping him out of trouble. At the same time he was thinking about how to get Burgess safely back to Britain, and conceiving a rescue plan for Maclean, who was to be tipped off by Burgess in person. It was important that Burgess be sent back to Britain involuntarily, otherwise eyebrows would be raised that Maclean had disappeared shortly after Burgess's return. To this end, Burgess had himself booked for speeding three times in one day, leading the US State Department to raise a furious protest at this flagrant abuse of diplomatic immunity; a few days later the British ambassador regretfully informed Burgess that he would have to leave.

Philby was not done with bluffing. He reminded his superiors back in London of the information supplied by Krivitsky: Homer, the FO mole, was of 'good family', educated at public school and Oxbridge, an idealist working for no pay. In response M15 drew up a shortlist of diplomats in Washington in 1944–5 that met the criteria. The list included a number of names, including that of Maclean. Things then moved faster than Philby could have anticipated. He knew that Maclean would fly. But it was a genuine shock to him that Burgess flew as well. That put him in the frame – was it not Burgess who had recruited him into SIS? Had Philby not offered his old friend accommodation in Washington? And now Burgess, having flown with Maclean, had as good as confessed that he too was a Soviet mole.

It was this realization that led Philby to bury the incriminating physical evidence in the dark wood on the way to Great Falls. But he knew there was also much circumstantial evidence that might implicate him, and had already prepared a range of defences. He also counted on the fact that many people would, he felt sure, be inclined to give him the benefit of the doubt. It would be inconceivable to them that a figure such as himself at the heart of the British intelligence establishment, educated at Westminster and Trinity, should be anything but loyal to king and country. Be that as it may, within a few days the expected telegram arrived from the Chief. He was to return to London immediately.

Back in the UK Philby survived a series of interrogations, but in the end he was asked to resign, with a golden handshake and 'a great black cloud over my head'. His resignation was followed by a 'secret trial' – a judicial inquiry conducted by a barrister possessed of considerable forensic skill, H.J.P. Milmo, KC, whom Philby knew to be 'the man whom MI5 usually brought in for the kill'. The kill didn't come; Philby had an answer for everything – or nearly everything. When asked to explain a dramatic increase in NKVD radio traffic between London, Moscow and Istanbul at the time of the Volkov affair, and another burst just after he had been briefed about the Washington Embassy leak, Philby simply replied that he could not account for it. At this point, Milmo appeared to give up. The judicial inquiry was over, but the interrogations by MI5 and others continued for a while, and Philby had to surrender his passport. He was still under suspicion, but the authorities could turn up nothing conclusive.

> I have no reason to conclude that Mr Philby has at any time betrayed the interests of his country.
>
> Foreign Secretary Harold Macmillan, in the House of Commons, 1955

After an unsuccessful spell in the City, Philby returned to journalism. When the press got wind that he might be the Third Man, the traitor who had tipped off Burgess and Maclean, he threatened to sue. Then, in 1955, Colonel Marcus Lipton MP, sheltering behind parliamentary privilege, asked the prime minister, Anthony Eden, if he was determined to go on 'shielding the dubious Third Man activities of Mr Philby'. In response, the foreign secretary, Harold Macmillan, cleared Philby in Parliament:

> While in government service he carried out his duties ably and conscientiously, and I have no reason to conclude that Mr Philby has at any time betrayed the interests of his country, or to identify him with the so-called 'Third Man', if indeed there was one.

Subsequently, Philby held a press conference and challenged Lipton to repeat his allegations outside Parliament. Lipton declined to do so, and issued an apology. 'I think that Colonel Lipton has done the right thing,' Philby told the press. 'So far as I am concerned, the incident is now closed.'

Having had his passport returned, Philby now embarked on a career as Middle East correspondent for *The Economist* and *The Observer*, based in Beirut. This was in fact cover arranged by SIS, to whom he continued to supply intelligence. At the same time, he was also feeding information to the Soviets. This happy arrangement

'In the last instance, Philby is driven by the incurable drug of deceit itself.'

John le Carré, reviewing Philby's memoir, *My Silent War* (1968)

might have continued undisturbed had Major Anatoly Golitsyn of the KGB (the successor to the NKVD) not defected to the CIA in Helsinki in December 1961 and spilt the beans. The beans took some digesting: it was not until January 1963 that SIS and MI5 offered Philby immunity if he returned to London and made a full confession. But Philby had other plans. After letting it be known that he *was* a Soviet agent, but adding nothing more, he disappeared from Beirut on 23 January, probably on board the Soviet freighter *Domatova*. In his memoir, Philby is teasing:

> So, after seven years, I left Beirut and turned up in the Soviet Union. Why? Maybe I was tipped off by a Fourth Man. Maybe someone had blundered. It is even possible that I was just tired. Thirty years in the underground is a long stretch, and I cannot pretend that they left no mark …

The person who turned out to be the Fourth Man, the art historian Anthony Blunt, was by this stage Surveyor of the Queen's Pictures and thus probably out of the intelligence circuit, so it is unlikely that he was in a position to give Philby the nod. The Fifth Man, John Cairncross, was also out of the loop by this time. More likely the warning came from Yuri Modin, the top Soviet handler and controller of the Cambridge Five, who had visited Beirut in December 1962.

The spy who stayed the course

In Moscow, Philby was awarded the Order of Lenin and the Order of the Red Banner, but his life seems to have lost something of its former meaning. He smoked and drank heavily, and his private life continued to be turbulent: he had divorced Litzi in 1946, having already fathered children by Aileen Furse, whom he later married, but who died in 1957. Two years later he married an American divorcée, Eleanor Brewer, who joined him in Moscow, but returned to the USA in 1965. In Moscow Philby seduced Melinda Maclean, wife of his fellow-spy Donald Maclean, but the affair was short-lived. His final marriage, to Rufina Ivanova, lasted until his death

СОВЕТСКИЙ РАЗВЕДЧИК

КИМ ФИЛБИ
1912—1988
5 ПОЧТА СССР 1990

After his death in 1988 Philby received a hero's funeral and many other honours. This commemorative postage stamp was issued two years later, shortly before the Soviet Union itself collapsed.

in 1988. He was given a hero's funeral by the KGB. Within three years, the Soviet Union was itself history.

Whether Philby ever found contentment in retirement is a moot point. In his waspish memoir, written in Moscow in 1967, he displays a strong degree of callousness and disdain towards those he regards as his intellectual inferiors; after all, these were all men and women whom he had duped. To what extent one should accept his assertion of ideological commitment to a world made better through communism is difficult to assess. Reviewing *My Silent War*, John le Carré wrote: 'Philby has no home, no women, no faith. Behind the inbred upper-class arrogance, the taste for adventure, lies the self-hate of a vain misfit for whom nothing will ever be worthy of his loyalty. In the last instance, Philby is driven by the incurable drug of deceit itself.' Graham Greene took a different view, asking 'who among us has not committed treason to something or someone more important than a country? In Philby's eyes he was working for a shape of things to come from which his country would benefit.' Philby himself wrote of the ends justifying the means: 'It cannot be very surprising that I adopted a Communist viewpoint in the Thirties; so many of my contemporaries made the same choice. But many of those who made their choice in those days changed sides when some of the worst features of Stalinism became apparent. I stayed the course.' Whether in the end Philby believed that history had justified his actions is unknown.

OVER THE DMZ

JOE DRESNOK
The GI who walked to North Korea

At noon on 15 August 1962 Private First Class James Joseph Dresnok, stationed with the US army in South Korea, picked up a shotgun and entered the Demilitarized Zone, the most heavily fortified border in the world. Roughly following the 38th parallel, the DMZ, which separates the two Koreas, is some 2.5 miles wide, guarded on both sides by large numbers of tanks and artillery pieces.

North and South Korea were then – and still are – technically at war with each other. The Korean War had been precipitated in 1950 by the invasion of the South by the communist North, and the conflict quickly escalated to include both the USA and communist China. By 1953 the fighting had ground to a stalemate, and a ceasefire was negotiated. But no peace treaty was ever signed, and great enmity continued between the two sides and their respective allies. The DMZ is in effect the last front of the Cold War.

> JAMES JOSEPH
> DRESNOK
>
> *Born* 1941, Richmond, Virginia, USA

Dresnok, a tall, heavily built man, appeared oblivious to the fact that he was running into a minefield. 'Sure, I knew about the personnel mines, maybe I could lose a foot or a leg,' he told the *Guardian* journalist Mark Seddon in a rare interview in 2008. 'But I just went, straight.' Nicknamed 'Comrade Joe', Dresnok has made a life for himself in North Korea. The fact that he has also allowed himself to be used as a propaganda tool by the North means he is regarded by many Americans as a traitor.

Life on the underside

But it wasn't ideology – nor was it money – that prompted Dresnok to defect. It was more that his life hitherto in the land of the free and the home of the brave had amounted to little more than a series of disappointments and knock-backs. His parents had split up when he was nine, and he had spent much of his teens running away from a succession of abusive foster homes in Virginia. It was a miserable experience, and the day after his seventeenth birthday, in 1958, he enlisted with the US army.

Dresnok had been looking for a home in the army, but the army viewed things differently. He was posted first to Germany, where, for a minor misdemeanour, he was forced to clean a truck with a toothbrush in bitterly cold conditions. He considered at the time defecting to communist East Germany, but rejected the idea. He had learnt that the East Germans simply grilled absconding US soldiers, and then sent them back over the border.

OPPOSITE **This still from the documentary** *Crossing the Line*, released in 2007, shows Joe Dresnok in North Korea in 2006, 44 years after his defection.

After his two years in Germany, Dresnok's wife left him for another man. 'I wanted to go to the most dangerous place in the world,' he recalls. His next posting was South Korea. Here he became attached to a local woman, but this led to more trouble when he forged an officer's signature on a pass to leave his base to meet her. Threatened with a court martial, he decided to go for a new life on the other side of the DMZ.

A new world

When he entered the minefield Dresnok heard voices behind him yelling at him to stop. He let off a round from his gun. He went on running. Intercepted by North Korean soldiers – some of whom wanted to kill him – he was taken to Pyongyang, the capital of the North, and interrogated. Here he met another defector, Private Larry Abshier. 'I opened my eyes,' Dresnok remembers. 'I didn't believe myself. I shut them again. I must be dreaming. I opened them again and looked and, "Who in the hell are you?" He says, "I'm Abshier." "Abshier? I don't know no Abshier."'

> 'I was fed up with my childhood, my marriage, my military life, everything. I was finished. There's only one place to go. On August 15th, at noon in broad daylight when everybody was eating lunch, I hit the road. Yes I was afraid. Am I gonna live or die? And when I stepped into the minefield and I seen it with my own eyes, I started sweating. I crossed over, looking for my new life.'
>
> Joe Dresnok, interviewed in 2006 for the documentary *Crossing the Line*

Over the next two years they were joined by two more US army deserters, Sergeant Robert Jenkins and Specialist Jerry Parrish. All four ended up living together in a single room, and every now and then they were wheeled out to bellow through megaphones across the DMZ to their former buddies, encouraging them to join them in the workers' paradise that was the People's Democratic Republic of Korea. They had all thought more about what they were running from than what they were running to, and hadn't realized how hated Americans were in the North, which was still in ruins after the US bombing during the war. Dresnok recalls that he felt everyone in the street was thinking, 'Oh, there goes that American bastard.' Before long the four men were regretting their decision to defect: their living conditions were poor, they were forced to memorize great tracts from the works of the 'Great Leader', Kim Il-Sung, and every aspect of their lives was subject to close control. In 1966 they tried to seek political asylum in the Soviet embassy, but were immediately returned to their North Korean overseers.

Rather than shooting them, the authorities set about converting their reluctant guests. The four men were allowed to find, or were provided with, female companions, to act as cooks, minders and mistresses. Jenkins later married a Japanese woman abducted by the North Koreans to train their agents in Japanese ways, but in 2002 she was allowed to return to Japan. Two years later Jenkins was

> 'This is a man who disappeared off the face of the known world in 1962. And I went into this … dark brick room. This … tall man in a black uniform came in. And he sat down, said, 'Hello Boy. I gather you wanna talk about making a film about me.' And it would have been less surprising to have met Elvis Presley.'
>
> Nick Bonner, who interviewed Dresnok in North Korea in 2006 for the documentary *Crossing the Line*

allowed to join her. He reported to a US military base in Japan, and was charged with desertion and aiding the enemy. He was sentenced to 30 days in jail, and later wrote a book, *The Reluctant Communist*, in which he alleges that Dresnok, whom he portrays as a North Korean stooge, had beaten Abshier and himself when instructed by their hosts – something that Dresnok denies.

According to official North Korean sources, Abshier had died in 1983 and Parrish in 1996, both of natural causes, so that left Dresnok the only one of the four still in North Korea. It was not until 1996, more than a decade after Abshier's death, that the US Department of Defense acknowledged that its four missing soldiers had been living in North Korea.

From private soldier to celebrity

Dresnok has no regrets. He married twice in North Korea. His first wife there was a Romanian called Doina Bumbea, by whom he had two sons. After her death he married the daughter of a North Korean woman and a diplomat from Togo. She gave birth to a son in 2001. From the late 1970s Dresnok became something of a celebrity in North Korea after playing the evil American in *Unsung Heroes*, a 20-part TV series directed by Kim Jong-Il, now the 'Dear Leader'. 'The Dear Leader takes care of me,' Dresnok says. 'Great man.' It is certainly unlikely that he would have made the jump from private soldier to movie star if he had stayed in the USA. As well as acting, he taught English and translated some of the works of the Great Leader. He is now retired and in poor health, due to excessive smoking and drinking, but he likes to go fishing, and bowling – a strange irony, that this most American of sports is so popular in perhaps the most vehemently anti-American country in the world.

> 'I start to learn English to become a diplomat. I would like to make the world which has no war at all and no terror at all.'
>
> James Dresnok, Joe's Korean son, interviewed in *Crossing the Line*

Dresnok denies he is a traitor. 'I love my country,' he told Mark Seddon. 'I love my town. In his teachings Kim Il-Sung wrote: "Those who really love their country and their home can become communists." I'm not a communist, but I would like to be one.' A couple of years earlier he had told documentary makers Dan Gordon and Nick Bonner: 'I feel at home. I really feel at home. I wouldn't trade it for nothing.'

A TALE OF
TWO GERMANYS

MARKUS WOLF

The spymaster of Berlin

As Markus Wolf faced five judges in a fortified, high-security cellar under Düsseldorf's main courthouse, he reflected on what he called the central irony of his life: that it was his very success that had been his downfall. 'I was in the dock,' he ruefully recalled, 'for running the most successful espionage service in Europe, East or West.' But it was not espionage he was charged with; it was *Landesverrat*, betrayal of country.

Until 1979, when he was covertly photographed and the picture identified by a defector, Wolf had been known to Western intelligence agencies as 'the man without a face'. In fact, he was a strikingly handsome – and cultured – man, who liked to quote Goethe and Brecht and who had a taste for the good things of life – the antithesis of the typical grey East German apparatchik.

For over three decades, until his retirement in 1986, Wolf had been the head of the foreign intelligence service of the German Democratic Republic – communist East Germany – and had directed the bulk of his efforts against the capitalist democracy of West Germany. 'It was widely believed,' he later boasted, 'that I knew more about the secrets of the Federal Republic ... than the chancellor in Bonn himself.' It was not something that many in the West, following unification, were prepared to forgive or forget. With the end of the Cold War, they felt, it was time for victors' justice.

> MARKUS JOHANNES WOLF
>
> *Born* 19 January 1923, at Hechingen, Württemberg, Germany
> *Died* of natural causes, 9 November 2006, in Berlin, Germany

Fighting fascism or destroying democracy?

Wolf was not by birth an 'Ossi' – a native of East Germany. He was born in Württemberg in southwest Germany in the small town of Hechingen – by a stroke of fate also the birthplace of Klaus Kinkel, who was to become Wolf's counterpart in the West German intelligence service, the BND, and who was to appear as a witness at Wolf's trial. Wolf's parents were Jewish and both were members of the Communist Party; his father, Friedrich Wolf, was a doctor and prolific dramatist, while his younger brother, Konrad, became a noted film director. When Hitler came to power the Wolfs fled to France, and thence to the Soviet Union, where they were granted asylum. It was not the last time that Markus Wolf was to seek asylum in Moscow.

As committed communists, the Wolfs were welcome in the Soviet Union. Young Markus – who became known by the Russian name Mischa – was given a good education, and trained as an aeronautical engineer. Following the defeat of Hitler and the division of Germany into Allied occupation zones, Wolf, then aged 22, was sent into the Eastern – Soviet – zone with other exiled German communists to set up a radio station in the ruins of Berlin. As a journalist, he also covered the Nuremberg Trials, where he came face to face with the men who would have exterminated him and his family, if they had had the chance. It was a transformative experience: 'I hoped that after the Nuremberg Trials,' he told the BBC in the year before his death, 'there would be a time without war, aggression or crimes against humanity.' As a young idealist, he welcomed the establishment of the communist GDR in 1949, seeing it as a bulwark against the re-emergence of fascism in Germany. 'How could anyone who fought against Hitler's barbarians have considered himself a traitor to Germany?' Wolf wrote in his 1997 memoir, *Man Without a Face*. 'My own contribution, and that of my family, to the fight may have been small, but I am proud of it nonetheless.' He continued:

> I feel the same way about my attempts after the war to publicize and make the world aware of the causes of Nazi tyranny, its terrible crimes against humanity, and the existence of former Nazis in the West German power structure. Hitler's long shadow was one of the reasons I agreed to the idea of working for a secret service. This was not treason.

Wolf was made head of the GDR's foreign intelligence agency, the HVA, the *Hauptverwaltung Aufklärung* ('main intelligence directorate') in 1952. He was still not yet 30. The following year the HVA merged into the State Security Service – the notorious Stasi. Wolf's boss was the minister for state security, the brutal and unimaginative Erich Mielke, who, like his fellow ministers in the GDR, was convinced that a US-backed West Germany was intent on crushing and absorbing its smaller eastern neighbour (in much the same way as many Western governments were convinced the USSR was intent on global conquest, while for their part the Soviets were in a constant state of defensive paranoia). In the belief that the GDR was inundated with spies, saboteurs and subversives, Mielke established the system by which one half of the population was set to inform on the other half, and the GDR became one of the most repressive countries in the Eastern Bloc. Wolf later claimed that he disapproved of much of the Stalinist thuggery of his Stasi colleagues; indeed, his third wife, Andrea, had as a young woman been imprisoned for four months for attempting to flee the country. 'I considered my own work in foreign intelligence to be a separate and more defensible sphere of activity,' he later pleaded in mitigation, 'but I could not help but be ashamed at the brutal tactics against internal opposition and those whose only desire was to leave the country.'

> If I go down in espionage history, it may well be for perfecting the use of sex in spying.
>
> Markus Wolf, *Man Without a Face* (1997)

The task of Wolf's HVA was to report on the threats from outside the borders of East Germany. It set out to learn about the Federal Republic's intentions vis à vis

Wolf (gesturing) sits behind Nikita Khrushchev during the Soviet leader's visit to East Berlin in 1957.

the GDR, and at the same time to garner what information it could about the military capacity and planning of NATO as a whole. In carrying out these tasks, Wolf was extraordinarily successful, running an estimated 30,000 agents and other sources within West Germany during his 34 years in office.

The Romeo agents

One of the techniques pioneered by Wolf was a variant on the honey trap, one that exploited the shortage of younger German males in the wake of the slaughter of the Second World War. The imbalance was particularly marked in Bonn, the West German capital, where large numbers of unattached female secretaries were employed in government service. Seeing an opportunity, Wolf suggested to the more handsome of his younger male agents that they set about charming and seducing these lonely women, especially those who worked for senior officials or ministers. The women – always out of love, sometimes also out of conviction – would then trustingly hand over confidential information to their new 'Romeos', information that soon found its way back to Wolf.

Sometimes there was a happy ending: for example, Helga Rödiger, a secretary at the West German finance ministry, married her Romeo, codenamed 'Gert', after they were both withdrawn back to the East in 1979. Wolf was guest of honour at their wedding. But Wolf sometimes tricked the women: when Dagmar Kahlig-Scheffler insisted on marrying her 'Romeo', Herbert Schrötter, she was flown from Bonn via neutral Vienna to East Berlin, where a wedding ceremony was staged in a registry office. Only after her arrest in 1977 did Dagmar find out that the wedding had been a sham: it turned out that the page that they had signed in the register had immediately been torn out and destroyed. As Wolf himself admitted:

There were cases of women whose love was abused, who for a certain time procured important documents or information, not knowing who for, or what service they worked for, and for a variety of reasons, were tried and jailed.

The outcome could be even worse – in his memoirs Wolf does not mention the tragic case of Leonore Heinz (see box).

The Guillaume affair

The most successful of Wolf's agents were his sleepers – young agents infiltrated into the West who stayed dormant, often for years, working their way up the political or government hierarchy, until they were in a position to provide significant intelligence, and even to influence policy. The most famous of these sleepers was Günter Guillaume, who in 1956 emigrated with his wife Christel to the West, with orders from Wolf to penetrate the SPD, the Social Democratic Party. Eventually in 1970 Guillaume – who had identified himself with the right wing of the SPD – became a close aide of the SPD chancellor, Willy Brandt, responsible for liaison with parliament, government agencies and the churches. The irony was that it was Brandt who initiated West Germany's new policy of *Ostpolitik*, by which the Federal Republic sought rapprochement with the Eastern Bloc, and for the first time recognized the GDR as an independent sovereign state. So when Guillaume was exposed in 1974 as an East German spy and Brandt was forced to resign, it was something of an own goal for Wolf. His organization, he later admitted, had 'unwittingly helped to destroy the career of the most farsighted of modern German statesmen'.

There was a further irony: Guillaume's son Pierre, with whom he was very close, was a Young Socialist, on the left wing of the SPD, who had regarded his conservative father as a traitor to the socialist cause. With Pierre's parents both in prison, Wolf did his best to see to the boy's upbringing in the East, but the disciplined, anti-individualistic

THE BITTER TEARS OF LEONORE HEINZ

IN 1959 LEONORE HEINZ, secretary to an official in the West German foreign ministry in Bonn, opened the door of her apartment to find a handsome stranger holding a bunch of roses. He claimed to be looking for another woman, but ended up giving the roses to her. Unbeknownst to Leonore, the man, whose name was Heinz Sütterlin, was one of Wolf's Romeo agents. The two were married the following year. Leonore brought home thousands of documents for her husband to photograph, before returning them to their files back at the ministry. Sütterlin's cover was blown when his controller defected, and the couple were arrested. When Leonore learnt at the trial that Sütterlin had been ordered to marry one of three secretaries, she hanged herself in her cell.

> 'Our methods worked so well that we unwittingly helped to destroy the career of the most farsighted of modern German statesmen, Willy Brandt.' Markus Wolf, *Man Without a Face* (1997)

ethos of the GDR was not to Pierre's taste, and in the end he returned to the West. His parents were released in 1981 as part of an exchange. At Wolf's own trial in 1993, Guillaume was to appear for the defence, telling the court: 'I have respected and served two people wholeheartedly in my life: Markus Wolf and Willy Brandt.' It was a statement symptomatic of the divided loyalties that prevailed in a divided country.

Betrayers betrayed

Infiltrated agents and their amatory conquests were not Wolf's only sources of information. Many of his best sources were key figures in the West German intelligence and security communities, who for one reason or another gave the GDR many years of devoted service.

In 1968 a young woman called Gabrielle ('Gaby') Gast visited East Germany for her doctoral study on the political role of women in the GDR. While there, she

West German Chancellor Willy Brandt, with his close aide Günter Guillaume (in sunglasses). Brandt was forced to resign when Guillaume was exposed as one of Wolf's agents.

fell for a mechanic called Karl-Heinz Schmidt, whom she dubbed Karlizcek. At the end of a passionate summer he told her that he was in fact an intelligence officer, and asked if she would cooperate with his service; when she hesitated, his superior told her that if she did not she would be prevented from seeing Karlizcek again. So she agreed to work as an East German agent, partly through emotional blackmail, and partly out of a belief that the political establishment in the Federal Republic was failing to face up to its Nazi past. Back in the West, quite by luck, her doctoral supervisor turned out to be a recruiter for the BND, the Federal intelligence agency, and in 1973 she started to work for the BND as a political analyst. Over the years, her ideological conviction increased, and at the same time her brilliance saw her rise within the BND to the position of deputy chief of the political department dealing with the Soviet Union and the Eastern Bloc. Her perceptive reports were read with great interest not only in Bonn, but also in East Berlin.

> One may wonder at times if the end justifies the means. It would certainly be the simplest thing to say, "No, certainly not." But that wouldn't be the full truth. With intelligence methods, you can't apply the same yardstick as with ordinary morals.
>
> Markus Wolf, interviewed for the CNN documentary *Cold War* (1998)

After he retired Wolf was often asked why such upper-middle-class Westerners, with strong and complex personalities, flocked to work for him. 'What we offered them,' he wrote in his memoir, 'was the chance of mixing idealism with personal commitment, something that is missing in many modern societies.' Gaby Gast was eventually betrayed in 1990 in the run-up to reunification by a senior HVA officer who was hoping thereby to avoid prosecution. Karlizcek, her lover of over twenty years, also betrayed her in a bid to save his own skin: telling the world that their affair was over, he refused to testify on her behalf. As a citizen of the former GDR he was given a suspended sentence, while Gaby, judged a traitor to her native West Germany, was sentenced to six and a half years. Karlizcek celebrated his freedom with an expensive meal in a restaurant opposite the courthouse.

Another of Wolf's top agents, 'Topaz', was also betrayed by a member of the HVA in 1990. 'Topaz' was the codename for Rainer Rupp, a West German who became a senior official at NATO's headquarters in Brussels. Rupp had been a student radical in the 1960s, and was recruited following his involvement in street protests during a state visit by the Shah of Iran. As he rose up the NATO hierarchy, Rupp was able to pass over streams of valuable military documents regarding the alliance's military planning, documents that were forwarded by Wolf to the KGB. In 1994 Rupp was sentenced to twelve years and fined 300,000 deutschmarks. 'How can it be,' Wolf protested in his memoirs, 'that after the peaceful reunification of two states recognized under international law, the spies of one state go unpunished, are even given indemnifications if they are imprisoned, whereas those who worked for the other state are sentenced to long prison terms and hefty fines?'

Endgame

Wolf too was to have his day in court. In 1980 he had been promoted to the rank of general and awarded the Golden Order of the Fatherland – but by the middle of the decade he had had enough. He admired the policies of perestroika and glasnost that Gorbachev was initiating in the Soviet Union, and in 1986, frustrated that the GDR's own leadership set itself against all reform, he resigned. At his farewell party he wryly quoted Brecht: 'A good communist has many dents in his helmet. And some of them are the work of the enemy.' General Secretary Erich Honecker, the top man in the GDR, himself told Wolf that he would 'never allow here what is happening in the Soviet Union'.

In the end it was Gorbachev himself who pulled the plug on the old regime in the GDR, when he announced in October 1989 that the Soviet Union would not stand in the way of internal reform if its allies in Eastern Europe chose to follow that course. Shortly afterwards the borders opened, the Berlin Wall fell, and within a year the two Germanys were reunited. For some, it was going to be an opportunity to settle old scores.

In May 1990, a few months before reunification was due to take place, Wolf received a visit from a CIA officer, who offered him money, a new identity and a home in California if he gave his cooperation. It is likely that the Americans wanted Wolf to tell them the identity of the CIA mole who was leaking the names of US agents to the Russians (this turned out to be Aldrich Ames; see p. 161). Wolf refused, although he realized that it was not safe for him to stay in Germany, especially after the Federal parliament refused to pass a bill granting an amnesty to former members of the GDR intelligence services. For two months he and his young wife Andrea wandered around Austria incognito, before following up on an earlier KGB offer to exfiltrate him to Russia. Wolf thus sought refuge in Moscow, as his family had in 1933, but he was tainted by association with the old regime, and Gorbachev did not want to endanger his good relations with Chancellor Kohl in Bonn.

In September 1991, after elements of the KGB had been discredited by their failed coup against Gorbachev, Wolf decided to return to his homeland. He was arrested at the border, and spent eleven days in jail before he could raise bail. It was not until May 1993 that his case came to court, and he was tried in the same high-security cellar that had witnessed the trial of Günter and Christel Guillaume in 1975. Wolf faced 389 pages of charges, and the trial lasted seven months. Wolf's defence was that he could not be guilty of *Landesverrat*, treason, as he had not been a citizen of the Federal Republic of Germany, but of a separate sovereign state, the German Democratic Republic. The prosecution argued that Wolf had conducted his operations from Berlin, which was now the capital of Germany; they also argued that the Federal Republic's 'Basic Law' gave it sovereignty over all former German territory. On 6 December 1993 Wolf was found guilty of treason and sentenced to six years' imprisonment.

His lawyers appealed, and the case went from the Supreme Court to the Constitutional Court, which in June 1995 ruled that Wolf and his colleagues could not be guilty of treason, as in 1972 the Federal Republic, under Willy Brandt, had recognized the GDR as a separate sovereign state. Wolf's conviction was squashed – largely thanks to the actions of the man whose downfall he had inadvertently brought about twenty years previously.

Brandt himself had stated, when he first became chancellor in 1969, that although two states existed in Germany, they could not be a foreign country to each other. This was the central paradox of the decades in which the two Germanys danced around each other, decades when citizens of either side wondered which side they were on. Many in the Federal Republic were sickened by the West's rampant consumerism, its toadying to the USA, its tolerance of former Nazis in positions of power, its lack of social and economic security in comparison to the East. At the same time millions in the GDR yearned for democracy and freedom and the West's cornucopia of consumer goods, and in the end it was they who brought about the change of regime in the East by mass peaceful action. But following reunification they found that, just as the GDR was never the workers' utopia its leaders portrayed it as, neither was the Federal Republic – with its lack of jobs for 'Ossis' and its lack of state provision – the heaven they had dreamed of.

Looking back, Wolf was ambivalent, acknowledging that things had gone horribly wrong in the GDR: 'Our side fought against the revival of fascism. We fought for a combination of socialism and freedom, a noble objective that failed utterly but which I still believe is possible.' He faced further prosecutions: for ordering the kidnapping of people from the West, for contempt of court when he refused to testify in the prosecution of a West German politician accused of spying for the East. He received a suspended sentence for the first charge, and was sentenced to three days in jail in 1998 for the second. While he was in prison his young grandchild sent him a drawing of a birthday cake with a file attached to it.

Wolf lived out his days modestly in Berlin, on the sixth floor of an apartment block without a lift, looking back on a life that had been 'richer in good and bad than I could ever have imagined as a young child'. He died on 9 November 2006 – on the seventeenth anniversary of the fall of the Berlin Wall.

THE REAL KARLA?

IT WAS OFTEN SAID that Markus Wolf was the model for John le Carré's fictional Russian spymaster Karla in *Tinker, Tailor, Soldier, Spy* and other novels. This is something that le Carré has always vehemently denied: 'The only Wolf I was familiar with, when I wrote the books in which he apparently claimed to have appeared, was a lawnmower,' le Carré has put on record. 'I repeatedly refused to appear on public platforms with him, and I have no admiration for his achievements.'

'For many men the Cold War was a game, and he was very good at the game.'
Peter Osnos, the editor of Wolf's memoirs

INDEX

Page numbers in **bold** denote a major section devoted to the entry.
Page numbers in *italics* denote an illustration/illustration caption.

AUTHOR'S ACKNOWLEDGEMENTS

In writing this book I have drawn upon a wide range of sources. In particular I would like to acknowledge the following authors and books:

Ackroyd, Peter, *Ezra Pound and His World* (Thames & Hudson, London, 1980)

Clive, Nigel, 'Harold Adrian Russell Philby', *DNB* online (Oxford University Press, Oxford, 2004)

Cookridge, E.H., *The Third Man: The Truth about 'Kim' Philby, Double Agent* (Arthur Barker, London, 1968)

Dumbach, Annette, and Newborn, Jud, *Sophie Scholl and the White Rose* (Oneworld Publications, Oxford, 2006)

Fahey, Curtis, 'Benedict Arnold', *Dictionary of Canadian Biography Online* (University of Toronto, Université Laval, Library and Archives Canada, 2003)

Farquhar, Michael, 'Rebel Rose, A Spy of Grande Dame Proportions', *Washington Post*, 18 September 2000

Fraser, Antonia, *Marie Antoinette: The Journey* (Weidenfeld & Nicolson, London, 2001)

Fraser, Antonia, *The Gunpowder Plot: Terror & Faith in 1605* (Weidenfeld & Nicolson, London, 1996)

Freed, Edwin D., 'Judas Iscariot', in Bruce M. Metzger, Michael D. Coogan (eds), *The Oxford Companion to the Bible* (Oxford University Press, New York & Oxford, 1993)

Gildea, Robert, *Marianne in Chains: In Search of the German Occupation 1940–45* (Macmillan, London, 2002)

Greenhow, Rose O'Neal, *My Imprisonment and the First Year of Abolition Rule at Washington* (London, 1863)

Haynes, Alan, *The Gunpowder Plot* (Sutton Publishing Ltd, Stroud, Gloucestershire, 1994)

Inglis, Brian, *Roger Casement* (Hodder & Stoughton, London, 1973)

Ives, Eric, *The Life and Death of Anne Boleyn* (Blackwell, Oxford, 2004)

Linder, Doug, *Trial of the Rosenbergs: An Account* (online, University of Missouri–Kansas City, 2008)

Livy, *Roman History*, translated by John Henry Freese, Alfred John Church and William Jackson Brodribb (1904)

Loades, David, *Henry VIII: Court, Church and Conflict* (The National Archives, Kew, 2007)

Loades, David, *Mary Tudor: The Tragical History of the First Queen of England* (The National Archives, Kew, 2006)

Martland, Peter, *Lord Haw Haw: The English Voice of Nazi Germany* (The National Archives, Kew, 2003)

Morris, Christopher, *The Tudors* (Batsford, London, 1955)

Nicholas, Siân, 'William Brooke Joyce', *DNB* online (Oxford University Press, Oxford, 2004)

Nicholls, Mark, 'Guy Fawkes', *DNB* online (Oxford University Press, Oxford, 2004)

Ousby, Ian, *Occupation: The Ordeal of France 1940–1944* (John Murray, London, 1997)

Parker, R.B., Introduction to *The Tragedy of Coriolanus* (Oxford University Press, Oxford, 1998)

Philby, Kim, *My Silent War*, with an introduction by Graham Greene (MacGibbon & Kee, London, 1968)

Plowden, Alison, 'Lady Jane Grey', *DNB* online (Oxford University Press, Oxford, 2004)

Stanley, Alessandra, 'KGB Agent Plays Down Atomic Role of Rosenbergs', *New York Times*, 16 March 1997

Stock, Noel, *The Life of Ezra Pound* (Routledge & Kegan Paul, London, 1970)

Sullivan, J.P. (ed), *Ezra Pound: A Critical Anthology* (Penguin Books, Harmondsworth, 1970)

Warner, Marina, *Joan of Arc: The Image of Female Heroism* (Weidenfeld & Nicolson, London, 1981)

Wolf, Markus, with McElvoy, Anne, *Man Without a Face: The Autobiography of Communism's Greatest Spymaster* (2nd edition, with a foreword by Craig R. Whitney, Public Affairs, New York, 1999)

In addition, I would like to thank the following: Richard Milbank, my publisher at Quercus, for welcoming my suggestion for a book on traitors; Emma Heyworth-Dunn, managing editor at Quercus, for overseeing the book through to press; Jackie Strachan and Jane Moseley of JMS Books for project management and layout; Jenni Davis, for editing the text with tact and a great eye for detail; Austin Taylor for the page design; Caroline Hotblack for the picture research; and the staff of Hornsey Library, for their ever-cheerful willingness to plunge into the dusty darkness of the reserve collection on my behalf.

PICTURE CREDITS

akg-images 8 akg-images/Electa; 16, 136, 166-167 akg-images; 34 akg-images/Jerome da Cunha; 78 akg-images/Nimatallah; 140 akg-images/Wittenstein; 143 akg-images/ Juergen Raible.

Ancient Art & Architecture 27 © Interfoto/ AAA Collection.

Alamy 71 © North Wind Picture Archives/Alamy.

Art Archive 20 The Art Archive/Scrovegni Chapel Padua/Alfredo Dagli Orti; 23 The Art Archive/Eglise Saint Sébastien Plampinet/ Gianni Dagli Orti; 29 The Art Archive/Eileen Tweedy; 61 The Art Archive.

Bridgeman Art Library 36 Hever Castle, Kent, UK/The Bridgeman Art Library; 46 Musée Rolin, Autun, France/The Bridgeman Art Library; 55 National Gallery, London, UK/The Bridgeman Art Library; 96 Private Collection/The Bridgeman Art Library.

Camera Press 181 Gamma, Camera Press London.

Corbis 88, 112, 114, 131, 134, 155, 159, 162 © Bettmann/CORBIS; 93 © Corbis; 103 © Underwood & Underwood/CORBIS.

Getty Images 56, 65 Getty Images; 77 National Geographic/Getty Images; 85 Roger Viollet/Getty Images; 150 Time & Life Pictures/Getty Images.

Lebrecht Music & Arts 149 © Leemage/ Lebrecht Music & Arts.

Library of Congress 68 Library of Congress (LC-USZ62-68483).

Mary Evans Picture Library 42–43, 49 Mary Evans Picture Library.

PA Photos 104, 109 PA/PA Archive/PA Photos; 145 AP/AP/PA Photos.

Photos 12 81 Photos12.com – Oasis.

Rex Features 106, 125 Rex Features; 120 Roger-Viollet/Rex Features; 174 © Kino/Everett/Rex Features; 183 Action Press/Rex Features.

TopFoto 14 Butler Henrietta/ArenaPAL/ Topfoto; 178 © Ullstein bild/TopFoto.

Quercus Publishing Plc
21 Bloomsbury Square
London
WC1A 2NS

First published in 2009

Editorial and project management: JMS Books LLP
Design: Austin Taylor
Picture research: Caroline Hotblack

A catalogue record of this book is available from the British Library

Printed case edition:
ISBN 13: 978 1 84866 011 3

Printed and bound in China

10 9 8 7 6 5 4 3 2 1